ON THE MERSEY BEAT

ON THE MERSEY BEAT

Policing Liverpool between the Wars

MIKE BROGDEN

OXFORD UNIVERSITY PRESS
1991

Oxford University Press, Walton Street, Oxford OX2 6DP
Oxford New York Toronto
Delhi Bombay Calcutta Madras Karachi
Petaling Jaya Singapore Hong Kong Tokyo
Nairobi Dar es Salaam Cape Town
Melbourne Auckland
and associated companies in
Berlin Ibadan

Oxford is a trade mark of Oxford University Press

Published in the United States
by Oxford University Press, New York

British Library Cataloguing in Publication Data
Brogden, Mike
On the Mersey Beat: Policing Liverpool
between the wars.
1. England. Police, history
I. Title
363.20942
ISBN 0-19-825430-X

Library of Congress Cataloging in Publication Data
Brogden, Michael
On the Mersey Beat: Policing Liverpool
between the wars/Mike Brogden.
Includes bibliographical references and index
1. Police—England—Liverpool—History—20th century   2. Police
Strike, England, 1919   I. Title.
HV8196.L5876   1991   363.2'09427'5309042—dc20   90-49131
ISBN 0-19-825430-X

Photoset by Rowland Phototypesetting Ltd
Bury St Edmunds, Suffolk

Printed in Great Britain by Biddles Ltd
Guildford and King's Lynn

To

My Father

and Robert Tisseyman

born 1869, South Hetton Colliery, Durham; educated Minton Colliery School, Durham; represented Edge Hill Ward on Liverpool City Council (Labour); Agent for the Co-operative Insurance Society; Chairman, Edge Hill Branch, Independent Labour Party; Committee member, National Union of Police and Prison Officers; Police Sergeant (1st Class) 24¾ years' service; Liverpool Police striker, 1919; dismissed 1919.

ACKNOWLEDGEMENTS

Many people have contributed to this narrative. Primary thanks is due to the twenty-four men of the Liverpool City Police who provided its core. The anonymity which many of them requested—secrecy was ingrained—is respected in the text. Harry Marshall of NARPO was an essential figure in guiding me to them. Brian Hilliard of *Police Review* was helpful with the illustrative material. Comrades in the ILP pointed me to the wit and wisdom of Yaffle!

The text would not have developed without the positive comments of Clive Emsley and the publisher's anonymous readers. Similarly, major, hidden, contributions were made by Richard Hart and Jane Williams (and the unknown but extraordinarily efficient copy-editor) on behalf of OUP. Much of the work was initially collated through the hospitality of Gertie Weinhart of Toronto Island. To her, and to Dany Lacombe and Maeve McMahon, and the other residents of 17 Borden Street, Toronto, I send my greetings. The long days in the Colindale Newspaper Library (where the title 'Keeper' means *Keeper*) were softened by the tolerance of Robert Reiner and Miriam David.

In Liverpool, many people have sustained this work since its inception. Comrades such as Roger O'Hara, Keith Black, Bob Golden, and Frank Carroll gave more support than they knew. From Snowden to Skiddaw, Terry Caslin, Dave Kermode, Bob Morley, and Steve Smith, endured many weary recountings of the eventual text. Ron Noon, a professional social historian as well as a 'scouser' has made several sage interventions in my historical understanding of policing and Merseyside. Don Jenkin and Bill Dunford contributed ideas and sustenance. More generally, I owe much to my colleagues—Pete Gill, Joe Sim, and Sandra Walklate. Their academic work and our students in Liverpool have jointly created a base for the development of critical criminal justice studies in the UK.

Finally, the major contribution has been unstintingly bestowed by Marcus and Sasha. Even the cold terraces of Goodison Park on a wet Saturday afternoon, did not diminish my parental appreciation of their tolerance in this enterprise.

M. E. B.

Institute of Crime, Justice, and Welfare,
Liverpool Polytechnic.

CONTENTS

Introduction

On the Mersey Beat is an account of policing with a difference: unlike the many official and academic histories of policing, it tells the story of police work through the words of its practitioners. It offers a picture of street policing between the wars that combines the verbatim accounts of former police officers with contemporary records.

It is not, however, intended as an *alternative* history. Its major thrust is sociological, seeking to understand how men—and they were all men—throughout their working lives survived draconian discipline and appalling work conditions. It seeks to understand how they could be detached from a class from which many of them had come, and carry out the imperatives—social, economic, moral, and political—of their betters. Centrally, it is concerned to understand how they survived those pressures, and what mental and physical resources they drew upon to maintain some self-respect.

Several paradoxes emerge. These officers of the Liverpool City Police possessed immense power over the lives over the traditional objects of public-order police work, the lower classes of the city streets. But they were, themselves, workers in gainful employment, who suffered severe indignities and humiliations at the hands of their commanders. Rank-and-file police officers in the inter-war years were no angels in the way they exercised authority on behalf of a smug urban middle class over the people relegated to the bottom of the social pile. However, they were also working men, subject to extraordinary and often perverse demands from their superiors. Policing involved facing both ways.[1] Police officers were both oppressed and oppressors.

The account in this book debunks the notion that police work is about crime—as popularly conceived. The mandate of these officers was to keep the Liverpool streets clean, as a kind of uniformed garbage-men. Its most common manifestation was that of 'moving on' any person, young or old, who committed the sins of playing pitch-and-toss on the street corner or chatting outside the public house after licensing hours. Arrests, other than for minor misdemeanours, were rare.

On the Mersey Beat contains other paradoxes. Beat policing with its quarter-hour points represented the ultimate in disciplined, supervised, timetabled work. As a practice, it had changed little since the inception of the Victorian forces.[2] A constable patrolling a particular beat could make a fair guess as to what street he would be proceeding up, at an identical time, a year in advance. However, for the policed, the situation was reversed. Liverpool was still the largest seaport in Western Europe, with twelve miles of Mersey docks and three-quarters of a million people. Its economy was dominated by the practices of *casual* employment. Men would queue fatalistically for hours, day after day, for a chance of a few hours' work on the docks. Relatively few of the people whose activities dominated police encounters on the street had regular jobs. Time, like control, had a different meaning for police and policed.[3]

Class relations were messy, confused. The young constable recruited from the Fifeshire coalfield found himself waving a stick outside a local pit during the 1926 General Strike. At the same time he supported his striking kin back home out of his police pay. Nor was the individual constable's behaviour necessarily consistent or easily stereotyped. An officer who regularly 'moved on' prostitutes would carry sweets for children on a street-crossing patrol. In part, these differences were a function of geography or physique. If heavily built, he would find himself on the city's Scotland Road, regularly batoning Irish labourers on a Saturday night. Another constable, differently endowed, might serve most of his thirty years in the city suburbs where his only problem (although that term grossly understates the deprivation) was the pervasive loneliness and tedium of the night-time perambulation.

Inevitably, the memories of the two dozen nonagenarian and octogenarian ex-officers that are recounted here cannot provide a total picture of policing a lower-class city between the wars. Hindsight teaches lessons about the wider social relations of policing. Whatever their own microscopic perspective, these officers were the *State* for the people they policed. The street people, themselves, have had less opportunity to speak. Women, given the antipathy of the city force to the future prospect of female police, appear almost entirely as 'wives' or 'whores'.[4] Personal recollections of events some sixty or seventy years ago contain their own frailties.[5]

Secondary material, however, is sporadically available to support and intersperse this oral history. There are the official accounts, which reflect the views of those who spoke much of the thin blue line but saw little of its daily drudgery. More important are the rank-and-file accounts. In their occasional journal, the *Bull's Eye*, the remnants of the Police Union, smashed by the Police Strike of 1919,[6] offered a rare glimpse of city policing by police who were also committed trade unionists. Supporting these views are the mock-humorous, subversive doggerel and illustrations which crept into the official journals—the only way that serving officers could voice their discontent in public.

The Liverpool City Police has been of critical importance in the history of policing in the UK. It was the first major police institution to be developed in mainland England outside London. For a more than a century, it was the largest—and the most expensive—force outside the metropolis. Its chief officers figure prominently in the constitutional histories. The City Police pioneered changes in style—from 'Gladstone's police shield' to the mobile (bicycle) radio. It was also a force that was bitterly and violently involved in industrial conflicts, such as the Transport Workers' Strike of 1911. On several occasions it laid heavily into the city's minority ethnic groups—the 1919 race riots in the city were a foretaste of the 1981 Toxteth troubles. It was regularly called on by the Home Office to break strikes outside the Merseyside precincts, from Welsh miners to Burnley cotton-mill operatives.[7] It was also a force that straddled the sectarian divide of Orange Order and Hibernian marches; the Commission of Inquiry into Police Conduct following the Toxteth riots of 1909 was the high point of its involvement in Belfast-style disturbances.[8] Critically, Liverpool was one of two major sites of an especially bitter struggle, the Police Strike of 1919. In itself and in its aftermath, this was both a catastrophe and a watershed for British policing. That strike set the stage for some of the experiences documented in this book.

The officers whose memories are presented here were policing a city in dramatic decline from the days when it had lorded over Britain's mercantile empire. It was predominantly a lower-class city. As one survey noted in the early 1930s,[9] roughly one-third of its inhabitants had lived—that euphemism for surviving—below the contemporary poverty line (Seebohm Rowntree's 'human needs' scale) for most of the previous decade. Unlike the Northern industrial capitals of Manchester and Leeds, Liverpool lacked a manufacturing base. The predominance of casual work (over half the working population are recorded as working in shipping, on the docks, or in related transportation[10]) ensured a classic lumpen proletariat, low-skilled and outside the disciplines of industry and the predictable security of a weekly wage packet.[11] Social amenities were at a similar level. Some families were still in cellar accommodation in the early 1930s. Up to a third of the inner city dwellers were concentrated at more than two persons per room, and central-city wards had the second highest population density in the country.[12] In such areas, public houses were scattered every fifty yards or so.[13] Consequently—apart from the period of the General Strike—policing the city invariably meant policing the lower-class streets. The police cordon sanitaire drawn around the disreputable slums ('rookeries') of Victorian Liverpool in the mid-nineteenth century, when Charles Dickens had spent a week as a voyeur in the temporary uniform of a Liverpool police inspector, had now become patterned, incursive, patrolling of the lower-class city. *On the Mersey Beat* centres on this class-control relationship—beat policing as the social control of the Liverpool lower class.

As its central model, however, it takes a form of control of both police and of policed—that of the Panopticon.[14] The term derives from Jeremy Bentham's design for the new model prison in the late eighteenth century. This was intended as a revolutionary break from traditional practices of punishment by altering the inner person, the conscience of the prisoner. Moral reform was to be obtained by several devices: segregation—the inmate was to be separated from other prisoners and from outside influences; total observation—no deviant relapse could occur unseen; an impersonal and incorruptible, rule-bound authority structure; and timekeeping—the prisoner was to live a day tightly regulated by the clock.

This vision of the new prison influenced the stampede to build prison buildings in the nineteenth century—from Strangeways to Liverpool's Walton Gaol. Some of its elements also affected a range of other institutions, from the workhouse to the New Police—control by surveillance, by the clock, and by impersonal authority. The Panopticon came to symbolize not just a form of prison architecture but also a new means of discipline and control of the urban lower class. In this text, that model is used to identify some of the experiences of being the constable, a controller as well as one of the controlled.

Chapter 1 focuses on twin themes—origins and families. Despite mythical ideas of local policing, these officers were selected like colonial levies to impose somebody else's social order on the lower classes of the city. Secondly, policing was not just a job. It was also a way of life. In an entirely male occupation, wife and kids were stuck with the shift system of the beat patrol, and tarred with the brush of isolation imposed by the husband's occupation.

The beat was the centre of the humble constable's existence. Chapter 2 documents its rituals, its frustrations, and the various subterfuges that officers contrived to ease the burden. Police forces are highly disciplined organizations —in fixed rank structure, in uniforms, and in instructions—and (since 1919) lacking any effective rank-and-file representation. Internal order was maintained by a draconian discipline combining the carrots of a better wage than that of most working men and a unique pension scheme. Chapter 3 documents the disciplinary obsessions of between-the-wars police work and the way some constables fought back.

Concentrating on the internal problems of policing distracts attention from the primary police function—imposing moral puritanism on the street people. Chapter 4 portrays that reality and its sundry incidents. Street control was managed in various ways—from the 'bottle of beer' backhander to the ubiquitous authority of an array of omnibus street legislation, or the 'stick' and the fist.

Police work, of course, is not all beat work. In its surveillance of urban life and leisure, there were two specializations. Plain Clothes departments stamped on, regulated, and often connived at, bookmaking, gambling, and prostitution. CID selectively creamed off the rare 'real' offences of the city—from bank robberies to incest and suicide. Chapter 5 conveys the insiders' account of the complexities of such practices.

Finally Chapter 6 deals with the 'troubles'—the unusual but memorable incidents. They range from the 'domestics' (where the pressure-cooker of connubial relations could often blow up in the face of the beat officer) to the confrontations of General Strike and unemployment marches, to the curious differentiation between the city's black and Chinese people, and to the injury that could suddenly cut short the thirty-year endurance.

1

Strangers Policing Strangers

We like to take them straight from the plough and mould them to any shape
we please.

(Commissioner of the Metropolitan Police, 1914)

JIM HAWKINS ended his career at the age of eighty-six, as a turnkey at Spandau.
A country lad from Cheshire, he had joined the Liverpool City Police in early 1914
as an escape from the drudgery and poverty of Edwardian farm work.[1] Becoming a
police constable was an act of desperation, not a career move: it was a way out, a
release from an endless prospect of agricultural toil.

His police service was to be disrupted immediately. Answering the patriotic
call of 'King and Country' at the outbreak of war, he joined the colours. After
experiencing mustard gas at Ypres and all the privations of the foot-soldier in
World War I, like many others of his ilk, he found himself jobless in 1919. With
the convulsion of the Liverpool Police Strike and the summary dismissal of half of
that force, he seized the opportunity and rejoined. After years on the beat, by
1945, he had graduated to Station Sergeant at the Main Bridewell.[2] But with the
all-important pension in reach, he had had enough. The experiences of a humble
functionary in the Liverpool City Police—as recounted in the following pages, in
the testimonies of Jim and his colleagues—was painful, with few rewards.

For Jim, there was an alternative. The incarceration of army deserters in the
Main Bridewell required the presence of Redcaps (Military Police). Their gossip
offered him a new future, in the German Occupation Police. When that force
folded in 1952, there were few further options. Spandau employment was the
outcome. He talks of growing old in that grim, unique institution, custodians and
prisoners—Hess and von Speer—together.

Jim's work-life was exceptional only for its later variety. Policing the lower-
class city was not an especially pleasant or stimulating experience for either police
or policed. The accounts of the recipients of that policing represent one side of the
coin. In the language of the previous century this group would have been known as
the criminal or dangerous class. It was the residuum of the Victorian rookeries
—the army of unemployed, the street kids, the under-life of a declining merchant
city that through its main industry had spawned a variety of deviant pursuits. The
experience of being the 'scuffers'—the rank and file police who often saw
themselves between the hammer of their superiors and the anvil of a pragmatic
distrustful public, is the other side of the coin.

The beat officers who policed Liverpool streets in the 1920s and 1930s came from a range of backgrounds—most from the provinces and a few from local 'police families'. Their accounts of police life are unique. Our knowledge of that street policing in the inter-war years conventionally draws on only two sources. There are the rose-tinted official histories of policing, written from the top down. In such accounts, policing has all the substance of an annual Chief Constable's Report. Secondly, there are several histories of a relatively organized working class, accounts that have focused on the antagonism between police and public in the General Strike and during mass demonstrations of the unemployed. Few of these ex-officers, now in their late eighties and nineties, saw that larger picture. Their memories are of the day-to-day and relatively humdrum individual encounters of the streets. They are perhaps more meaningful, in attempting to understand the class relations of the police institution in Britain.

That day-to-day experience, till now unchronicled, ranged from the sheer slog of the 'updo', 'downdo' street patrol, the arbitrary and absolute discipline imposed by their superiors, the contact with the street people in betting, prostitution, and in the 'doing-nothing' pastime of the city's street corners, to the occasional esoteric incident (the horrendous domestic slaughter) or the race or anti-police riot. These accounts, in the words of their participants, support cynicism over popular memories of the supposed golden age of policing. They also provide a vivid picture of a unique occupation under stress.

ORIGINS

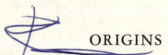

Conventional British police history contains much mythology. Nowhere do the orthodox accounts wax more lyrical than in the notion of preventive policing. The police officer is portrayed as a citizen-in-uniform. He polices *his* fellows by their consent, is elevated by them to a position of legal authority, and is representative of the community that he polices. This is convenient folklore, promoted from on high, seeking to demonstrate a direct affinity between the police and the policed.[3] Historically, as far as the city forces are concerned, policing was in fact normally 'policing strangers by strangers'.[4] Whatever its stated intentions, preventive policing came to amount to 'moving-on' the lower classes on the city streets.

From the first recruitment to the Metropolitan Police, when the new 'blue lobsters' came predominantly from Ireland, Scotland, and rural England,[5] policing was often conducted by officers who had little—from dialect to customs—in common with the people who were the primary focus of preventive police work, the denizens of the city slums. In many cases, this was a deliberate policy. It was implicit in the first justifications for the Metropolitan Police from the Commissioners, Rowan and Mayne. It was a policy continued by successive chief officers, in London and the provinces. It discouraged discretionary law enforcement in favour of the policed. It also made the new recruit directly subject to his superior's unchecked contrivances.

There were push and pull factors in the recruitment of strangers. Force policy promoted it. But especially in the between-war period, poverty, unemployment, and near-starvation wages in the provinces of the British Isles drove many young men to seek employment that offered a relatively high wage and, critically, a unique pension. In 1919 police pay had been well below the level of semi-skilled workers. In Liverpool, immediately after the war (with the prospective withdrawal of a war bonus), police pay had declined both in actual and relative size. Even ordinary labourers were said to despise police pay.[6]

Earnings of typical semi-skilled workers, Liverpool, 1919

Police constable	£2. 13s. 0d.
Scavenger	£3 7s. 6d.
Cotton packer	£3. 8s. 0d.
Dock gate man	£3. 8s. 0d.
Carter	£3. 12s. 0d.

Source: Desborough Committee on the Police Service, *Report*, 1919.

The post-Police Strike Desborough Committee introduced a commencing wage of £3. 10s., rising by ten yearly instalments to £4. 10s. In addition, allowances were made for critical items such as housing and clothing. The committee also confirmed retirement on half pay after thirty years. By 1924, police constables in England and Wales were receiving (including allowances) more than half as much again as the average male worker in industry.[7]

After 1919, nowhere else in state or private employment could a working man provide so well for his future. Consequently, city forces in the 1920s and 1930s were a shifting blend of Norfolk farm labourers, Irish crofters, Scots miners, and a mass of rootless men cast adrift by service in World War I.

There were some exceptions: occasional local recruits could be accepted, especially from the 'safe' stratum of clerks and the lower fringes of the middle class. A distinctive source of recruitment lay in the emerging inter-generational police families. Police fathers commonly begat policing sons.[8] But the principal impetus for joining the police was that of cash—not a Samuel Smiles self-improvement motive. It was a bleak prospect that pushed most new recruits towards the City Police.

POLICING AS ECONOMIC SALVATION

Particular industries, hit by recession and by government-induced pay-cuts, were a major source for early recruits.

M. B. I was in groceries and provisions working in South Wales. Things were very bad then. The closing of the mines. No one wanted anthracite coal so that it affected businesses in South Wales. I was at a dead end. I applied then for various police forces. Liverpool was the first to answer. I had been apprenticed and trained in groceries and provisions and things were so bad that that was nothing in that particular line that I could foresee for the future. So looking around for something else—and of course you get people saying, 'You're tall, lad. Go in the police.'

The lock-out of a million miners in 1921, at a time when 11 per cent of insured persons were already unemployed, was a major impetus for seeking police employment. One estimate placed miners' pay after that dispute at less than half the pre-war level.[9]

W. S. I come from Falkirk, a pit-village, Armadale Colliery. My two brothers were called up for the war. I was raised on a croft and my father was a ploughman—walked behind two horses. He earned a pound a week to keep four. I started in a coal-mine at thirteen and a half years—earned fifteen shillings to a pound a week. I was involved in the big coal-strike in 1921. The coal-miners were out for sixteen weeks—the dole wasn't out then. We had to walk from our village to Falkirk three times a week, six or seven miles each way. After the strike, I was getting ten shillings a week for six weeks.

When I went home, my mother said: 'Old Jim Taylor, the farmer, is ill—go along and see if he'll give you a job.' So I went along to Jimmy Taylor's farm. 'Thirty shillings a week and your food.' So I had to get up in the morning, to walk two miles for seven o'clock. Go out in the fields. And the maid would come out at ten with tea and toast and again at four—more tea and toast. I got two duck eggs, and walked home the two miles. And that was my life! One day, I had to walk six miles with the sheep to the market and when I got there, the farmer gave you two shillings! So all those things filled you up and made me come to be a policeman.

The push to escape from one's lot was compelling, especially for young pit-men. Tradition-ally, the services have always been an escape route.

D. A. I come from West Lothian. I joined in February 1926. I was a miner and I hated it. I was determined to get out of it. So I was going to join the police force or the navy and the police force came up first. I hated the mines beyond description. Money was very scarce in those days. I was on part-time in the mines and only bringing home nineteen shillings a week. My mum had to keep me and give me pocket money out of that. My father was a stonemason by trade. The weather was so bad that he was practically out of work all winter. It was in January, and we'd had heavy falls of snow.

I was walking down to an adjoining village to get my hair cut and I saw the local policeman walking down the road in front of me. A policeman in the country is a man of substance and you only talk to him with the greatest respect. I thought to myself if I'd have the courage to speak to him, and I hurried up and caught up with him. 'Morning Davy.' 'Good morning, son.' 'I was thinking of joining the police force.' 'How old are you, son?' 'Nineteen.' 'Just the right age. Do you know how to go about it?' 'No.' He dictated a letter there and then and I could quote it to this day. He wished me good luck. And I was in the police force within a fortnight. I wrote to four forces in Scotland and four in England and I got replies back within two days. But Liverpool was about eight days coming. My mother said, 'Liverpool's ignoring you, son.' But Liverpool sent an application form and I was on the job before you could wink.

Desperation for a decent wage, a relief from the soup-kitchen, sent many young miners to traditionally alien occupations.[10]

B. T. I had been working in the mines—the miners' strike of 1926 was on at that time. I was only nineteen and a half. I left school at thirteen and ten months and went to be an apprentice joiner for six months. I got fed up. I was only getting half a crown a week. I was going to get ten shillings if I went into the mines. This was in West Lothian, between Edinburgh and Glasgow. I didn't take much interest in the strike. I followed everyone else. We were on strike and that was that. I didn't know the rights and wrongs of it. There was nothing very right about the mines. Any holiday you took, you didn't get paid for it and there were no Bank Holidays except in the New Year—but you didn't get paid for it. I was a full-blown miner and I was getting ten shillings a day and we were on a four-day week. What they wanted to do at that time was reduce the wages by five shillings a week—it was quite a lot of money.

There's a happy-go-lucky spirit about miners. You're like a lot of schoolboys and when you leave your work, you go and play football, or meet your girlfriends. You never had much money to spend but you enjoyed yourselves. But it was really hard working in the mines. I only came down to Liverpool because I was part of a large family. There was no dole money then. When I look back, I don't know how we managed. There was only soup kitchens to get any sort of food from during the strike and that wasn't very much. There was about six or seven of us and it would take some money to feed us.

I chose the police because there was nothing else to choose. What could you choose? There was no other jobs. One or two of you would start talking about what you were going to do—about two or three of us thought we'd apply for the police. I wrote to London, Liverpool, Ayr, and it only happened that Liverpool was the first reply that I got. They were a bit short of men just a few years after the Police Strike, and they were building up with younger men. They'd sacked quite a few of the older men. Wanted some young blood.

Contrary to many contemporary assumptions, few saw policing as an avenue of self-improvement.[11]

J. B. I was born in Dover in 1905. Education was based on what you got in World

War I and therefore a bit primitive. You try and improve that side. When I was fifteen years and nine months, I joined the sea school at Gravesend which was entirely free. I joined a ship in 1921—went on tramps and oil tankers until 1925. I signed off a ship in Glasgow on Friday night—I had been writing to a girl in Liverpool—and was sworn in as a policeman in Liverpool on the Tuesday. You meet many different opinions at sea about different walks of life and I was a pretty raw person. Somebody said, 'You should join the police.' In those days, the police was a very respectable job. You were looked up to. It was a better job than the labouring class.

In such cases, financial necessity was often coupled with some personal ambition.

A. T. I was an apprentice armature winder at J. H. Holmes and Son in Newcastle-on-Tyne. I had a cousin who joined the Leeds Police. My mother was a widow and I was the only one who could earn anything. My wage then was eighteen shillings a week and I thought I could help her out. When I did get in, I was able to send her more home a week than I was getting when I was living with her. I joined the police because it was the most money offered, and it was a chance to improve myself. I couldn't see any future working in the factory and securing a good job there because to become a foreman then was just a matter of sticking out a long time and I couldn't see myself staying that long.

A. M. I come from Ipswich. I visited my brother who was living in Wigan and, like me, trying to get on in the world. I was a gardener's labourer. I tried the Met. and Liverpool. Soon after I tried for Liverpool, they said, 'Come on and take an examination.' Came in the February and joined. Doubled my take-home pay by joining the police force in 1924.

The opportunity to transfer particular military service skills, such as cavalry experience, was an additional incentive.

K. M. I was born in Liverpool, in Everton, and went on the training ship *Indefatigable* (my father was drowned at sea as a seaman) and then on troopships during the war, the *Derbyshire*. When the ship was about to be laid up after the war, the ship brought back the British prisoners from Belgium, and then the Australian troops to Australia. Then I didn't know what to do—so joined the army, the Lancers, in 1919. Served in the Middle East and in India. Got married while on leave from the army, so I thought I had better settle down here. The police had horses, so I joined up in 1926—went up to see the chief inspector and was taken down to the riding school. They let me go round with the horse and the mounted, and so I was accepted for the police.

Most recruits had obtained only basic skills in their previous occupation. Economic necessity, the major 'push' factor, was occasionally coupled with a touch of ambition. There was little evidence that policing had any intrinsic attractions.

OUTSIDERS

In the colonial police forces of imperial days, the imperial state might deliberately recruit outsiders without any possible affinity to the locals to police the territory.[12] *It was assumed that such recruits would be able to overawe the natives by their physical presence, a characteristic deemed more important than specific skills or intelligence. In nineteenth-century India, for example, many of the British police were 'Hindustanis or Purdistanis. They generally possess considerable physical strength, they are proverbially honest and faithful, but their brain-power is very limited.'*[13] *Similarly, in Ceylon, the early police 'came from a sturdy stock of fighting men . . . they . . . created a fearful impression on the Sinhalese'.*[14] *Imperial tradition seems to have been maintained in the home country in the post-war years.*

P. H. Most of the recruits came from Scotland in those days—no work up there for them. The Liverpool Police advertised in the Scots and Welsh papers for recruits. They got a good track of young Scotsmen and Welshmen to come and join the Liverpool Police. What a bunch of fellers—you couldn't understand a word they were saying, especially those from up north and from Newcastle. It was a deliberate policy—they preferred them from outside. I remember one bobby —from Orkney—he had picked someone up at the bottom of Water Street. When he was giving evidence in court, the magistrate said, 'Send for an interpreter.' Too many relations and sweethearts hanging around—some of the young Liverpool policemen used to get their girlfriends to walk around the beat with them.

An announcement made at a recent meeting of the Birmingham City Council that Birmingham born men are not eligible to join the local force is said to have created surprise in some quarters. 'The Policeman is always more effective when serving away from original surroundings,' said the Chief Constable when questioned. There might be one or two small places where the rule did not apply, but it was in force in all the large towns.

(Police Review, 1920)

M. B. I did apply in Newport but they wouldn't take local lads there. You had to come from elsewhere. It was a fairly deliberate policy. In smaller places like Newport, Cardiff, Swansea, they followed it rigorously. You didn't have much chance of getting into the Newport force unless you were a rugby player. The whole of the Newport front forwards were policemen.

Alien police of large physique were deemed preferable to other recruits with urban, streetwise skills and possible local affinities and sympathies.

POLICE FAMILIES AND THE LOCALS

Exceptions were made for police families, after careful selection. Son might follow father, often after war service.

S. H. I joined the Guards in 1912—all six footers. I was six foot one. I was in the first battle of Ypres in 1914. Two of my mates were killed on either side of me. I got sent back home and was on guard duty at Buckingham Palace and St James's Palace for the rest of the war. I was in civvies for a few months after the war and then I joined the Liverpool Police after the Police Strike. My father's a policeman in Colchester and my brothers were policemen.

G. E. I'm a Liverpool man born and bred. My father was a Lancashire man, and he joined the local police when he came out of the army as a regular soldier. He was a cavalry man at the battle of Tel-el-Kebir—that was the time that 14,000 cavalrymen chased 60,000 of the fuzzy-wuzzies. I joined in 1919 at the time of the Police Strike. I was eighteen—mind you I didn't look eighteen, more like thirty. I was very dark, had a very stiff beard.

Since 1848, when 20,000 clerks from the city's merchant houses had enlisted as Special Constables, that clerical class had always been a police reservoir.[15]

T. D. I was a clerk in an insurance office in Liverpool before the war. My father was a sergeant in the Lancashire Police. When the war came, I was already in the Territorials, and was immediately called up at the age of eighteen. I was badly wounded in the head at Arras. It resulted in me being blind for three months. Finished the war as a lieutenant and rejoined the insurance company. But I suffered headaches, so I was advised to work out of doors. The Police Strike was on, so I was taken on although half an inch short in height.

Police connections eased the escape from unemployment.

K. R. I joined in 1925 as a twenty-one-year-old. I was serving my apprenticeship at the Automatic Telephone (now Plesseys). I'd been in Liverpool since a baby. I left the council school, Praed Street, and served a seven-year apprenticeship to scientific instruments—a glorified brass-finisher. Then at the end of the war, whereas we had twenty apprentices at the workshop, they gradually went down and down because we had the population of the armed services selling expensive telephones for coppers. The trade went right down and I was one of the last three apprentices and I decided to go. My dad was a policeman, a sergeant in the Warrant Office, and he could see I was getting a bit concerned about the trade. With his help, I went along to the recruiting office and got on.

T. B. I joined in 1924, aged nineteen. When I left college, I went to work in a cotton-broker's. You kept your nose clean and you were there for ever. I was posted to the cash department. Then suddenly we got a fellow named Mitty—he went and invested in dollars and all different sorts of currency, and metals, and he got us in such a mess that the firm wrapped up, and also because of the growing Wall Street crisis. So I was made redundant. My father was in the army—Secretary of the Old Comrades Association and knew a lot of policemen there. So he fixed it up.

Some local young men managed to sneak in, despite the policy of 'safe' recruitment. But it was not a case of self-improvement.

H. P. I'm from Liverpool and joined in 1928. My father was a pilot on the docks. There was no attraction for joining the police. It was just the chance of work. You were lucky to get into the police, especially in your own city. It wasn't just the money. There was nothing else. When the kids left school, there was no work. I went to the Liverpool Institute and when I left there I went to work for a firm of average-adjusters and I was there for four years. But they were making people redundant, and I was let go.'

T. D. I was in the merchant navy, came from near Liverpool in the Wirral. I joined the police in 1928 (twenty-five years of age). I never wanted to be a policeman at all. I tried to get in the Customs but I was too old. When I left the Merchant Navy, there was 386,000 out of work in Liverpool and the parish officers were giving married people thirty-five bob a week to live on, half a crown for each child. Inside the parish office, it was just like one big snake, went round and round, and as you went round you got five bob as you passed the window.

J. V. I came from round here unlike many of them who were from Scotland and so on. We were the idle rich (!) and I was due to start as an electrician in Tithebarn Street—a man named Captain Angus who was a big nob in the Corporation. Due to start at nine on the Monday morning. So I go marching up and there was a notice in the window: 'To Let'. That was my start in life. Joined the police when I was twenty. My dad ran a pub and I was unemployed except that I would be called into the bar to help. But that wasn't secure and I wouldn't have a barman's job in any case—their wages were ten shillings a week (six in the morning till eleven at night).

But, in general, recruits had to be sanitized, either by external supply or by parental connections.

JOINING UP

Joining was a shot in the dark. Few had any realistic idea of the city to which they were committed or of the nature of police work.

A. T. I had a girlfriend in Newcastle-on-Tyne and she'd asked me for tea and I was having tea with her father and mother, cousins and aunts, and we had just finished. They said, 'Come on, tell us his fortune!' And I looked askance at them—I couldn't believe it. 'Fortune?' 'Yes, she's clever at the cards and with the tea-leaves.' She says to me, 'You're going on a journey—by rail.' 'Oh,' I thought, 'somebody's told her I've applied for the police.' 'You'll go in front of three men and you'll have a talk with them and one will become friendly.' 'There's nobody I know in Liverpool, 200 miles away.' Well, when I got to Everton Terrace, I was led into the office and—God's truth—there was a chief inspector, and an inspector, and a sergeant, facing me. I couldn't help but believe it—coincidence or not. Then they gave me an address to go to—Mrs and Mr Sherman and their son Tom.

To raw recruits, travel from native town or village was bewildering. They were not being selected for their street knowledge.

D. A. When I came down here, I had never been in England in my life before and the Edinburgh train stopped at Carlisle. There was a feller sitting there, sat down beside him. So we started talking. 'Where are you going?' 'Liverpool.' Said, 'So am I.' 'Where have you come from?' 'The Lake District.' We both found out that we were joining the Liverpool Police. So he said, 'I have a friend that's in the police there from my village—we'll go there.' Went by tram-car from Lime Street. We finished in Jubilee Drive where his friend was.

B. T. Never been outside Scotland before. I came down here and if I'd been rejected, I didn't know how I would get back. Because of the pit-strike the family couldn't afford to give me any money. Just got the train fare down. Fortunately enough, on the way down, I met another chap who was coming down to join the police and when we arrived at Exchange Station, we were met by one of his friends who had already joined. He took us in a tram-car to the school. This was about five o'clock at night and they sent us to lodgings in Aigburth.

SCABS OR SAVIOURS?

Many joined, in Liverpool as in London, in consequence of the mass vacancies created by the Police Strike of 1919. In Liverpool, half the establishment of some two thousand police had been summarily dismissed. The strength of the Liverpool Police reaction to the strikes was due, in part, to several immediate factors. Police pay locally had suffered more than in most other forces from pay cuts and stringencies (some constables were working a 78-hour week for the basic pay); rest-day rotas and payments had been clumsily handled; and promotion prospects (and consequent pay) appeared to have more to do with 'connections'—Freemasonry and family—than with any more objective criteria.[16] Precipitated by the employers' attempt to destroy the fledgling police union and to divide the state's bodyguards from the working-class movement, the strikers elicited little support from other trade unionists, whom they had ferociously belaboured in the Transport Strike eight years earlier.[17]

This unique affair had both short-term and long-term effects. Instant recruitment of ex-servicemen filled the gaps. Establishment organs—from the Inspector of Constabulary, Sir Leonard Dunning, the former Liverpool chief officer, to the Liverpool Weekly Courier *(which praised the youthfulness of the intake and their apparent quality)—were fulsome in their tributes to the new officers. But for years they would be resented by some of those who had kept their jobs—erstwhile colleagues being replaced by 'scabs'. The city for some years to come would be short of experienced officers, as the force developed an unbalanced age structure (the 1919 recruits grew old together). Untrained newcomers were posted straight to the streets.*

S. S. I joined in 1919 during the strike. I'd served four years in France, demobbed back to Cheshire and at a loose end. One evening, at the cinema with a girlfriend, and at half time the chap in front of me opened up the *Liverpool Echo* and there was a big page advert—RECRUITS WANTED—LIVERPOOL POLICE.

G. E. I was a seaman, going away to sea, and my boat docked at Liverpool, just when the Police Strike happened. When I come off the ship in the Canada Dock, instead of policemen on the gate, there were soldiers. We asked about it. They said 'The police are all on strike.' I'd been trooping and the troopships were getting tied up because they had taken all the troops back—we were taking American soldiers back—so I was looking for a job.

Went to the police station and joined the police. They were taking on any young feller that could pass the examination—physical. So I was one of the gang that joined to fill up the vacancies. They wanted a lot of young fellers. We got no training—never went through the police training school because they were that anxious to get men on the streets. We were all sworn in by the coroner. He was the magistrate. We had to take the oath and we were given an armlet and a baton, 'Get out on the street in pairs.' Just to let the public know the police were back.

They'd smashed every shop in London Road. You had to walk all the way up London Road—inch-thick, broken plate-glass windows and tailors' dummies strewn about the street. First job was out collecting the loads of suits and things that had been pinched from the London Road shops. As soon as they heard the police were coming—we went out in fours and fives—they were bringing all the stuff up from their houses and throwing it on the streets. We had to go and pick that stuff up. They'd realized then that the police were back in control.

In a tumult partly complicated by simultaneous bakery and tramway workers' strikes, the London Road area of the city had been sacked. With a ludicrous over-reaction, warships docked at the city's pierhead, with their heavy armament aimed landwards. Retribution was feared.[18] 'They were panicking in case they were caught with the stuff . . . they were melting down sacks and sacks of sugar and pouring it down the drains.'[19] There was no love lost between the strikers and those who had taken their jobs.

G. E. Some of the men sacked had put in a lot of service. Bob Tisseyman, the sergeant who led it (he finished up as a councillor) had put in twenty-four years—just one year off his pension [see Chapter 6]. He lost the lot. Some fellers were three months off their pension. There was much hostility from ex-policemen. I remember going up to the top of London Road and the pub on the corner, and one of the leaders, one of Tisseyman's bully boys were there. He'd come out of the pub and he was full of drink. He started calling me 'scab!' and this, that, and the other.

He was calling me all sorts of things and making a fool of me. So I just turned round—I was in plain clothes but with an armband—and grabbed him by the scruff of the neck and it was easy to take him. One or two civvies came and helped march him up to Prescot Street station. I charged him with being drunk and disorderly.

No Ex-Policemen Need Apply

I was called to the Colours August 4th, 1914, and served throughout the war in Egypt, Dardanelles, Sinai, Salonika, France, and Belgium. I was demobilised three months ago and joined the Liverpool City Police, serving a month on actual street duty, when the strike started. Admitted that we did wrong, but we wanted fair play. I went to my pre-war firm seeking employment, having a dozen references, military and civilian, but the answer that I got was 'No ex-Police wanted'. It has been the same everywhere I have been.

(Letter, *Liverpool Echo*, 1920)

Ex-P.S. Miles introduced the deputation, which he said represented the whole of the Police who struck work, and they asked Sir Archibald Salvidge to use his influence as leader of the City Council in the financial straits in which they now found themselves. He mentioned the fact that unemployment was rife, and it was difficult for them to get employment, and the fact that they were Police strikers prejudiced their case. The men were practically faced with the workhouse or something similar.   (*Police Review*, 1920)

Open air meeting to support police strikers "45 of the police on strike served in the Great War, but what did they do when they returned?" Man in crowd "They locked me up for being drunk and disorderly and I was fined a quid".   (*Liverpool Daily Post*, 1919)

P. E. I stopped in because my father said so—he was an old policeman. I was on nights and got chased off the beat by the strikers but next morning I went to the station and stopped in the station all night.

The remnant of the Police and Prison Officers' Union had its own comment on those who had taken their jobs:[20]

Night Watches

Cast: A POLICE CONSTABLE
     A NIGHT WATCHMAN

Scene: A street under repair. Watchman seated in box with coke fire.

Time: The witching hour.

Enter Constable

CONSTABLE. What of the night, watchman?

WATCHMAN. Darned cold. Would be a sight worse without this fire.

The policeman, who has just seen his sergeant leave his beat, proceeds to make himself comfortable

CONSTABLE. Your mate round the corner is very deaf. I had to shout to make him hear.

WATCHMAN. Um! he's very deaf.

CONSTABLE. Wouldn't do for our job. They're hot on those points.

WATCHMAN. Oh! that's strange. I didn't think they were so mighty particular in the police.

CONSTABLE. Not 'alf! If they rumble a chap's deaf, he's fired. Medically unfit. I've seen a lot go like that in my twelve years.

WATCHMAN (*by the way, a police striker*). That's darned queer. I remember a call for a strike in '19. We that heard it got fired. There was a lot of deaf 'uns that didn't hear. Have they all got the sack because . . . ?

Policeman gets up quickly, collects his impediments, and exits hurriedly

WATCHMAN [*musing*]. Funny! Twelve years service. *His* hearing seems all right, anyhow.

(*Bull's Eye {Journal of the Police and Prison Officers' Union}, 1921*)

S. S. After being sworn in and the medical, we had a class for a day at the school, and Chief Inspector Mackenzie took us through the Instruction Book and gave us a rudimentary idea of what was expected of us. Six of us were pushed out on patrol straight away wearing an armlet over our civilian suits. We were in the charge of an old inspector, past pension age, and he stopped to talk to someone—a striker. We walked on and some people smiled at us and some didn't and two young ladies said, 'They're Specials' and one of us said, 'There's nothing special about us.'

There were contrary views of the newcomers.

M. B. Most of the new recruits were demobbed from the army—used to uniform and properly disciplined. The city was rather lucky to have us.

K. R. Most of them were ex-army men that had come back from the war. The bulk of their training was to put them in uniform and to put them outside immediately—pick your duty up afterwards. Then they started doing a bit of training later on. They had to—there were some queer characters in the police force. They got all sort of fellows in after the strike—housebreakers and shopbreakers signed on to the force. They weeded a lot of them out. You had all sorts of people come back from the army—no questions asked—they wanted policemen. They joined the police force, something to do, gave them the opportunity to do a lot of things they shouldn't do—many of them finished up in prison. You got funny sorts of sergeants too—they wouldn't have been sergeants but they had to find somebody who knew a bit of police duty so they gave them a stick to carry around.

P.C. Batchelor of the Liverpool Police, and one of those who joined in 1919, was discovered collecting mementoes of his Police service one hour before his resignation took effect. Six months' imprisonment with hard labour is really too bad after all the kind things Sir Leonard Dunning has said about the better class of men who have joined since the Police Strike. It appears that this individual had been dealt with by the Chief Constable on various occasions for disciplinary offences. We would say again to Sir Leonard Dunning that as bad as the characters are which *he gives* to the Police strikers they are as angels compared with the records of those whom he so consistently eulogises.   (*Bull's Eye, 1922*)

George Thomas Parry, a young police constable, who joined the Liverpool City Force in January, was sentenced to six weeks' imprisonment on each of two charges of theft . . . Prisoner was first charged with having a brace and four bits belonging to Thomas Kenny, a joiner . . . Parry, who was arrested after attempting to sell the tools to a contractor, said that he had bought them from a workman some weeks previously. He was also charged with having been in unlawful possession of two hammers, a spanner, plane, drill, a lock and key, and other articles supposed to have been stolen. Some of these tools bore the initials of the London and North Western Railway Company, in whose employ prisoner had been before joining the police force.   (*Police Chronicle*, 1920)

The strike had a long-term effect on relations within the force and on promotion prospects.

P. S.   There was a notice went in the *Echo* at night: 'All policemen who wanted to remain in the police should report to Hatton Garden in the morning'. Some fellers were on holiday, so didn't report in, thinking they were alright. Got sacked, the lot of them. So we come along and we were taken on. Those who got taken on after the strike had a bad time. The ones who had stayed in took it out on us—made it bloody miserable for the like of us because we'd taken the jobs that their mates had been sacked from.

S. S.   Because of the strike, you had men who had fourteen or fifteen years in—and then the young recruits. If you were a young recruit and you wanted to know something, you would say: 'Constable, what would you do in such-and-such a case?' And the only answer you would get was: 'You've got a bloody Instruction Book—get on with it.' There was a friction there all the time—the strike made one man jealous of another. You'd get a section sergeant who favoured two or three of his section of seven or eight men, and the others just had to get on with it. Some people just couldn't do wrong. I've seen a time when I've been going round the beat—section sergeant would have all the other men round him on the beat telling them dirty yarns and I've been kept going round. In some cases, you would be friends, but they would be telling tales behind your back.

Nearly a thousand officers had been sacked as a result of the strike. Those ex-officers were evicted from police housing, lost their pension rights, were effectively debarred from further local employment, and had to struggle for several years to obtain the return of their own superannation contributions.[21] *The bitterness of the strike pervaded the force for the next decade. It also left enormous manpower gaps, to be filled by desperate measures. By the early 1920s, rather more specific training had been established.*

TRAINING

For candidates who had reached the force in rather more peaceful circumstances, there was a major hurdle. Selection was tough. It was a long way back home for the majority after rejection for mis-spelling, flat-feet or colour-blindness. Four-fifths of the hopefuls who presented themselves at the Inspector Mackenzie's desk failed to pass. In 1926, for example, 8,000 men applied to the Liverpool Police. Five hundred and fifty were called for interview. Only 168 passed.[22] For those who survived the preliminaries, rote learning from the Instruction Book hardly induced enthusiasm for the job.

T. B. Old Mac was in charge of the Training School in Shaw Street. He said to me, 'What do you do for a living?' 'I haven't got a job.' 'What do you know about the police?' 'I don't know anything about them—never even spoken to a policeman.' (Both my father and family being in barracks, we'd never met the police.) He said, 'Have a word with your father.' So I spoke to my father about it. Father said, 'Take it as a temporary job.' So I got a note from Old Mac to go up to the school—passed all the reading and writing (it was only children's stuff). But physical was different. I was five foot nine and a quarter, and the limit was five foot nine and a half. This sergeant said: 'That's hard luck—go on home and do some exercises, and get your mother to buy you some thick-soled shoes.' Which I did and that gave me an extra half inch. They thought that was pretty good exercise.

A. T. I went to the Dale Street bridewell. There was a chap in there with a gammy arm and I said, 'Where do you go to apply?' 'Get the 13 tram and get off at Everton Terrace—you'll find someone there.' I walked to Everton Terrace. Chief Inspector Mackenzie came in to see me. Constable just took my measurements. He looked to see if I had my Discharge Book. 'Very good.' You always got that whether you were good, bad, or indifferent. He said, 'Do you spell "especially"?' I said I spelt reasonable. 'Well, spell it.' I only put one 'l' in it—sent me to the doctor in the morning and to come back if everything was alright. Went into Everton Terrace on the Tuesday and there was a big billiard table—gathered round it were about twenty men. 'Stand on the end of the line.' The magistrate came in—and that was it.

Fear of rejection was real, for those who had nothing to return to.

D. A. I come down on the Saturday and stayed with a fellow from my own district who was a policeman in Liverpool. He took me to Everton Terrace—men mountains in size and I was only a country boy then. I thought to myself, 'You stand no chance whatsoever.' The chief inspector was a Scotsman from up by my home, Mackenzie. We had the medical exam and the CI called us all together and said: 'The following men whose names I call need not stay because the doctor won't pass them.' I listened very carefully and I thought, 'For some reason he has missed me.' 'I'll go over those names again.' Still wasn't on the list. 'Those whose names I haven't called, go upstairs to the education examination.' Dictation—moderate difficult words to spell, the arithmetic up to decimals, vulgar fractions, and that was that. After that they sent us to get a bit of lunch to wherever we could find it and to come back and we would get the result. 'I'm happy to tell you that you have all passed the examination and those that are required to go home to work their warning at their work can do so, we'll call them. Those that don't have to work their notice can stay, and they're on the police force from this minute.' So I said, 'I can stay, sir.' Out of that bunch of a hundred, they only took thirteen. Some were turned down for flat feet and that kind of thing. It wasn't a desperate examination. But they looked at every feature.

It was a careful selection in which the most obviously fitted did not always make the grade.

W. S. We went to Everton Terrace to be examined. They said 'Where do you work?' 'In the coal-mines.' They gave us a bit of an exam. You had to do all the different things to pass the examination—there were about twenty or thirty of us. I didn't have the education of some of the fellows—some of them were bank clerks. Six of us were taken on out of fifty. The fellow that I had come from Scotland with wasn't. They were refusing men for all sorts of defects, such as eyesight. 'Could you start now?' Shocked me. 'I'll have to go back and work a week's notice.'

K. R. You had to pass the examination to join so you had to be educated enough to read and write, have a good style, and also they'd test whether you were colour blind or not. They had a book and they'd open it up. 'What colour's that?' 'Green'—when it was blue. You couldn't understand big fellows getting confused over that. Asked me to spell 'scientific'. I was a scientific instrument maker so that was no problem. 'You've got small feet, haven't you?' Size seven. I was five foot ten but I was small-boned. 'You'll have to pull that chest of yours out a bit.' But the CI, knowing my dad, pulled one or two strings—he never said so, but he undoubtedly did because I was on the list for the next school.

> . . . being of an ambitious mind,
> I sought the first policeman I could find,
> He listened and made this observation,
> 'You'll get all you want at the nearest Police Station.'
> I went to the Yard with most hopeful intentions,
> Where an amiable Sergeant took my dimensions;
> Raving at me as he tested my sight,
> Till I could see neither black, nor yet white.
> The doctor then thoroughly tested my chest,
> And I went home so thankful I'd braved the test.
>
> But that was not all, tho' 'twas no use complaining,
> I had yet to do six weeks of hard training,
> Before I was privileged my young self to view
> All togged out in uniform blue.
> Still hopefully dreaming of things yet to be,
> I resolved then to 'swot' up and wait patiently.
> Oh! the things they told me I would have to swallow,
> If the life of a policeman I would venture to follow.

Reports and summonses up to date,
'Swedish' drill at a terrible rate.
Marching, saluting and volumes of law,
Plenty to learn ere my training was o'er.

(*Police Review*, 1923)

Literacy, eyesight, and general physique were the combination of factors assessed. No one was asked about local knowledge.

CHANGING IDENTITIES: INTO POLICE SCHOOL

Police training, despite attention to rote learning and physical training, has always been more about socialization, a transformation of identities, than about the acquisition of specific skills.[23] *In colonial policing, where the 'strangers policing strangers' policy had achieved some success, public school ethic combined with imperial policy to insulate the new police from the locals, this practice had been brought to near perfection in the mandated territories of the Middle East.*

The position of the Palestinian policeman . . . may be likened to that of a boy learning to play cricket. First of all, he needs a good wicket to bat on. Confidence has to be established in the young player. He should not be put into bat on a bad and bumpy wicket. The good wicket the government must provide. The bowling must not be too difficult to start with and the lad should be given pads and gloves for his protection. The Palestinian policeman wants housing. He must have a good coach. This is essential. It is easier to train the young player to hold a straight bat than later in his career to get him out of bad style or habits. The Commandant is the coach. The team should not be comprised entirely of young players. The young players need some support. There must be a few more seasoned players in the side. Someone must go in first and break the bowling. The British police will do this. Someone who can go in and hit hard if necessary when runs are wanted. The troops can do this. Information about the other side is wanted so that the field can be set to stop them scoring. The C.I.D. should do this . . . There must be a good umpire who will give a reasonably correct and in any case prompt decision (the magistrate). A side will play all the better if they get encouragement and support from the public. So the young player is gradually trained and he may eventually become a Hobbs.[24]

The ritual of formal learning had to be undergone. But what was critical was the rite of passage in which an identity was transformed.

S. S. First day was not a very good day. Me and another recruit were detailed to collect all the spittoons that surrounded the parade room at Hatton Garden and wash them out. They gave us a couple of buckets each. Other chap said, 'Let's resign!' They issued us with a pair of police trousers and blue jerseys and told us to buy a pair of boots. We wore them all the time we were there. Inside the school—talk about Charles Dickens—there were narrow staircases and old-fashioned windows looking down on Shaw Street. It was a real reform-type school. We used to drill there and get alleged lessons. The doctor used to come and he'd go

'Rrr . . .' and then bang out again. He didn't want any part of it. The other staff just used to read straight out of the Instruction Book—it was dreadful, no effort to imbibe you with anything, and Saturdays you had to scrub out, and mop, and clean windows, polish the brass fittings, and clean everything. There for about a month. Given a vague outline of what you had to do and problems of working your beat and 'No Smoking' and so on.

M. B. We had two months at the training school. Inspector Crosby was the main tutor. My job there was principally scrubbing floors and that sort of things and when you came out you were an alleged policeman. We were taught first aid, police procedure, a little arithmetic, a bit of geography, and reading and that sort of thing. Went briefly through the Police Instruction Book from A to Z, page after page, just touching lightly on everything. No physical teaching such as fighting or wrestling. A little bit of marching. Swedish drill—up-and-down and in-and-out. Physical drill up and down the yard. The sergeant in charge (an ex-army sergeant, of course) snarled at you. In the second month, we were only at Everton Terrace in the morning, and on the beat with an experienced officer for three hours at night.

THE BALLAD OF BULLSNITCH
('Bullsnitch' is the gym
Instructor of a certain Police School)

Sing a song of Bullsnitch
'Swinging arms-begin;
A change is coming o'er the class,
The fat man's grown thin.

The thin man's grown thinner,
'Swinging arms-begin',
If it wasn't for his dinner
He'd pack the damn job in.

The thinnest man is going—where?
'Swinging arms-begin',
A moment since he stood just there,
A humanised hair-pin.

A draught has caught him. He has gone.
'Swinging arms-begin;
The rest of us must 'soldier on'
Until we're just as thin.

And when our backs and breast bones meet,
'Swinging arms-begin',
Perhaps they'll turn us on the beat,
A helmet, bones, and skin.

(*Police Review*, 1932)

GRADUATION

Graduation involved a formal examination in which aspiring constables were graded into three classes, affecting future promotion prospects.

K. R. There was quite a stiff examination at the end. Examination consisted of first four rules—money, avoirdupois, weights, linear measure, simple and decimal fractions, simple interest and mensuration, reading, writing, dictation, composition, geography, and general knowledge. You had to pass an examination in first aid. That was rather funny because Sergeant Culshaw was the instructor and Dr Pearce was the examiner. We used to line up outside the door. We knew how the questions went. If a chap coming out told what the questions were, he'd know what the next question would be—used to pass it on. Your question might be bandages or fractures and you would pass it on as you went out and you'd make sure you got through. We had three grades. First grade was very good and you were half way through the education examination for Sergeant, second was considered reasonably good, and third grade, you just scratched it. I got second grade and sat again a few months later, and got second grade again. I didn't bother again. If you didn't get a third grade, you didn't get on the job.

Physical and mental rituals were the surface manifestation of a socialization process that would reach its goal with the posting to an appropriate beat (determined by demeanour and size—physique was to match the level of expected resistance). The young—mostly alien—civilian recruits had been metamorphosed into constables of the Liverpool City Police.

BEAT ASSIGNMENT

M. B. At the end of the period, we were allocated to divisions and the tallest (and if anything the smartest) went to A Division [city centre] and then you had the other divisions coming down, the shorter men ending up in the outside divisions. A lot depended on your appearance, as with the Guards regiments. As you got smaller, they drafted you further out. They looked to the rough fellows like the miners to get jobs in tough divisions like Rose Hill—those were just the boys for the drunks and so on. Then there was another lot who were reasonably spoken and they were transferred to the nice districts. They hadn't much sympathy on where they placed you. When we started, we did a month of nights. Others had the soft type—traffic and things like that—you were all supposed to get a spell of it but you didn't.

> . . . my studies at last were completed.
> By the Chief's stern voice I was soon after greeted.
> Smiling a little, he said 'Jenkins, you may
> If lucky a Superintendent be some day.'
> Then smiling again with an air of precision,

He remarked 'Let me see, you're for O Division.'
Being naturally anxious, and most keen on knowing,
I inquired to what sort of place I was going?
'The Borough' said one 'and now to be sure,
That's where they kill the Police by the score;
Why, only last Tu'sday, they 'grained' poor old Griffin,
But cheer up, young fellow, they may not 'do you in'.
Feeling too full for words, I came to the Station
Which promised a thirty-years situation.
The Sub. fixed me with a cruel icy glare,
As if I had no right to be there.

Elated with pride, I at last got a beat.
Now a *uniformed Policeman*, the thought was so sweet,
With nothing to do, and plenty to see;
It was a red-letter day for me.
Looking upwards, I paused in my meditation—
Raining like fury. My cape at the station.
Well, I did what I thought was the best thing to do.
In a doorway I stood as the storm fiercer grew.
Up came the Sergeant, as wild as a bear,
Said 'What do you think you're doing there?
Remember, young man, you're not pushing the plough;
Just wake yourself up, *you're a Constable now!*'
Wretchedly wet I went on again,
Hoping the Sergeant got washed down the drain.

(*Police Review*, 1923)

With a little assistance from his older colleagues and from his superiors, the young constable was deemed fit to bat for his side against the hostile elements of the city.

REGULATING THE HOUSEHOLD

Unfortunately, however, to the City Police commanders the creature comforts of spouse and home—a sign of stability—were required before he could be deemed to have fully graduated, to be trusted.

With a (relatively) secure job and, critically, a guaranteed pension, policemen were a good prospect for a young woman wishing to guarantee her own economic future. But, as they settled into the city, police regulations—written and unwritten—impinged on every aspect of their domestic life. Police work was a total environment.

A Good Catch?

T. D. For a Liverpool woman to marry a policeman was a good catch because of the wage. All the ladies were most respectful to the police people. You were a step above other people so far as the money was concerned. When you first started, there were all sorts of girls looking for a police officer to put them in the family way. It was the best of the working-man's wages in those days because the average individual only got £1 3s. whereas a police officer got £3 10s. and marriage allowance was another 14s. on too. So it was a good thing from their point of view.

Women were seen by a male establishment as a problem for other reasons.[25] (*Ironically, the British police only acknowledged the need for women employees—apart from bridewell matrons—when Scotland Yard discovered typewriters in the 1890's.*)

H. P. We were well warned about women the day we came into the force. We had to avoid them. The trouble was, in a few cases, you got girls making certain allegations. Once the allegation was made, your name was mud. The police force was such that you never lived it down. You wouldn't get into an ambulance or get into a police van with a woman unless you had another witness with you. You daren't be with a woman alone—the allegations that might be made. Lots of allegations—I've had allegations made against me but absolutely unfounded.

A police force that opposed the idea of women police until the 1940s constantly, and deservedly, got its knickers in a twist over the arrest of females.

Vetting the Wife

Getting married was a little like becoming a Tory MP: your prospective partner had to be deemed suitable as well. She was taken on as an unpaid member of the Constabulary. Some of her problems were acknowledged. Police Chronicle offered cooking recipes in its weekly 'Mrs Policeman's Corner', together with an 'Uncle Bob's' column for the children. The Daily Worker had its own version—including one 1930 letter from a Liverpool child, complaining of being ordered off the streets by a policemen.

D. A. You had to make a report that you applied for permission to marry. It stated how long you had known her, her age, name, address, father's occupation, and that went to CID and then came back vetted—in case you were mixed up with the wrong type. Immediately I was married, I had to take my marriage licence along and that was enough for them. Fortunately, she had been a nurse and that was sufficient for them. I know of a feller. He was from B Division, Scotland Road. He got a barrow girl in trouble and he married her and the Chief Constable's Orders sent him right from Scotland Road to Garston. No buses and very difficult getting from one place to another. So they penalized him by sending him as far away as they could, hoping he would resign.

A. T. I got married when I was on leave—on a Saturday—and started my leave that day, and we went away on our honeymoon. When I returned I said to myself, 'This is the first chance I'll have to tell them I got married.' So I told the sergeant and he said, 'You'll be in trouble for not reporting that you got married.' I said, 'I couldn't tell you I was married because I was a single man.' I was told down on duty to see the superintendent. He says, 'What's this? You got married and said nothing about it.' I said, 'I reported I was married when I got back off leave. I wasn't married till the first day of my leave.' He said, 'How did your wedding go?' I said, 'Very well.' He said, 'Well, don't do it again,' and let me go, which I thought was very good of him because I was dead scared of the superintendent. They were normally worried about the wife's background—fortunately none of her people had been in trouble or likely to get into trouble. The wife had to be friendly with all the neighbours but at the same time careful as to who she was friendly with. We were advised not to hob-nob—never knew when you might be called to intervene as a police officer.

In some forces, celibacy was the rule for the first few years of service life, a monasticism that led to major complaints. Women were a distraction from police duties, and could hinder the husband's urban mobility. Her non-police affiliations were a problem and besides, she might not readily accept the role as an unpaid adjunct to the police service. In county forces, however, the wife acted as the station-keeper, without recompense, in the absence of her husband.[26]

LETTERS TO THE EDITOR

'I have been engaged to a P.C. for twelve months. It has always been my fiancé's ambition to be a policeman and last year he was appointed to a force in the South of England. I have a good job as a 'companion help' to a lady in the Midlands. Our meetings in the last year have had to be brief and far between and the Police Authorities will have it go on for three years more. Imagine a more indignant and unnecessarily cruel situation. Surely, if the marriage ban is necessary, two years is enough. Why must I spend four of the best years of my life looking after somebody else when I might be looking after my husband's needs. . . ?'

'Marking Time'

We have borne the trial for a year and it seems like ten. Our savings are being crippled by our efforts to see one another just once a month for a few hours, and the joy of these scanty visits is marred by the thought of the pending farewell. After each visit, we are embittered at the way our young lives are being controlled and wasted . . . I cannot afford to give up my job until I can marry.   'Buried Alive'

. . . In London, the term is now four years and in my own Force, it is five years, or on reaching age 30 whichever is the soonest. As for myself, I face the prospect of being engaged for five and a half years! I have 300 miles to travel to visit my fiancée. The fact that single quarters are truly a bachelor's existence does not mitigate the desire for a home of one's own. We have no wireless installed and we are obliged to do all our own housework. This may be good training but 'spring cleaning' isn't much to look forward to after 8 hours of duty. What enthusiasm has the girl of today for her young man to join the police force, when she finds that if he does so, she has five years to wait and during that five years she must be content to see him only when the exigencies of the Service permit? . . .

'Disillusioned at 23'

But some officers differed:

I am thankful that I had those [unmarried] years of experience behind me before I did look for a partner. The difference between the civilian and the policeman is so marked and the changeover so slow in effect that the novelty and glamour experienced by the recruit have been the causes of many a young man making a wrong decision . . . This is how I see it happening: The young man joins the police. His parents, brothers and sisters are all intrigued by the idea. He feels quite bucked up with the prospect of a settled life, and he simply cannot understand why he is not allowed to marry his young lady . . . Assuming that he is allowed to marry at this time, what next? The grim realities of the job bring a decided coolness. Different shifts and duties become irksome and interfere with his social life, and Police affairs are so often dragged up when he is in her company, that he is forced to consider himself more or less a social outcast. More importantly still to his wife is the almost hostile attitude of the neighbours and the ever-present fear of a report of their domestic affairs being made to her husband's superiors, with the inevitable semi-public enquiry.   (*Police Review*, 1939)

The urban police between the wars were confused about the marital relationship. Marriage was a sign of stability but it was also an impediment to divisional movement. The wife was necessary to service the constable on shift in inclement weather. However, she was perceived as a potential fifth column—able by her own relationships to undermine the deliberate isolation of the constable. The contradictions were not easily overcome. The Police Review *correspondence was one of very few devices by which the wife—the appendage of a male force—could articulate her own severe grievances and then only under the cloak of anonymity.*

D. A. A policeman's wife was not allowed to work in those days. She was looked on as the backbone of the force. She kept her husband happy and contented and the police force looked upon it with favour the sooner you got married. If you were unmarried, you were seen as unresponsible. Unpaid worker for the force. I think that the police force really recognized that because all the time the wife was pensionable—not the same as the man but always entitled to a pension. Your career in the police force was very bleak if you had domestic trouble. If you fell out with your wife that would be fatal. If you were divorced, and your wife was to blame for it, that could be the end of your career. It showed that you were unreliable. You had to think twice about your ideas for promotion.

Safe House

Domestic life was monitored in various ways. Housing allocation had several motives. Police travel time added to preventive patrol, so some areas were prohibited. On the other hand corner houses acted as mini-police stations.

B. T. Even if you got new lodgings, they had to send a police sergeant round to examine them, see if they were fit. They were interested in the type of people that you were going to live with. Wasn't much good them finding that you were going to lodge with a man who was in and out of Walton Gaol every five minutes. If your in-laws kept a shop, you had to get out. You wouldn't be allowed to stay there. That was one of the regulations. You couldn't live on business premises. So if you lived over a shop, you'd have to find digs in case you showed favouritism. There was plenty of people prepared to take you as lodgers because there was a lot of poverty then. I was out in Garston (they couldn't get me any further) and I had to go into digs (thirty bob a week). New houses were being put up off St Mary's Road and a Welsh widow lived there. It was reeking with new paint and it was only after the penny dropped that you realized that you had turfed the poor soul out of the main bedroom. She was probably stuck in the box-room.

> 'You'd better find lodgings,' he murmured, 'and then,
> In the morning be here at quarter past ten.'
> I discovered some 'digs' on a moderate scale.
> When I think of these lodgings, description would fail.
> Devouring at meals things a dog would not eat,
> Was not to my mind a Band of Hope treat;
> What with mutton like leather, and coffee like rain,
> And soup that would substitute furniture stain:

(Police Review, 1923)

M. B. There was always a possibility that you might be told to move house. I've known bobbies been told to get out of their house and move elsewhere because of who their neighbours were. Police could step in because they paid us rent allowance—12s. 3d. You couldn't buy much for that and you couldn't spare much over with two kids. If you lived on one side of the city, you often found yourself posted to the other side because that was extra policing. Going back and forth you had to wear uniform, you weren't allowed to change into civvies. During that time, they've got policemen crossing the whole of the time. You picked up many a job while off duty, going to and from work. You could have accommodation in your own division but you wouldn't be allowed to be on the beat around there—to stop you from going home or idling your time.

A. M. Policemen were given Corporation housing to make sure that they got housing. When I got my Corporation house, another policeman said, 'Is it a corner house?' 'Yes.' 'They always give policemen corner houses—makes a police station on every corner.' After I'd been there a week or so, I found a gang of young fellers—eighteen to twenty—sitting on the wall of our corner house and when I warned them, they all went away and never came back again.

Housing allocation and rent allowance have always been a major area of contention within the police institution. Only within the last decade has the junior officer won the right to live where he or she thinks fit—and even then at the Chief Constable's discretion. In some ways, police officers had the same status in rented accommodation as that of a tied agricultural labourer—lose the job and (as the police strikers found) lose the house.[26]

THE FAMILY ON SHIFT

Family hours were timetabled according to the demands of the beat, children's play stilled by the demands of the bobby's sleep.

P. P. Night duty is a terrible duty. (*Wife*: 'That twenty-five years he was in the police was the worst time of my life. Night duty was terrible—husband couldn't sleep and if anybody came to the door, my voice would go as low as a whisper and their voices would go higher and he'd get an hour in bed and down he'd come again'.) The least little noise woke me up. In consequence, you'd go round the beat half dead. Night duty is a terrible duty. I've known it to be perhaps three weeks before I've seen my kids, when you had to do extra duties. There was no way of contacting your wife when you should have been home at midnight after evening duty [in CID] to say why you weren't home. One night it was about 4 a.m. when I came home what with the arrests and the paperwork.

H. P. It was a hard job for a woman. My opinion that the woman had the worst part of the job. You went on all duties and when you left home, she never knew the time you would be coming home again. You could make an arrest. You could be in hospital, traffic accidents, anything. If they happened towards the end of the watch, you didn't pass it over. You had to attend to them, and if they were serious, you had to carry on making reports. If you made an arrest just before going off duty, you'd have to wait and see the thing through—may have to put a Report in for the Prosecution's Department for first thing next morning and your wife was at home waiting. She didn't know where you were, what you were doing, and they didn't encourage wives to ring up all the time to find out. Very few of us had telephones anyhow. And the woman was left there with perhaps a young family. She couldn't act like a normal woman. She was trying to be normal but had to live a policeman's life. She had to put up with all that shift duty and all that went with it. Your uniform all had to be dried and looked after. You had to get to bed while she was doing it—creeping round the house all day in case she'd wake you up (that's if you could sleep) if you were on nights.

T. B. It was very difficult working shifts because half the time the children were crawling around—'Don't make a sound'—when I was asleep, on nights. After-noon duties were out. There was only mornings when you were with the children and then you were that damn tired, getting up at 4.40 a.m.—so you had to go out of your way to be with the kids.

In a possession case at Romfort County Court, the applicant was a Metropolitan Police Officer. It was stated that he was unable to get his proper sleep after night duty in consequence of the behaviour of other occupants of the house. The annoyance consisted of jumping up and down the stairs, chopping firewood, and banging overhead while the officer was trying to sleep during the daytime. Judge Crawford said it was intolerable that a man who had been on night duty should be annoyed in this way. It was most essential that Policemen should be mentally and physically fit.   (*Police Review*, 1922)

The children were affected in other ways.

M. B. When the children got into trouble with other children (if you had someone come round complaining about your child—they'd thrown a ball in the garden or something like that), if you stuck up for your kids, it was immediately: 'I'm going to report you', and up they'd go to the station and report you over this silly business. They wouldn't do it to a baker or a grocer but, because you were a policeman, they'd report you.[27]

LETTERS FROM POLICE WIVES

Dear Mr. Editor . . . a four weeks of night duty is as trying for the Policeman's wife as for himself. Her household tasks must be performed as silently as possible; bedrooms must be 'turned out' at inconvenient hours and children home to their meals from school have to be kept quiet for fear of disturbing the slumbers of the weary representative of Law and Order . . . while the husband is out all night, the wife must assume the role of protector of her household. The net result of this is, with certain types of women, a frayed temper, of which the husband—already sorely tasked by the inconveniences of night duty—is the victim.

they are away from us so much. The life of policeman's wife is not a happy one because she never feels free to go out like other wives.

When a man is engaged as a Police Officer do the conditions of service state 'When he takes unto himself a wife that she as well as her husband becomes a servant of the Police Authority'? It is generally understood that a wife's duty lies in looking after the welfare of her husband not the interests of her employers, but it appears to be the latter.

Dinners at 2.30 p.m., teas at 6.30 p.m., suppers at 10.30 p.m., and the like all tend to cause the guid wife extra labour and a tying to household duties that no woman in any other walk of life realises. Of course, where there is only Mr. and Mrs. Policeman, the guid wife may go hungry for two hours and await the arrival of her spouse, thereby making the meal one affair, but if there happen to be hungry children coming in from school at 12.30 p.m. and 4.30 p.m. the guid wife must needs make two separate meals. Consequently, her life is one round of meal times . . . therefore one finds Mrs. Policeman getting nervy, run-down, and depressed periodically.   (*Police Chronicle*, 1934)

HOLIDAYS

Family holidays, too, were determined according to organizational whim—and sometimes through personal loyalties.

B. T. Fourteen days a year, and if you wanted a week at Christmas, and there were six of you wanted it, you had to toss for it. Say a sergeant had six men in his section, he'd only let one man off for Christmas or he might let two. And if you put down for August 8th, sergeant would say, 'I'm sorry but I've put Tom down for that.' They'd put a list for holidays, but that was only a shot in the dark. I remember we were going to Pontin's taking our family—young children. I said to my wife, 'I'm going to put down for those dates on the off-chance.' We were due to go on the Saturday and the Wednesday before that I didn't know if I was getting my leave or not. Once went to the Isle of Man—could get privileged tickets. But within two days, there was a telegram from the CC: 'Return immediately'. I lost my holidays for that period and you got no replacement.'

W. R. When I was a rookie, you had to go to the back of the queue, letting the married men and their children get away first. Later on, I always took mine early because I couldn't bother fighting to get the other holidays. A few of the blue-eyed boys managed the summer time—would be pally with the sergeant, so they would get preference. No such things as Christmas breaks—didn't have Christmas dinner in years. Same with Daylight Saving—you might be fortunate and miss an hour, or unlucky and have an hour added without pay.

Holidays were always a bone of contention. One of the causes of the Police Strike in Liverpool had been the refusal of the City Watch Committee to honour completely the Police Forces Rest Day Act, 1910, which gave the constable one day off in seven.[29] *The nature of police work—especially the inversion of working hours as compared with other occupations —requires that many officers be on duty when other people are at play. The 'unsocial' timing of rest-days and holidays, and the priorities of night beat work, added to the policy of isolating the constable from the public. It led to an inward-looking force, so that police officers mainly sought comradeship amongst others wearing uniform.*

MATES

Much sociological literature on British policing in the present day emphasizes the importance of the occupational or 'canteen' culture—the norms and values of a relatively stressful occupation in which immediate peers are the sources of comradeship, support, and social life.[30] *However, police life in the city between the wars was not quite so simple. You were explicitly sundered from socializing with civilians. But paradoxically, there was no necessary alternative venue within the police ranks. Friendships were determined by the imperatives of the beat. Leisure, too, was regulated. Some comradeship was possible—but only tenuously.*

The only real social life available was with one's peers: housing allocation, civilian suspicion of police, and the shift system, determined the constable's social circle. For some, social isolation was ameliorated by a council-housing allocation that designated certain streets as police housing, and by contact with the marginal stratum of the lower middle class.

W. P. Round here was a real police community. It was the kind of area that was seen as 'approved'. They had good police organizations for police dances and that. Would be held in stations. At Prescot Street where I was, there was a police dance every fortnight in the parade room, which made a lovely dance-room. You mixed amongst a decent set of people. Usually the shopkeepers and that would come and join the police dances.

Even social life might require a uniform.

D. A.   You weren't allowed to drink in your division. If you wanted a drink—an unwritten law—you had to have a regulation dress outside duty—a blue suit and a bowler hat. I never was one for going drinking. But when I did go, I went up to the Bath Hotel and you usually met a clique there of police officers. Some policemen off duty used to 'live' in the Fairfield Police Club. But you always had the idea that the bosses were watching. It was all right for the bosses to drink but not the policemen. You had to choose who you drank with. You weren't allowed to be friendly with people such as licensees. Usually mixed just with the relations—had a brother-in-law, a detective sergeant. Used to play cards at each other's houses.

G. E.   You'd have to belong to a good club to get a game of snooker. I belonged to Sefton Park Conservative Club. You weren't allowed to belong to a Labour Club or anything like that, so you had to keep it quiet. I joined the Conservative Club in 1919 in the name of Gee—my initials, G.E.E. You weren't allowed to belong to a political club. I was very fond of bowls and I couldn't join the Brookhouse Bowling Club because it was on licensed premises and you were barred—so that I joined under the same name—Mr Gee.

But for many officers, colleague relationships had to be tenuous.

A. T.   I knew no one. I got to know this policeman, Jack Drummond, from Dundee—but we were all on different shifts. You couldn't make friends with anyone for the simple reason that you were on nights. You were on ten to six. The man you might know would be on mornings, six to two, and the next friend would be on two to ten.

A. M.   It was an isolated work-life. But there was a good camaraderie amongst the men—mixed with one or two of them off duty. But that again was handicapped. I picked up with one of the acting sergeants. We spent the same duty for twelve months as friends—went out together. But very soon he got shifted to another division and from then on we were just nodding acquaintances. It was most difficult to keep friends.

Social ostracism bore most heavily on the woman.

P. P.   My wife had rather a right time here. She came to Liverpool with me and she didn't know anyone. For a while, you couldn't get a house and we were in rooms. I think a policeman's wife had a pretty rough time. She was more or less tied to the house. (*Wife*: 'Never marry a policeman. Your relatives and friends would be going out for the day. He's off work only once in a blue moon and different times on. He's out all night, no good for a wife. You've just married and you've got to live. Had one child and then another one—you've got to put up with it. What other job could he do?—he's only done the police force!')

Either you accepted other officers as friends outside duty—if that were possible—or you were on your own with only the wife's family (if she was local) to fall back on.

S. S. I think that the only friends I had outside the force were my brother-in-laws and my sister-in-laws. It wasn't as though they were stopping you mixing with other people, except the problem of the times you were off duty. When you were on nights, you weren't much good to your wife as regards outside interests—going to the theatres and so on didn't happen very often. In mornings you could do. But you had your breakfast about half-past three and you'd sit around talking and within an hour you'd fall asleep and you'd be glad to go to bed soon after. Wife soon got fed up with that. Most of my time my wife was on her own at nights—must have been a big strain on her.

D. A. I packed the force in after twenty-eight years. I couldn't see any betterment of conditions in the police force. Our social life was deteriorating into nothing—still on a six-day week. There was one night I came home from duty and something had annoyed me and it was eleven o'clock at night, and I said to my wife, 'I'm fed up with this job. I'm going to pack it in.' She never left me alone. She kept at me . . . She said, 'Won't you resign when you go back in today?' 'No, I won't pack it in today until I get another job.' She was fed up. We were very fond of old-time dancing and there was a church at the bottom of the road and we used to love to go there and I could only make it once in six weeks and whereas she loved to go on a Friday, she was partnerless. If you were invited out anywhere you had to go to the calendar and work out what duty you'd be on. Then you'd finish up by saying, 'Sorry, I can't come.'

The only time of genuine sympathetic relationship was in time of trouble on duty, a relationship paralleled throughout police history.[31]

T. D. If one of your men was in trouble down in Byrom Street, anybody going up, a tram-conductor perhaps, would shout, 'Your mate's in trouble'—and some of them would come with their sticks in hand, waiting to muck in. There was comradeship on demonstrations—one-for-all and all-for-one. All shoulder-to-shoulder then. There was very good support when you were in difficulty.

But normally, friendships were things that civilians had. Even police contacts were often shunned.

A. M. Didn't mix with other police officers off duty—your wife took a good part of your time as she was entitled to. You didn't mix with other policemen off duty, for a very good reason—you left your work behind. I'd seen enough of police on duty.

Individual circumstances, personal idiosyncrasies as well as organizational imperatives dictated the limitations of social life and consequent exposure to peer-group influence. In the end, you were often a real social outcast.

'ONCE A POLICEMAN, ALWAYS A POLICEMAN'

The low social status noted by observers in Edwardian days might have been slightly diminished.[32] *But there was no apparent lessening in the alienation from the general public.*

A. T. Wife had come from a big family. She was seen as a policeman's wife. I've gone off duty to her house in uniform. Pick her up and the whole family's there—dead silence for a minute or two—a policeman in the house. I felt it very much because it wasn't just once that it happened. Whenever I went, 'he's a policeman', and that's it. The only time that people were antagonistic was when they had a snide remark to pass about your pension. They always used to resent that you were getting a pension at the end of thirty years' service.

> A Policeman's lot is not a happy one,
> Truth that only few people realise,
> Whatever comes, he has to carry on,
> Human feelings hidden from their eyes.
> 'Service first—the home takes second place . . .
> If maybe, he goes out on pleasure bent,
> Perhaps calls in a pub to have a drink.
> Conversation drops—they've got his scent.
> 'Drink up'—how they can tell, you cannot think.
> He drinks his gill mid looks that plainly say:
> 'We know you're one and so not wanted here.
> Slip off, my lad, be gone, be on your way.
> You're not to trust.' It's all too true I fear.
> Within the narrow circle of his friends,
> Who know him well he's voted quite 'O-Kay'.
> But he is quickly snubbed, perchance he lends
> His ear to conversation 'gone astray'.
> A social outcast, that's just what he is.
> (His wife, his kids too, to some extent.)
> Not wanted when it's fun, or drinking 'fizz',
> Trouble brewing makes him heaven sent!
> Respected more than in days gone by.
> But 'fear of consequences' makes this state.
> Should he 'speak out of turn', you'll hear them cry
> 'I'll see your Chief—you'll likely 'get the gate'.

He's patronised by those who have the dough.
'Aw, yes! I'm friends with Super. So-and-so.
Report me!—Pooh! you'll never get me fined.'
A man must be thick-skinned, it's understood,
For pin-pricks, gibes, and jeers he must endure.
From people much enlightened since the Flood.
From 'New-rich' to the 'incidentally poor' . . .

(*Police Review*, 1931)

Social separateness of police officers in Liverpool thus stemmed from a combination of policies and the pressures of the job: the national urben practice of 'strangers policing strangers'; the local effects of Police Strike dismissals; housing and domestic rules; and duty rotas. Although many of the social values displayed by officers of the Liverpool City Police in the succeeding pages—in particular, their attitude to women, and in their contact with the lower classes and ethnic minorities—were similar to those found in recent studies of the police elsewhere, they are not so easily explained. Social and occupational isolation was one factor likely to give rise to that particular conservative constellation of attitudes. 'Canteen' culture can only develop where social intercourse with other police officers is the norm. Beat life in particular provided few such opportunities for social immersion in the world of one's fellows.

2

The Nightly Round: Updo, Downdo

IN May 1919, a Metropolitan police officer was sacked for misconduct. He had 'paraded at 10 p.m. for beat duty until 6 a.m. Before 1 a.m., he was noted missing from his beat and could not be found. At 5.10 a.m., an officer purposely posted outside his lodgings heard an alarm go off. At 5.30 a.m., the police constable appeared in uniform ready to resume duty, with a view to leaving it at 6 a.m.'

The central feature of police work between the wars was the beat, the cornerstone of police practice, the crucible of the constable's experience. To the outsider, the civilian, beat work was directed at controlling the street population.[1] Its regulated, preventive surveillance features, in practice meant 'moving on' those civilians who dared to stand idly at the street corner. To the insider, to the lowly constable, however, it was an insidious device of control and discipline. From his perspective, it was intended as much to control his own actions as to cow the lower classes of the street. The beat was the site where police control of the urban population was felt most acutely. It was also the crossroads at which the constable felt most subject to authority.

Every officer spent some years on the beat. For 90 per cent of them, it was the reality of their normal working day in the Liverpool Police. The beat, a hangover from the early Metropolitan Police as well as from the older watch system, had clearly defined features. It was carefully controlled by time and by geography—a day divided into three eight-hour slots. Each hour in turn was subdivided into quarters, at any one of which the feared 'sergeant' figure might appear. It was also measured in yards. Neighbourhoods of terraced streets, shops, and warehouses were segmented into one-hour slots. Clock and distance, in confining police work-life, were reinforced by the dictates of superiors in a quasi-military organiza-tion. It was an isolating experience with penalties for those constables who wished to exchange civilities with their peers or with passers-by. Time, distance, and social isolation ensured that each patrolling constable carried a mobile Panopticon with him.[2]

It was a process studded with ritual—from the initial parade, the displays of truncheon and Beat Book, in a curious combination of coercion and submission, to the final signing-off in a weary station-house or bridewell. It was generally hated by its subjects for its tedium and excruciating monotony, as the isolated officer patrolled the city streets at night, and was physically separated from both peers and public.[3] It was a practice requiring the submission of the lower classes on the street, yet at the same time reflecting subordination of the constables to the whims of senior officers and to a manipulative body of law.

Inevitably, it gave rise to both unthinking acceptance—the weary, slow plod from point to point—and resistance, as a variety of easing devices were contrived.[4] The beat was the core of police practice, the hub of policing around which other activities revolved. Beginning and ending with formal parades, it displayed all the paradoxes of an occupation whose function was simultaneously to be both the controllers and the controlled.

RITUALS

Rituals are a central feature of police work. From careful staging of interments for officers killed on duty to the daily parade for beat patrol, police work is played out on a stage to both internal and external audiences.[5]

B. T. When you were going on duty, you had to parade at the station at half past, as a rule—a quarter of an hour before the beat. You looked through the Order Books that were posted to us—read the Inspector's Orders, the Superintendent's Orders, the Crime Orders, Complaints Books, Families Away from Home Books. Then you went on parade.

A. M. We fell in like soldiers in a square. When the sergeant had been to every man, made sure that he had his key, his baton, boots were clean, and all the rest of it, then he told the man when to take his refreshments and what beat he was on. The sergeant stood in front of his men and when the Inspector came along, all the men stood to attention, and the sergeant said, 'All correct, sir.' Then the inspector said, 'Stand at ease.' He read the Orders that we had already read, in case we hadn't read them. Some of the old inspectors tried to catch you out. They read out a complaint at perhaps, 22 Dale Street, and you would say, 'Aware of it, Sir,' and he would turn around and say, 'What is it?' and if you didn't know, you were in lumber. Inspector was very annoyed if you didn't say that you were aware of it when he read things out.

However, the uniformed, sixteen-legged crocodile was an easy target for ridicule.

K. R. Then you had to produce your appointments—which was your baton and brass keys [for the police telephone boxes], hold them in your hands, and then you were issued with the Beat Book on parade. It contained quite a bit of information —the position of the police telephones, the infirmaries, the hospitals, fire brigade, fire boxes, and so on. That finished, he gave us: 'Attention. Right turn, and quick march,' and we all marched out of the parade room by the left foot. When we were out on the street, we followed section by section, and each section went to its own beats. We were marched out in a crocodile, just like schoolgirls—weren't allowed to go out two-by-two or in threes or fours, but all in a line so we wouldn't disturb the pedestrians. Young kids used to quack at us as we went past. When we reached our beats, we dropped off the crocodile. There'd always be an extra man who had a different beat every day. Finish, there was only one man, the sergeant, who had come out with us, and then went back to pick up his correspondence and what not.

In the parade, detailed knowledge of the day's work was required, the raw material for the day's duties.[6] *The line-up, like the singular march to the beat, also had the symbolic function of dramatizing the ordered hierarchy, the disciplined Panopticon structure, of the police organization. The police audience, the constables, had their status and office dramatized. The public—even the kids who mocked—were confronted with disciplined state power on their doorsteps.*

Proceeding in the Direction of—

Rituals have to be learned, rites to be imparted to the novices, with curious rationalizations.

T. B. You're walking slower than the average person, when you're first about. When you do your first beat, you're walking with the sergeant and suddenly a voice will call out, 'Where are you going, son?' and you're about ten yards ahead. His idea was that if you come on the scene and there was a right old set-to, you wanted to be as fit as you can to get into the set-to.

THE BORED 'UN OF THE BEAT

Joe Soap up to the city came,
His hands were large, his feet the same,
To join the Police Force was his aim,
 Tho' tired, so tired.

Joe's chest was measured, 'twas not too bad,
Inside him Joe felt quite a lad,
Though outwardly he looked most sad,
 And tired, most tired.

He tackled the tests with commendable zeal,
Then in front of the M.O. he did peel;
But yawned when asked 'How do you feel?'
 So tired, so tired.

Joe got allocated to the beat,
Then out was sent on the night treat,
The Sergeant said 'You're rather beat',
 Said Soap 'I'm tired.'

Joe's feet they felt like lumps of lead,
His helmet hurt his poor fat head,
'Great Scott! young man' the Inspector said.
 'You're tired, too tired.'

Soap, went on duty in the Mall,
Soon scotched himself against a wall;

The Super. then did him call,
  'You tired? You're fired.'

The Chief his record marked—ah, me!—
'Dismissed, with much ignominy,
Because as far as we could see,
  He was born tired.'

The moral comrades, is quite plain:
If in the Force your bread you gain,
Tho' hard the duty, great the strain,
  Don't show you're tired.

(*Police Review*, 1927)

For the novice, who had spent a mere two months in training in the city, far from home in Scottish pit village or Norfolk town, the introduction to beat work was like plunging into a cold shower.[7]

W. S. I was posted right away on nights. I came out into a strange city—hardly knew my way around. You were simply given a lamp and told, 'Your beat starts here. Off you go.' I promptly got lost. When I first started, I got a paper to go to Rose Hill Station on Scotland Road. The boss said, 'You go to Scotland Road and come in here for your tea, Bill.' I couldn't find my way to Scotland Road. I see a van coming up. 'Stop, mate. Where's Rose Hill Police Station on Scotland Road?' I arrested one man early on. I had only been in the force five weeks. I had to ask him the way to the police station.

Normal policing meant night-beat policing. For eight days on end, beat officers, half the rank-and-file establishment, saw little daylight.

There are in this force a number of young men who have fixed hours of duty—8.30 a.m. until 5.30 p.m. with every Sunday off. These men are comparatively young in the Service. In contrast, the Constables who do alternate duties and have rotary leaves with one Sunday off in seven are, during the week-ends, called upon to do extra work. This happens when a man's ordinary hours of duty are 6 a.m. to 2 p.m. and when one likes to look forward to spending a few hours with one's family. During the football season (eight months of the year!) the early turn men parade at 6 a.m. to 2 p.m., return for a few hours, then re-parade 6 p.m. to 10 p.m., and sometimes have to go on duty at 6 a.m. the following morning. Having regard to the time taken up in travelling, to and from the place of parade, the time taken to perform twelve hours' duty is spread over seventeen hours. The night duty men are also called early from their beds to parade for the football matches, therefore with insufficient sleep, coupled with hours of standing in the cold within a short space of rising from a warm bed, it is not surprising to have a heavy sick list . . . can not matters be arranged more conveniently for the family man?   (Letter in *Police Review*, 1935)

T. D. The day beat was twice as long so, in effect, there were twice as many men on night duties as on days. The parade I had to lead down from the station to the beat was much longer on nights. You did a fortnight of mornings—6 to 2, a fortnight on afternoons—2 to 10, and a month on nights—10 to 6. It was a six-day week—one day off in eight. So if I was working a full week, Sunday to Sunday, the next day would be my rest day, and the next week, it would be a Tuesday. Otherwise, it would be continuous duty.

Whatever the official view of police work, to those on the ground, it was above all else a job. As a working man, your concerns on beat patrol were mundane but real—above all else, the unsocial hours and the peculiar daily rota.

Keeping the Points

Point-to-point, with its connotation of upper-class steeplechasing, had quite a different meaning to the patrolling officer, whose work-life it structured. The discipline of the points made constant supervision unnecessary, with the sergeant able to strike randomly at any one of sundry crossroads, an arbitrary arrangement whose authority was backed up by the total recall of the Beat Book record.

K. R. Not even shown round the beat first time. Given a Beat Book. You made quarter-hour points and you didn't know where the sergeant was going to pick you up. If he couldn't find you, he wanted to know where you had been. He wouldn't report it unless it was deliberate and too often. My beat went up Duke Street, turn left on Great George Street, up past the David Lewis Hostel for Seamen, down Park Lane, back to the bridewell and the quarter-hour point at the top of Duke Street.

'Milking' (checking) locks was a key practice. It was assembly-line production without a product.

K. R. In that time, I had to do all the side streets, milking padlocks. You had to run up the warehouse steps. Half-hour point was by the David Lewis, and then three-quarter-hour point down Park Street. Ridiculous making them quarter-hour points—because the burglars knew where you were. If the sergeant got there before you and didn't find you, he would tap with his signalling stick and it goes for miles in the middle of the night—give him a little tinkle, and you walk towards one another. He doesn't say, 'Where have you been and why are you late?' because you're on your way immediately. If you don't see him, you've got to make all your points religiously until you see him, and having found him, he makes a note in his diary, and you make a note in yours and you're away.

The Police Union expressed the rank and file's perception of the contradiction between the reality of beat patrol and the expectations of superior officers.

Theoretically a constable when taking up his beat is to concentrate on preventing crime. In practice, however, the young constable soon learns that it is a more paying proposition from his point of view so to work his beat that the time-table is not deflected from.

Sergeants and Inspectors know almost exactly where an officer can be found at a certain time, and woe betide the constable who keeps his superior officer waiting. A constable who in the course of patrolling sees something which in his opinion is of a suspicious character, should satisfy himself one way or the other before proceeding to work the remaining portion of his ground. To delay half-an-hour means that his Sergeant is kept waiting half-an-hour, so that the latter is compelled to work the P.C.'s beat in the opposite direction in order to find him. A sergeant with a large area to cover and under the necessity of visiting each constable, which visits have to be duly recorded, becomes testy if one or two of those under his charge are late arriving at certain points on their beats. It is not that the Sergeant really objects to the constable having a legitimate excuse for being late, but it is because he too has to satisfy his superior officers that his omission to visit all the constables regularly is due to efficient Police duty.

Dialogue

P.C. All correct, Sergeant.

SERGEANT. All correct, eh? Where have you been?

P.C. Working my beat, Sergeant.

SERGEANT. You are three minutes late. Haven't you got a watch? If not, you had better get one.

P.C. Yes, I've got a watch, Sergeant.

SERGEANT. Well, where have you been that's made you so late? Hanging up somewhere?

P.C. No, Sergeant. I have worked my beat as near as possible to 2 and a half miles an hour, and I don't think there is much to complain about.

SERGEANT. Well, don't keep me waiting another time, or you'll find yourself on the Report for improperly working your beat. I don't believe what you say.

(*Bull's Eye*, 1921)

Managing, massaging time is central to beat work. Where timekeeping signifies authority,[8] *the overseer's watch and chain, the ability to organize time to one's own advantage is a subtle form of subversion as well as a device for self-preservation.*

Preventive policing, the backward and forward travails of the patrolling constable, summed up in the police clerk's jargon of 'updo, downdo', was a repetitive assembly-line process in which locks, shop doorways, and street lamps marked the passage of time.

A. T. I was posted to D Division, Scotland Road, night duty round Great Howard Street leading to the Northern Hospital by the big tobacco warehouse and I had to patrol round there and along one street, up the next, down Dixon Street, up the next, down Regent Street—downdo, updo, updo, downdo all the time, trying shop doorways and all the locks. We used to call it 'milking locks'. It's the only thing you did. On nights, it was a constant checking of locks.

You started off at the beginning of your beat—set out on the north side of Lime Street—took a quarter of an hour to walk round and try all the locks. When you tried all the locks and doors, you were responsible. If one was found unlocked, you were responsible and in trouble. So you made sure, all your locks, doors, were made secure, no lights left on because if there was a suspicious light, you had to report it. And having done that, you repeated it all night.

I was on Mill Street for a bit and some of the padlocks there on the fish shops were filthy—you had to be very careful to wash your hands before you had your refreshments. I started Chisenhall Street on first quarter points, then I would walk along to the next very scruffy part—all broken down garages and yards and things. The only thing I heard was dogs and rats. I'd go down to the bottom and try all the locks, come up, go along the next street. On the right hand side—the full length, from Howard Street to Gardner's Row—was the stables for the Corporation drayhorses.

S. H. We were held responsible for property and we had to go round and test every doorway and that would occupy the first time round—say an hour and a half—and then usually you had to go round and test them a second time, just to make sure. What we used to do—you know in the olden days, the ladies used to use stays. They had whalebone in these stays and we used to cut pieces about half an inch long and in the daytime, I used to make a bag full and put them in between the doors and I'd go round the first and time and put them in and when I went round later, if that whalebone was missing, I'd make enquiries. One unlocked and you got in touch with the station and they would contact the key-keeper and they would come out and lock the place up. In those days, you used to have special police telephones and you would ring in direct to the station.

A Liverpool Police Constable stated that his beat included the Communist Party offices in Hope Street. In consequence of a previous burglary, he placed a secret mark on the street door, and on the morning of May 23rd, he found that the mark had been interfered with . . . the accused descended . . .   (*Manchester Guardian*, 1925)

The institution had its own ideas about how to relieve the monotony of the beat. Occasional breaks in routine were available, to be undertaken either as a sign of enthusiasm, or as a momentary release from tedium. Some locations, such as the city centre, A Division, offered more release than others.

H. P. You had to go round keeping your eyes open for various things. There were all sorts that we dealt with in those days. For example, we would get into trouble if we failed to notice that there was a blocked gas lid in the wall that someone could fall over. If we missed anything on the beat, even sunken flags in the roadway —and we didn't report them, we'd get a report back wanting to know why. If it started to snow, say at four o'clock, we would have what we called snowmen—and we would knock them up and they would come running to get a day's work in the snow. Other times, in the outside divisions, we would often have a list of people to call up in the morning—such as our own men for early morning duty. There were also other things such as places where people were away from home—the Plain Clothes could have as many as twenty or thirty places where people were away from home, and he was expected to pay attention and he would have to go round and visit them all.

Now I'd had quite enough of my duties by day;
How I welcomed Night Duty, I need hardly say.
One hour after midnight. All is quite calm,
But hark! Oh! Great Caesar; a burglar alarm.
Very soon several Policemen had answered the call,
Surrounding the building. I stood near the wall.
Lonesome I waited, 'twas as silent as death,
When a sound in the darkness made me catch my breath—
Like a flash I had laid him all out on the ground,
He fought like a fiend, but made not a sound.
I was feeling around for his safe-wrenching tool,
When he gasped, 'Off my chest, you great blundering fool',
The voice was the Sergeant's. Upset he was too!
And the names he called me turned the air blue!
I could only stand quietly and scratch my poor head.
'Out of my sight, do you hear?' he said.
As a P.C. I felt I was not a success.

(*Police Review*, 1937)

B. A. In B Division, during the day, there were so many things happening all the time. It was a good division for learning police work. But it was quite different at night. We learnt by practical experience—that a chimney on fire is an offence or a dog without a collar. If a chimney was on fire, you couldn't just let it burn away. My first traffic accident was someone walking into a horse.

There are obvious similarities between beat supervision and a more recent form of Panopticon control—the probation 'tracking' system in which convicted offenders can be 'supervised' in the community by random checking, at any one of a series of timetabled points during the day.[9] For the constables, this clock discipline was reinforced by more severe castigation—perhaps for missing an unlocked door or newly broken window. Like tracked offenders, the beat officer between the wars carried his prison with him. Surviving that mental control led to improvisations.

ALIENATION

'TIME WASTED IS EXISTENCE, TIME SPENT IS LIFE' *was the inscription read every night by a constable on the Picton Clock. On the beat, the officer conducted an array of largely meaningless and low-status tasks—checking, checking, and checking again. Patrol officers rarely encountered any 'action'.[10] But beat duty was of course not the only punitive experience for the rank-and-file policeman. The immobile custodian of the Dock Gates did not have even the dignity of movement. Worse still was the permanent flapping of the scarecrow on point duty, directing traffic.*

J. V. Night duty was what got me off the job. The beat I had started in Garston village went right through to Speke. Your principal job was trying doors and keeping your eyes open for anything suspicious. There was nothing more boring than flogging around, looking for something like a bike without lights. Some areas were very boring, especially in the suburbs. You could go all night and not see a single soul and the same in the city on a Sunday morning. You wouldn't see anybody walking round these big buildings and not a soul in sight. There was no crime, nothing. Time dragged terribly, you had to keep going round, but it was bloody awful.

M. B. On Dock Duty, you'd stand all night and not see a soul and the Liver Building up there with the clock gradually going round and you'd think: 'I won't look at it, I won't look at it at all.' Then after one chime, you'd think: 'It must be three o'clock now.' But it was one o'clock.

> . . . We see a smart 'Pointsman' stand waving his hand,
> And to the onlooker it all seems so grand;
> But 'jam' made of traffic is not very 'sweet'
> And 'tastes' rather sour to 'him' on the beat.
>
> There are tourers and 'buses, lorries and trams,
> All have to be guided by one pair of hands,
> And if by confusion you make a mistake,
> Your kit to headquarters, you'd soon have to take.
>
> Then take the bad weather and out in the night,
> Of course in the summer it all looks alright;
> But 'on point' even then it is not quite all fun,
> Being melted and scorched by the heat of the sun.
>
> (*Police Review*, 1931)

M. B. Point duty was pretty hard work, particularly on a busy junction—the Legs of Man, bottom of Scotland Road. You could stand there with your arms and legs like lead. You got half an hour plus ten minutes relief for your refreshments and that would happen at ten in the morning and you'd been there since seven. When you came back, you stayed there until three. Later on, they encouraged the beat man to take over for five minutes—for a man to go and stretch his legs. A very tiring job it was, particularly in winter, when you had a heavy overcoat on.

The Liverpool Stipendiary the other day confessed he had upon more than one occasion watched members of the City Police Force on point duty in various parts of the city, and he admitted he had been extremely confused at some of the signals given to traffic. When a policeman raised his hand as a signal to approaching traffic to halt, there was no definite indication as to which vehicles were requested to move on when the Officer waved his other arm.   (*Police Review*, 1921)

Most police work, the daily grind, was similar to many repetitive tasks—from the treadmill of the Victorian workhouse and prison to the modern-day assembly-lines—both physically tiring and mentally tedious. That endurance was not a quality that induced ready sympathy from a class that still looked on the constable as a kind of public flunkey.[11]

'It Always Rained'

Troubles have a habit of being compounded. It always seemed to rain more at night. Snow rarely fell hard during the day. The weather God had it in for the night patrol. Rain could shape every incident on the beat.

P. P. It was a tough life, especially in wet weather. I've gone on duty with clothes drenched—you'd have night uniform on, and a cape. Now that cape, it would be raining on it all night, and we had no means of drying it so that cape was left on a hanger in the house and the next coat was taken and that was worn but for some reason it seemed to be always raining on nights and you had coat wet and you came to go out it was still damp.

> Dark is the night and stormy the weather,
> Cape drips water on dubbined boot-leather,
> Overcoat skirts on wet trousers flap,
> Helmets are watery from spike to chin-strap.
> Rubber heels squelch and rubber soles squish
> Rain water from buildings descends without.
>
> As watchful and wary, in lanes, roads, and streets,
> The Policemen patrol the lone night-duty beat,
> From slates in the city, from tiles in the town,
> Unendingly, unceasingly, it gurgles pipes down.
> On highways and pavements rain splashes and streaks,
> As though it would turn them to watercreeks.
>
> While sodden and sopped in lanes, road, and streets,
> The Policemen patrol the long night-duty beats.
> Then the wind round high chimneys in eddies and whirls,
> Up streets and round corners, its cold fingers curl
> Shaking and shuddering most buildings small,
> Shrieking at others, broad, solid, and tall,
>
> Uplifting light litter, downhurling loose slates,
> Slamming and banging on all unfastened gates;
> But with ears on the listen, in lanes, roads, and streets,
> The Policemen patrol the weird night-duty beat . . .
>
> Oh, townsmen, so smug and warm in your bed,
> Oh countrymen, blanket drawn up to your head.
> Did you give a just thought 'ere you dropped off to sleep,
> To slumber and snore till day doth again peep,
> That on nights such as this, the burglar or worse,
> Might slit your windpipe for the gain of your house,

Were it not for the fact that in lanes, roads, and street,
The Police are patrolling the night duty-beats.

(Police Review, 1928)

P. P. You're looking for anything such as traffic accidents that were no bother except that you're worn out walking. But then came the bad weather and the frost—they didn't allow for you being knee-deep in snow—they expected you to be where you should be.

W. R. At night, out in the rain, you put your greatcoat, cape, and water leggings on. Back home at six in the morning, then out again for the football match duty at half past twelve (you got 7s. 6d. for it), then back on again at night. They still expected you to come nice and clean with your leggings nice and clean.

Weather was a hazard for which the organization had little to offer—apart from a heavy serge cape, and a stout pair of boots or 'scuffers'.

ORGANIZATIONAL SOLUTIONS

Present-day patrol work is relieved through peer-group contact, the occasional camaraderie of the cigarette or the joke in the back of a Panda car, the crackling spontaneity of the personal radio.[12] *To save on personnel and consequently to minimize undesirable social contact, the original Metropolitan Commissioners had submitted the personal qualities of 'forbearance' and 'calm demeanour' as the major responses to the threat, as the inhibiters of opposition, and as a substitute for colleague support.*[13] *Solidarity in time of threat, support when problems emerged, was to be provided by some notional public 'front' and a tin whistle.*

M. B. You could rely on your colleagues if they were there. But the only means of communication we had, apart from the police telephone boxes which were far apart, was a whistle that didn't carry miles. It's no use blowing a whistle asking for help, if you know the policeman is a couple of miles away. I remember a little kiosk outside Allerton Cemetery. It had been bust. First thing you've got to do is inform CID about the chocolates and cigarettes that had been stolen. Nobody in at CID, and I had to get someone to secure it. I blew my whistle till I blew the pea out of it. Then I had to go down to the station to get somebody and by the time I came back, most of the stuff had gone. You were normally by yourself and sometimes you were lucky if some of your colleagues came or even if members of the public came to help you. There was a lot of support from your colleagues if you were in trouble for the very reason that they knew if they gave you help, you'd automatically give it them. We used the police telephone boxes when we were locking somebody up and you had to handcuff them to a railing while you rang up for the van. We all carried a key but the boxes were a long way apart.

Inside the Section Box he lay,
His key grasped to his breast;

His head was bare; his greying hair
Against the kerb was pressed,
With tunic burst, and trousers torn,
He sprawled there, half-undressed.

Benumbed, exhausted, spent and done;
There in the dirt he lay;
He'd run in answer to the Light
Full thirty times that day.
But peacefully now he dreamed a dream
Of green fields far away . . .

While sobbing, he made up his mind.
'Today I shall resign.'
He'd never had such a peaceful sleep
Since Nineteen-twenty-nine
With signal-boxes came the dawn
Of his torment—and mine!

(*Police Review*, 1937)

Improvisations and improvements came slowly, from those who had also suffered.

D. A. Later on, a fellow named George Menzies was good on radios. He tried to make a set which could be taken on a motor bike. They put them on pedal-cycles. The pedal-cyclists only had receiving sets and a little loudspeaker that you clipped on the handlebars of the bike. The cyclist had a big leather bag strapped on the bicycle frame and they kept the set in there. I remember the call sign. It would start off with 'GBO calling MBO. Constable 192F'. They gave you the message and told you where to go. But the ordinary man on the beat had nothing like that.

Technological changes came about as much by rank-and-file initiative as by management innovation. It was those who suffered the isolation of the front-line patrol who demanded changes. When Menzies opened the door to radio communication, he could have had little appreciation of one aspect of its future impact. While it might be used by management to deploy resources more effectively, it could also give opportunities for diversions from tedious duty—for example, by allowing outside officers to join in dramas outside their own subdivisions.[14]

HUMANIZING THE MACHINE

Contact with colleagues can serve several functions. It allows a repetitive task to become tolerable; but it can also threaten the ordered hierarchy of an organization where discretion is to be minimized by directive communications. Social interaction between the rank and file can subvert the organization and breed resistance.

T. D. There were men on the opposite beat and sometimes you could spend a little time talking to them as long as you weren't caught. It was looked on as a very serious offence. Gossiping, it was called under the regulations. You'd do anything to break the boredom of the beat. A man might go off his beat to have a chat on the Docks, and have a smoke in the Dock bobby's hut, when you knew the sergeant wasn't around.

T. B. I couldn't go across the road to speak to another policeman if I saw him, never spoke to anyone. You'd be reported—three charges: failing to work your beat, idling your time, and gossiping. They would do you on one charge but they always laid three against you and you would have no escape. Occasionally, after refreshments—two would go in at two o'clock, two more at half past two, and so on—the only time you could have a natter with your colleague was when you left the station and you saw the sergeant going in for his refreshments. Perhaps another chap would come along and stop on the other side of the road. He would be in as much danger as me because if he shouted across to me, he'd have been done for idling his time and gossiping. They would have got two of us.

Communication between constable peers was a threat to the discipline of command. Isolation of those at the foot of the pyramid of authority, the Panopticon principle, was central to maintaining the image of the force on the street. All time on duty was the property of the Chief Constable.

'STEALING POLICE TIME'

Time was a precious commodity. There was no dilly-dallying when you went to book in for your break at the bridewell. The adage 'time equals money' ruled. The ratepayers and the Home Office wanted their penn'orth. The bridewell sergeant would book you in and out. It was on his head that you returned to the beat on time. Even the toilet was timed.

H. P. Just prior to my joining, all policemen had to have their refreshments in shop doorways. Only allowed twenty minutes. There was a mini-rebellion about that just after the Police Strike and then they allowed policemen to go in for half an hour's and eat breakfast. Later, you had half an hour break to have your meal. It was very inadequate at times, especially in winter if you were on point duty. You'd go in and have to queue up, wait for the chance to get the frying pan to put bacon and egg in it, and your hands so cold you could hardly hold it, and that would take up a quarter of an hour. As soon as you got in, and your foot crossed the threshold, you called out your number. I would say, '74D in for refreshments'—recorded in a book and in that half hour, I had to make my tea, eat my sandwiches, wash my cup, put on my coat or whatever I was wearing—cape if it was raining—and be out for that half hour.

P. H. One time I came on duty at Rose Hill and left my cape at the bottom of the stairs—on the banister. When I came for refreshments, I rushed through down the stairs and back again, walked into the bridewell, and called out for my refreshments. The inspector was there. He says, 'What are you doing here?' 'I've come for refreshments, Sir.' He says, 'You're stealing police time.' 'But I've only been down to the banister to pick up my coat.' 'It doesn't matter. You're stealing time.' And I had to come out a minute early to pay it back. In our station, the only facility was an iron cauldron of boiling water. No cooking possible. On one occasion, the wife gave me a tin of beans, small kettle, and I put it in the cauldron. I was told to go to the telephone. There was a terrific bang. The tin had blown up. I went back and there was pork and beans covering everyone.

A. T.   I was reported one day. I came out of the station, having had my break and was putting it into my notebook—'refreshments at such-and-such a time, leave such-and such a time'. Sergeant came round the corner and he said, 'Where have you been?' So I said, 'Just coming out of my refreshments.' 'Well,' he said 'it's now six thirty-two. I'm reporting you for idling your time for two minutes.' And that's exactly what he did.

D. A.   On the Dock gates, you were allowed into the police hut for refreshments. But if it was breakfast, you had to cook it within the half hour and get out. If you were in for 9 in the morning, you were out at 9.30 and the other fellow must not book in till 9.31 a.m. A lot of them brought bacon and eggs but you had to cook it and they had to leave the pans and things clean when they left—so it was always a rush job and all policemen suffered from bad stomachs.

A meal-break is not just a response to a physical urge. It is also a time for sociability, a release from the tedium of the job. In the Liverpool City Police, no such considerations were possible in force orders. Time wasted equalled theft. The eight hours' duty was the property of Watch Committee and Chief Constable. Using a couple of minutes for private imperatives was a serious violation of property rights.[15]

'THERE'S TROUBLE ON T'BEAT'

Traditionally, the beat in the city had been the area for serious mischief—the dread of young men playing pitch-and-toss (the first such incident is reported in 1839,[16] and the latest in 1979[17]), and the perils of children flying kites.[18] In the 1920s, the incidents were a little more prosaic—but useful if they gave the patrolling constable something to chuckle over for an hour or two.

K. R.   There were mainly annoying types of things—such as lads playing football in the street and that sort of thing, and the drunks coming out of the pub, and on the corner. An awful lot of indecent exposure used to go on. You were pleased to find a hand-cart on your beat. You should take it in but you didn't—just rolled it on to the next beat.

You took everything in your stride—walking up Henry Street, a bucket of water went right in front of me. I wasn't annoyed except that it was bitterly cold, freezing. I put my head round the corner: 'What if a horse came and broke his leg on the ice?' 'Oh, I'm sorry.' 'Well, go and brush it into the gutter.' Then you went on your way. When something happened, you were delighted. If the [bobbies] heard there was a break-in, or anything, they'd all be in a rush to get there.

A bit-part might be played in somebody else's drama.[19]

T. D. I was on the beat round Stanley Hospital and I got to this point at four o'clock on the Saturday morning. I walked round the front of the hospital. The gates were all closed and there was a mother and a daughter who was pregnant and walking around it. All of a sudden, the baby starts to come. She got hold of the railings and all I could hear was screams. There was no traffic about. I ran round to the Casualty Department, rang the bell, couldn't raise anybody. Thought, 'What am I going to do?' We had a system of telephone boxes that connected you to the bridewell. I rang from the nearest box to the station where they controlled the ambulances. I couldn't convince them at the other end that I needed an ambulance because I was outside the hospital. When I ran back to the girl, there were a couple of railwaymen on their way to work and another policeman carrying her to the Out-patients. Suddenly, all the lights came on in the hospital and they eventually opened a side-door and let her in.

Other duties, of course, could also be pretty tedious, especially when you were stuck carrying out a rotten job against your own sympathies, your loyalties divided.

A. T. I once did a month on the canal bank, looking after Tate and Lyle's coal that was brought in when there was a strike on. People were trying to pinch it all the time. It was a terrible job, standing there for eight and a half hours—because you didn't finish after eight hours. No refreshments, you just kept straight on. The barges used to come down the Leeds and Liverpool canal right down to Tate and Lyle's, where they had chutes that came down from the building into the barges and the coal was sucked up because the coal was very fine; and the poor people there—they'd be on the other side of the canal and one would perhaps get on a barge and throw two or three pieces of coal and then scamper up. I had about five barges to look after and you couldn't see everyone—not that I cared so very much, to tell the truth. I got one, one day and he had a sackful—four stone of it.

One of the few differences between beat policing and assembly-line work was that it contained a measure of unpredictability. While 'real police work', crime, was almost non-existent,[20] *other dogsbody incidents could provide a measure of relief.*

Encounters in the Night

Social contact was vital, if you were to retain your sanity and some vestige of independence from the 'job'. A friendly encounter gave a glow which lasted through the night. Even an awkward meeting with a tiresome drunk, or a disputed stop-and-search, was a desirable break from the pedestrian routine. Some beats had more to offer than others. The occasional encounter with someone who seemed out of place was a relief. There was a class of 'night-people' with life-styles far removed from the humdrum daytimers.

B. T. If there was a night-watchman, you could stop and have a little talk with him—they had these coke fires. Lime Street was the place for drunks and policemen were always keen. A drunk turned up and he was wheeled up the road to the station. Drunks, men coming from the clubs, occasionally a seaman coming home with a kitbag on his shoulder and you would say good night to him. But beyond that, you would never stop.

A. M. If the road was up and there was a night-watchman with a bit of a fire, you went up to him. You used to look in and see if he was awake. You could smell the gas from the coke and 'Are you awake there?' and then you might have a little natter with him—but only for a couple of minutes because if the sergeant saw you, you'd be 'on the peg'. Once you had been visited by the sergeant, you'd go for a scrounge, somewhere you could get a smoke—a bakery where there was a bit of heat in the winter-time. You'd be glad to get in there for half an hour but you wouldn't risk more than half an hour. Stand around the fire, talk to the night-watchman but all the time taking a risk that the sergeant might have doubled back on you, to see if you were working your beat. At two o'clock in the morning, you would find two men with a hose back of Rose Street, hosing round a big pile of fish entrails as high as this—the retail fish market was just there. You knew everyone who went to work in the early morning—the chappie who came round on his bike and rod to put out the gas lamps or to light them.

On A Division, it was comparatively lively. During the night, there was always something about—vehicles, mail-vans stopping about the station, and occasional people. One person I always remember was a window-cleaner—about half past three in the morning, I walked along Lime Street, trying my doors, locks, and windows. Suddenly I saw a man cleaning windows in the dark. 'Oh,' I said, 'what a lark.' I thought he was a burglar. First I quizzed him: 'Who are you? What are you doing?' 'Oh, I'm cleaning windows.' I was a bit stumped then. 'How long have you been doing this and where do you go afterwards?' Ultimately, the man convinced me he was in fact a window-cleaner, starting about half past three to four o'clock. He worked till nine o'clock and that was his day's work.

B. T. In those days, the days of tram-cars, there were always gangs of men. You'd hear them clinking all night. They would come around at about ten and place their lamps out. Doing the overhead wires and lines. Down Lord Street, they'd have big hose-pipes out—not just one or two men but big gangs of men. Then there'd be the Corpy watchmen all the way round, wherever there was a hole in the road.

W. S. On night duty on Scotland Road, there was always something moving. When I went there, the Corporation men used to come and wash the whole of

Scotland Road. I'm at the top of Hornby Street one night/early morning. I could see an image moving. Go along and have a look at this. And it was an old woman—she was a religious maniac and she was rushing out of the house in her nightie and praying in the gutter.

Urban life depends upon an invisible stratum of people who repair the city's infrastructure while all the rest are abed. In a sense, the patrolling constable blended in as part of this hidden social group, of whom most of the city's population were largely ignorant. Night-time contact had a levelling quality, in which night-watchman and beat constable could meet as relative equals, sharing the strains of isolation and tedium.

CREATIVITY

In the absence of such contacts, excitement had to be manufactured.

D. A. Round where I was it was particularly deserted. There was very little night-life except a fellow coming home on his bike. I used to tell him off for riding a bike without a light—summonsed him in the end and he was fined about ten bob. People didn't speak to you. There was a Masonic Hall in Island Road. Many a time, I sat outside waiting for someone to come along but it was never bust while I was there. If the sergeant had caught you there, you'd have been in trouble because you weren't flogging the beat. It was just walk, walk, walk.

> . . . why should he light up his front lamp to time?
> An errand boy must have his fling, you know.
>
> Faster he fled along the quiet street,
> And boldly glanced around this way and that;
> He did not hear the sound of heavy feet,
> Or in the gloaming see a spiked top hat.
>
> From out the dark, a blue clad figure appeared,
> Stolid and stern, it almost blocked the street,
> The cyclist saw one mighty arm upreared.
> He jammed his brakes, and stopped his circling feet.
>
> Then from his bike he almost fell with fright,
> And on his lips there died the cheery lay.
> Gone was the pride he felt as through the night
> He dashed, without a lamp to light his way.
>
> Then boomed the voice, 'My boy, just what's your game?
> No light, Good Lord! no red reflector? Now,
> Come on young man, I want to know your name,
> And tell the truth, for truth is best, you know.'
>
> A still small voice, that seemed so strangely small,
> In contrast to the loud and blatant tune.

With eyes downcast, he did not seem at all
The youth that winked defiance at the moon.

With sinking heart, the errand boy replied,
'I'm Harry Smith, of Baker Street, Walsall.
I'm sorry, sir, I did not mean to ride
Without a front lamp on my bike, at all.'

'Now then, my lad, your tale I don't believe;
I'm too old, boy, I know your little game.
Come on—the truth—it's useless to deceive;
Inside you go—or—What's your proper name?'

The youth looked up, shame showed upon his face,
Repentant tears welled quickly to his eyes.
Sadly he spoke, 'Yes sir, to my disgrace,
I've told you nothing but a pack of lies.'

'I'll tell the truth, I'm Willyum Shakespeare,
Hathaway House, or 9, Ann Arden's Lane,
Stratford-on-Avon, in Warwickshire;
My Aunt lives there, Jane Harvard is her name.'

Then said the Law, 'My boy, that's what I want,
Your proper name; you see you can't fool me.
Now get that lamp of yours alight in front,
And never tell more lies to a P.C.'

(*Police Chronicle*, 1932)

If you weren't to be turned into a zombie, a walking automaton, in the absence of other night-people, incidents had to be manufactured. That process was not easy. Potential suspects were a little difficult to come by. Civilians at night, threatening little damage to the fabric of society, might be taken aback at being suddenly confronted with the majesty of the state in the form of a bored constable.

RESISTANCE

Various strategies, individual and collective, were developed to combat the organizational pressure. In Liverpool, resistance was not as co-ordinated as it had been in Chicago a decade earlier, where the implementation of a quarter-hour telephone call-in system collapsed when all the police call boxes immediately developed mysterious malfunctions.[21] Scrounges —unofficial ways of resisting the uniformity of the beat—often meant little more than an illegal cigarette or a beer, forms of resistance accompanied by their own surreptitious rituals. Too much control and predictability might eventually subvert the organizational goals.

T. D. You could always have a cigarette if you wanted it but if you got caught, you were in trouble. On night duty, there's always plenty of deep doorways. A lot of them used to catch it. The sergeant would appear from somewhere and you'd dash the cigarette quickly, but the smoke aroma hung around the doorway. The sergeant would go sniffing around so that he showed he knew what you were doing. Sometimes you'd get a nasty sergeant and it was painful. You were watching him and he was watching you, so there were less catches than when the easy-going feller was on.

A. T. If you wanted to have a smoke—we used to have smokes: we weren't angels by any means—you had to get into a shop doorway, put your cigarette in your mouth, strike a match, shield it with your hand, and then blow the match out and then your hand would go up your sleeve. The smoke was coming down your sleeve, standing in the doorway, watching for your sergeant coming out from his refreshments. You'd meet the chap on next beat and have a smoke somewhere. You'd make arrangements beforehand, perhaps with the station-keeper, who would say to call down and he'd have a cup of tea made when the sergeant was out.

T. D. A woman in Kent Street used to come to the corner with a bottle of beer. Used to chat to her, standing in the door. With one sergeant I had then, I used to make up stories about keeping an eye on thieves if he didn't find me at the points.

P. H. George Low was very fond of a midday noggin. The Tuebrook Funeral Parlour, belonging to MacDougalls, had the franchise for everybody killed on the streets. George had a standing order there. A certain inspector, not very friendly to George. He watched George going into MacDougalls, let him settle down for three minutes and then he'd strike. One of the funeral fellows said: 'George, what you do is to lay in one of the shells [coffins], take your helmet off, and we'll drive round back of the cinema, and you're on your own.' Inspector was standing there and George came up behind him and threw him a beautiful salute. The inspector couldn't believe his eyes. Both of them were discharged two years later.

Of course, all gamekeepers were once poachers. Every sergeant had served his time as a constable. Few strategies of resistance were unknown. But even gamekeepers can find the rules restrictive.

K. R. One night we had a strange sergeant in from the South End of the city who was filling in for our missing sergeant. I waited and waited for him at the points and eventually met him about three or four o'clock in the morning for the first time. He signalled me from Pitt Street and I met him and he gave me the peg [the notebook entry you both make]. 'Which way are you going?' 'I'm going down to the Customs House.' 'I think I'll go up to the Cathedral,' says the sergeant.

We separated, and as soon as I got into a side street, I went down it and there at the bottom was Cuttle's Bakehouse. I went in as usual, took off my greatcoat and tunic and tie and made some small pancakes and dipped them in boiling fat—used to take me a quarter of an hour every night. There's me turning over the pancakes, hear the door moving. It's the sergeant. Now he'd told me he was going up to the Cathedral. But he didn't. He waited for me to get out of his sight, and then he worked his way down to Cuttle's Bakery. (I found out later this was his old beat.) I felt terrible. He says, 'All right, 125'; and then after ten minutes he says, 'On your way,' so I got dressed and went out and thought, 'Now I'm for it,' but I heard nothing more.

The Sergeant and the Constable.
Were walking round the beat;
They wept like anything to see
Such quantities of street.
'If this was only cleared away'
They said, 'It would be sweet.'

If seven cops with seven mops
Trod it for thirty year,
'Do you suppose,' the Sergeant said,
'That they would get it clear?'
'I doubt it' said the Constable,
'Unless it was filled with beer.'

The Sergeant and the Constable
Walked out a mile or so,
And there they rested in a pub,
Inspectors didn't know;
And all the half-pint measures stood
And waited in a row.

'The time has come,' the Sergeant said
'To have a little talk
About Inspector Crabface
Ere we resume our walk.'
And so they started whispering
With one eye on the clock.

'Hot boiling oil', the Sergeant said,
'Is what he really needs;
In fact, no punishment could fit
That bad old man's misdeeds.'
And thus and so, they whispered low,
Forgetting how Time speeds.

'Have one on me,' said Sergeant Stripes;
But Hanifeet turned blue!
'Old Crabface has arrived,' he gasped,
'Whatever shall we do?'
'The night is fine,' old Crabface spoke.
'Do you admire the view?'

'It was so kind of you to come,'
Said Sergeant; 'really nice.'
Inspector he said nothing, but

.   .   .   .

'Wish you were not quite so fat,
I'll need the barrow twice.'

'It seems a shame,' the Sergeant sobbed,
'To play us such a trick;
After we've brought you out so far,
And made you trot so quick.'
Old Crabface shook his head and said,
'Your speech is much to thick.'

'Although I weep for you,' he said,
Undoing the barrow straps,
'I've plenty handkerchiefs at home,
I'll need them all, perhaps;
But Discipline must be maintained
And not allowed to lapse.'

'I see,' said Crabface, counting,
'You've had a pleasant run;
Fourteen—fifteen pints you've had—';
But answer was there none,
And this was scarcely odd, because
They'd finished every one.'

(*Police Review*, 1938)

In developing surreptitious techniques to break up the beat monotony, superiors were not always what they seemed. Some sergeants, heading for promotion, would clamp down heavily on minor infringements. Others, serving their time, recalled that they, too, had once been constables.

Weighing up the Costs

Resistance took different forms. Wherever the pressure occurred, a different tactic had to be developed to release it. Techniques of avoidance, easing strategies,[22] *were especially important to prevent unpaid overtime. Discretion in law enforcement could be a two-edged weapon. Before initiating an incident, you weighed up the pros and cons of the costs in time.*

A. T. In those days, if you locked somebody up at night, you might be let off duty at three o'clock in the morning. But if they were short, they would keep you on until they could get another man from a different station, so that you might only have two hours off. And you had to walk home, go to bed, and set your alarm, and you had to be up at the court at 10 a.m. What made it worse, was that the police had the time of the tram-cars and the time it took to get to a certain stop. They allowed you five minutes from your house to the tram-stop they had selected, and then five minutes to walk to the courts. Then when you arrived, you might be there an hour, two hours.

At your first court, you got a ticket when you arrived from one of the men, gave you the time you got to the court. When you had finished there, there was somebody on duty to give you a slip. You had to keep this slip to show the time you had left. And they had the time worked out for every policeman the length of time he was allowed to travel from court to home and back again and you added that time to the time you were engaged in court and it was worked out to the minute—worked out officially how long it took the tram. So if you were on night duty, it wasn't much use getting off early and going to bed for a couple of hours and then going to court—you might be engaged in court for a long time. So whatever duty you were on—morning duty, that was all right, it was in the firm's time, but if you were on afternoon duty, you would have to attend court and maybe go straight on afternoon duty.

T. B. I was about to lock a fellow up at ten to the hour I was going off at. I thought, 'I'll be kept in the station for an hour dealing with all this.' So I waltzed him across the road and put him in a doorway and left him for somebody else to find.

S. H. I'm going along Scotland Road one night, going home, and I could hear someone smashing a lot down and this woman came saying, 'Bobby, come quick. He's smashing the home up.' Her old fellow's smashing the place up and so I says, 'Listen, there's a bobby standing in the next street.' We didn't tell her we were going home. 'Go tell that bobby on the street there.' And as soon as she disappears, we beat it as fast as we can. We weren't going to get mixed up in a job, when we were going home off duty. And there was no bloody bobby there at all.

Painful experience taught you when to use an avoidance tactic.

T. D. I was on duty on Lambeth Road junction one day when a feller came up to me and said, 'There's a body floating in the canal.' I said to myself, 'Christ, I'm due in for breakfast in another quarter of an hour.' So I went down to the canal. There's a man's body there. Oh, you should have seen it. The stench! I don't know how long it had been there.

There was no axiomatic concern with the call of duty. Easing actions were subject to an instant cost–benefit analysis.

Law as a Two-Edged Sword

Law enforcement has always had mythical characteristics—the notion that infringement always results in some corresponding reaction by the enforcing agency. In the same way that the discretion 'not to arrest' was a means of avoiding punitive extra hours, the power to arrest could also help the other way round—coping with the tedium.

T. D. You might be glad to lock up a drunk to get out of the rain for a while.

Sometimes, we'd lock two or three up—sometimes only one. When we were six to two on evening patrol, to be truthful, we used to go out looking for drunk and disorderlies—just to stop the bloody boredom. We'd say, 'Come on—we'll see what we can find.' We'd go round the corner and perhaps there'd be a couple of fellows fighting or drunk. We'd say: 'Bugger off—we'll give you five minutes.' Chances are we'd run them in. It all helped.'

But it could also operate the other way round.

A. T. You used to accumulate this time you worked over and try and get off the last four hours when nobody was about. If you had a section with only five men, only one could get time off because two other men would have to share the beat. Then you were given so much time to get back home again. Collected up. So you didn't get any benefit from locking someone up—it was discouragement if anything.

Constables were subject to contrary impulses. Depending on the particular circumstances, the use of legal discretion was creative. The unique features of the time and place structured the use of discretion.

Rebellion

Resistance could take several forms. There was always the ultimate alternative. When the going gets tough, the rough get going.

S. H. The worst part of the job is when you had to go round that beat at four o'clock in the morning and it's teeming with rain. I've come and I've took my boots off and poured the bloody rain out. I've seen fellows with nine or ten years' service, saying: 'I'm leaving you. I'm chucking the job in, though I've got no job to go to.' I've seen one sergeant with fourteen years' service chuck it and go to Australia, saying: 'I've had enough of this bloody job.' The worst part of the job was going on the beat in winter. It's not a pleasant thing to be walking up and down those side streets off Soho Square and those neighbourhoods on your own on a dark night in the winter. It broke a lot of people. It broke their nerves. I can remember several policemen being reported missing at the police station where they were on duty. I can remember at least three who disappeared and nipped home. I remember one Welsh fellow up from the Valleys—he run home at night-time. It broke his nerve. Went home to Wales and he had the police uniform on. That's where he made his mistake. They sent up to bring him back.

Other resisters took the risk of long-term career damage, without having to pay the ultimate price.

P. A. I got called as a witness in a motoring case, and it came up when I was on nights and I had to get up and call in the solicitor. They let me off at four in the morning and I had to be in court by nine. The case didn't come up and by two in the afternoon, they said it would probably be tomorrow. So I rang up and told them in the office. 'What about my duties?' It lasted three days in court and I had to do night duties and then, finishing between 12 and 2 a.m., going on nights again, going off early, going to court. The third day, I struck—said, 'No, no more,' to the office. 'Shan't be doing no duty tonight.' 'Why?' 'Because I'm tired. In fact, I'm exhausted.' That's that. I don't go on duty. Knock comes to the door and there's this bobby. 'We want to know what's happened to you?' 'Tell them I'm not coming.' So he goes back and I heard no more of it. But it was a rotten experience. I was seething.

Desperation might result in final defiance. However, there was one further technique of resistance.

The Other Alternative

You could either buckle under the strains of the beat, find an avoidance tactic, or give up and head for the home town. But for some beat constables, there was another possibility. Whimsy might be an outlet.

A. T. I remember one night, one chap. He was in the first Section I was in. He came out from refreshments, and we were all bored to death, waiting to go round again, flings his cape round his shoulder, took his helmet off, and started dancing down the road, throwing flower petals about.

Later on, some of the policemen—I didn't see it, I heard about it because I read the reports of complaints. A lot of people in those streets (they were very poor, but they were very proud) and on the steps leading up to the house, they'd have laid a little piece of lino, three pieces or two. These fellows for fun would pinch one and put it on another step, and do this going all down the road. This caused friction amongst the people—course everyone kept their mouth shut amongst the bobbies. In fact, on one occasion, a very close friend of mine found this step with a piece of carpet on it. So his mate with him said, 'Let's change this.' And they pulled this and it must have been leading right under the doorway through the house, and they pulled it right across the roadway, still sticking under the door. That did cause a bit of friction, because the bosses used to try and find out who it was.

Colleagues who used unusual avoidance and resistance tactics achieved a certain folklore status with their colleagues.

P. H. Crystal sets were new. Nobby Clarke instructed on the cat's whisker radio. There was a ventilator in the wall of the office where he worked. The crystal set could be pulled into a ventilator by pulleys to avoid the sergeant knowing he was listening when on duty in the station. George used to sprinkle nuts on the floor to warn himself of officers coming in. Inspector comes in—up goes the radio to the ventilator out of sight.

There are many accounts, sometimes apocryphal,[23] *of how shop-floor resistance to management operates within authoritarian organizations. Even in police work, with its severe sanctions for resisters, subversion was both necessary for survival as well as feasible, given the right knowledge of the rules of the game.*

END OF THE BEAT SHIFT

In the police service there was no simple end to the day as there had been no simple beginning. You couldn't just clock off after your beat. A day that had begun with the parade affirmation had to terminate in the same style. But even then you remained at the beck and call of the organization. For example, in the 1920s there were no civilian domestics at the station-house. Cleaning was the prerogative of the lowly beat officer.

T. B.   There was a station-keeper and he was in there answering the calls. He had a lot of power. You had to hop to it—it was considered to be a privilege from the sergeant and you had to go in here and strip down, and scrub windows and that sort of thing. It took a lot of mental pressure.

K. R.   Whenever they had a raid on the Chinese gambling, they took them all in the cells and they all sent out for Chinese meals, and when they'd all gone to the Main Bridewell in the middle of the night—'125, scrub out!'—and I had to take my tunic off and scrub out after the Chinese had been.

W. S.   We'd got into Rose Hill station at the end of duty, and if one man didn't come in, they'd send a search out. You were still kept on until he was found. Then you had to sit there and the sergeant would say, 'Fall in,' and you'd fall into line, 'Section correct, sir,' and he might be another ten minutes before he decided to say, 'Dismiss!' and by then you'd lost an hour. You never got it back, of course.

In the late 1930s the Liverpool Police brought in a new 'discretionary movement' in which constables made half-hour points, which gave them relative freedom on the beat. The justification was to make police patrols more unpredictable to potential malefactors. But its major effect was to make life slightly more tolerable for those at the sharp end of the beat system.

In Jeremy Bentham's Panopticon, the authorities utilized several key control structures. Similarly, subservience of the beat constable was maintained by social isolation, by timekeeping, by surveillance, and by the specifics of detailed regulations and instructions on parade. However, subversive survival strategies were possible. As in the Victorian prisons and asylums, the retention of personal sanity required some deviant dodges. But then appeared the formal disciplinary devices of the institution to counter such improvisations.

3

Discipline: More Sticks than Carrots

'FOUND drunk in privy with prostitute. Dismissed!'[1] The Watch Committee's dismissal of one Liverpool constable in 1843 illustrates the orthodox explanation of the rapid turnover of police officers in the early years, when a force such as the Metropolitan could lose one-third of its work-force annually.[2] Those Victorian forces had apparently enrolled too many inadequate individuals, susceptible to the kaleidoscopic temptations of street life. Personal pathology, individual incompetence, were easy excuses for the inability of many officers to stay the course. Constable failure not organizational failure was the cause. The answers were more selective recruitment and yet more discipline.

But there is a rather different interpretation, one that was quite apparent in the city of Liverpool between the wars, for voluntary and involuntary resignations.[3] The strains of beat life were bad enough. But the discipline that backed up that solitary duty was—even by the standards of the 1920s—extraordinarily harsh and pervasive.

There were some compensations. Pay was better than that for the average working man, more substantial than the ten-bob dole which was the experience of many of their compatriots. The pension scheme was remarkable for its day. Promotion—and consequently more freedom from disciplinary restraint—was a further carrot. Control of the beat officer through formal organizational sanctions had both negative and positive attributes.

THE PUBLIC IMAGE

For most city dwellers, there were two images of policing. On one hand, there was the ubiquitous picture of the officer plodding the beat: a figure armed with omnipotent powers and, as such, to be deferred to or to be avoided. Then there was the mass impression: the city's rituals and festivals—the visit of a monarch, the launch of a warship from the Mersey shipyards, or the personage of Her Majesty's Inspector annually reviewing the assembled ranks over tea and buns for the dignitaries of the Watch Committee.[4] There were occasions to admire the police *en masse* as they marched in serried ranks to patriotic tunes from the Police Band. Displays of police horses, motor cycles, dogs, and dress marching were a dominant image of policing as a uniformed institution in the city. Police pageantry was a symbolic rite.

This second image reinforced the first. Behind the solitary constable was a vast army of *doppelgänger*, wheeling and cavorting in the city's Sefton Park, ready and available to reinforce the power of the patrol officer, a force to be reckoned with for those who might dispute the territory of the street. Police on parade, in the absence of marches by a peacetime army, was both a major civic celebration and also a symbol of untrammelled power. The police on parade dignified a pretty grubby calling.

There was a parade of the Liverpool City Force in Sefton Park on the occasion of the annual inspection. The force mustered 1,209 strong, comprising 1,068 Constables, 98 Sergeants, 34 Inspectors, 7 Superintendents, and was commanded by Chief Constable Francis Caldwell, C.B.E., M.V.O., accompanied by Assistant Chief Constable Everett, O.B.E.

They paraded in three battalions. There was also a squadron of 29 Mounted Police, 24 police cyclists, 5 motor cyclists, and 6 Airedale police dogs. To the strains of the Police Band, the men marched past, first in column later in fours. Their fine physique and smart appearance made a very favourable impression. The mounted squadron subsequently executed several movements. A number of policemen under Instructor Clinton gave a display of Swedish drill.

The movements were watched with keen interest by the guests of the Watch Committee. Quite a garden party atmosphere prevailed, which was emphasised by the serving of tea and ices at small tables.   (*Police Chronicle*, 1921)

M. B. I remember when I was an inspector. They were launching the *Ark Royal*. An order came out from the Chief Constable: 'The following inspectors (there were three of them—I was one) and sergeants and men will parade at such-and-such a yard at Birkenhead at eleven o'clock for the launching of the *Ark Royal*. The yard is near Hamilton Street station. They will be in best uniform, white gloves . . .' and so on. Sure enough, I went over there with the other inspectors and we said to the sergeants: 'Fall in the men.' There wasn't a single man who wasn't there all spruced up and well turned out at this awkward hour. This was the type of thing we were proud of.

Membership gave one status, an accolade of civic success. Pride in the uniform was real, tangible, and central to the display of personal worth.

M. B. In those days, the police were almost like an élite force because if you joined, people would say: 'He's joined the police. He's achieved something.' We had silver plates on our helmets, silver buttons, whistles, chain. They were not chromium-plated and they had to be cleaned regularly, every day. They were cleaned until you could see your face in them and fellows were so keen that when they got a new tunic, they would cut all their new buttons off, and put their old buttons on that were beautifully shined. Same with the helmet. Then they brought out chromium-plated badges and buttons. And it took you all your time to get them decent again with a wet rag. All the pride gone. We had pride in our uniforms, pride in the way we kept them.

I used to work alongside a man who was very proud of his handcuffs. This man's annual visit to the Police Court was eagerly looked forward to . . . a case of an unlicensed dog, or a chimney on fire . . . he was noted for his handcuffs; they were, in fact, thought to be the 'finest' in the country—they were silver-plated. I knew yet another man who always possessed two pairs—one for everyday, and another pair were for formal occasions.

(Police Review, 1925)

The unarmed, stern-looking bobby proceeding at regulation pace down the street embodied the virtues of respectable Britain.

T. D. If the sergeant saw you with your hand at the back, he would come up to you: 'What do you think the public will think about you? Get your hands away from there and get them down by your side.'

Like the beat parade, from the public ceremonies to the appearance of the individual uniform, the public face of city policing was unblemished. It embodied the power, majesty, and efficiency of the state in the finery of police uniform.[5]

THE WARTS BEHIND THE PUBLIC FACE

There were, of course, one or two things that police officers kept to themselves, that the public never saw or heard, and that with the death of the Police Union there were no channels to articulate.

T. D. After being on morning duty [6 a.m. to 2 p.m.], we had to parade at 2.20 p.m. at Sefton Park. Mr Hignet [the tobacco baron] was holding a fête for charity. So we marched round with different bands, and at 8.45 p.m. we were told to escort the bands to various parts of the city. One constable had the temerity to state that we had had nothing to eat since 9.30 a.m. He was told that he would be reported for insubordination. The superintendent was told and his excuse was he thought we were all on the Afternoon Section. The constable was transferred to a division as far from home as possible.

We had finished a tour of night duty [10 p.m. to 6 a.m.] and a telephone message came to hold us back. At 7.10 a.m. we were instructed to go home, change into day uniform and parade at Sefton park at 8.45 a.m., which left no time for any breakfast. On arrival at Sefton Park, we were transported by bus to Church Street, as the late King and Queen would pass through on their way to open the Gladstone Dock. Afterwards, we were taken by bus to the Essex Street bridewell for a free meal. This consisted of a milk bottle filled with water to which had been added some lemon juice, and four rounds of Vienna bread, which should have contained beef, but it had run out. So the bread was deposited in the slop bucket. Thence to the Dock Road and from there to East Prescot Street, as the Royal Family were staying with Lord Derby. Then back to the corner of Blackmoor Drive and then we were told to parade at 10.45 p.m. for night duty. Time off would be allowed providing the Police Service would permit it. In other words, if you couldn't get it in the next three months, you could forget about it!

And woe betide anyone besmirching the uniform for improper ends.

W. S. We had tunics with two pockets there and two pockets here, where kept our 'fixings'. We used to go on a tram-car and have a smoke, and a councillor was on there once, and noticed us having a smoke. He complained, so they took those two pockets off us. So we had tunics with just two pockets, one for a book and one for a whistle.

The uniform was the visible symbol, the tip of the iceberg, of a formidable body of sanctions. It signified a disciplinary code of considerable imagination, a vast armoury of Chief Constable's powers, both petty and absolute.

H. P. I remember one time, the inspector coming round—we didn't always see eye-to-eye—telling me I hadn't polished my buttons. In those days, we hadn't got chromium buttons—I had gone home soaked to the skin, after eight hours' rain, dried the stuff and was coming out next morning. My buttons had been polished all right—I was keen on them. I was keen on the uniform, being smart. The inspector came along: 'You haven't polished your buttons.' You had to take it from the inspector, you can't answer back.

Remember the old bachelor button? When we wore braces, you'd get a card of them . . . in two parts . . . the top part and the underneath part [with] a stud [which] you had to put in your trousers. You had to make a tiny hole to push it through—I've seen men reported for using them—making a hole in their uniform.

As in other aspects of police life, detailed regulations governed the minutiae of dress.

H. P. All the uniform was stamped at the time it was issued. You had to wear them at certain times. Old duty was worn for light duty and, for Sunday, you had your latest uniform—be out on Sunday with white gloves, and on special occasions. You had them for quite a long while. They were all stamped. You might have to show the inspector the stamp to show that you were wearing the correct trousers—every now and then, you had to bring all your uniform in and all your uniform was an awful lot of uniform. You'd have two capes and three uniforms. You had an Instruction Book, all your various accoutrements at home. You'd have to take them all in to be examined, then see if there was any fraying around the trousers and you hadn't reported it, for ordinary wear and tear had to be reported and then taken in for repair—you couldn't repair it yourself. If you were in a bad accident or been into the slums with lice and things, you had to report it and bring your uniform in. It would either be destroyed or cleaned officially.

The public façade of the mass ceremony and the individual uniform concealed the blemishes, organizational and material, to which civilians were not privy but which bore heavily on the ordinary constable.

The Clockwork Man

The pettiness over uniform repairs epitomized the way control by the Chief pervaded the working—and the non-working—day. Social control of the rank and file, in its formal disciplinary guise, had a multitude of possibilities. An array of sanctions—'fizzers', 'on the peg'—informal and formal, regulated the beat in an attempt to produce a display of robotic precision and efficiency.

W. R. You weren't allowed to talk to a girl in my time. I've known myself disciplined because my mother spoke to me in Bold Street. On another occasion, a woman cousin met me there and we stood talking, 'Who was that woman you were talking to?' And I got told off for it.

S. H. One night, I was on duty in town and my mate and I was in Renshaw Street and the Chief Constable came along in civvies and said: 'Report yourself, gossiping on the beat.' If you were talking to a prostitute on the beat, you'd get booked for gossiping—for idling your time. But if you were locking up or cautioning, that was different—but you had to put it in your book that you had cautioned her. If I was talking to you on the street and you had asked me where such-and-such a street was, that was all right. If I was talking to you as my pal, I'd get done for idling my time.

D. A. I used to be on an adjoining beat in Cressington Park and I started at the park gates at one side of the road and there was a policeman on the other side of the road—you wouldn't cross the road to talk to him . . . you weren't allowed to talk to the public—that was gossiping, idling your time, failing to work your beat—three charges straight away and soon as the sergeant reported you. Whatever happened to you, you were on a charge if you weren't at the point that the sergeant expected you. But if you're looking down a back entry or something, you can't always be there.

M. B. On the beat, discipline was severe. If people had been in a building after we had been round testing it and seen it secure, they'd come out and leave it open. Quite a lot of PCs got into trouble for that sort of thing, 'being reported for neglect of duty', 'failing to keep the premises secure'.

In many cases, whatever decision you made, you had much to lose, little to gain.

D. A. A friend of mine was posted to a beat in Allerton and one summer's afternoon he saw a young lad—about fifteen years of age—getting into a car. He took the hand-brake off and just moved it about thirty yards. Then he got out of the car. He caught him and it turned out it was the assistant chief constable's son. He was in a terrible dilemma. He didn't know whether to lock him up or what to do. So he walked him round the beat until the sergeant found him. The sergeant instructed him to take him into the police station and charge him with taking a vehicle without consent—the offence as complete by moving it thirty yards. He was reported on a discipline charge for failing to arrest the boy at the time. Instead of walking him round the beat, he should have taken him straight to the police station. The boy was cautioned—never went before the court because of his father being the ACC and this fellow went before the Chief Constable and he had ten years' service at the time. He lost the ten years' increments. Went right back to the rank of probationer. Fined £1 a week until he had done his penance. Had to go back to the school—had to sit amongst the probationers, and then after the school, he was posted right from one side of the city to the other. He appealed against the punishment to the Watch Committee, lost it, and resigned. A terrible punishment.

To the charge of pettiness, the organization—as elsewhere—had a reply. The Panopticon principle required an eventual acceptance of these justifications.

T. D. The discipline was tyranny but it wasn't bad for us—two policemen walking along the road together, talking about women or football like everybody else, and they can't keep their eyes for crime or for offences being committed under their noses.

A. M. Discipline was very tight. In fact, it was a sort of petty tyranny. But there was one thing about it—it made men of us. It made us able to stand up on our own two feet, to sharpen us up in many respects. But it was a little too much.

Survival in the force meant in part learning to accept as legitimate some of the City Police's more peculiar idiosyncrasies and arbitrary discipline.

'You Mustn't Make a Mistake'

Like beat duty, on shift around the clock, discipline never let up. It was a total environment. It governed the minutiae of affairs, ready to strike wherever weakness showed up.

P. P. Sometimes, when we were going in at night, when it was wet, we would try and put a mac on and slip down to A Division parade room—hang the mac up quick and dive into your coat. If you were caught, you'd be charged for being improperly dressed—you had to be in uniform. I was late once, got there at ten instead of half past and was put on a discipline charge by the superintendent. You mustn't make a mistake—just like the army. Some trivial thing—say if an accident happened, three or four people injured in a car crash, pages of statements to take, and then a Report would come back; 'Had the driver signed his driving licence?' That was very easy to overlook.

Some superiors were more zealous than others to enforce the disciplinary code.

H. P. I've seen inspectors go round the police huts and examine the First Aid Kit. When you used anything, you had to put it in the Book. I've seen a bandage worth less than a penny and an inspector, he'd go in and find one missing. If someone didn't own up to it, he'd get all of them who had used that particular hut over the previous month, trying to find who had used that bandage and not reported it.

P. E. A man dropped dead in front of me on the street and I took him to the mortuary and I got into trouble over it because I didn't search the body properly. I forgot about the back pocket. His people complained that he always carried a five pound note in his back pocket. They sent one of the detectives around to the mortuary to search the body and they found the note in the back pocket. I got 'crimed' for it, got into trouble for not searching it. I got fined two classes [a class was half a crown] a week for twelve months, so it mounted up.

On Saturday, 15th May, an Acting Sergeant was in charge of an area near Muirhead Avenue, Liverpool . . . under him, there were on duty two Police Constables . . . between 11 p.m. and 11.30 p.m., observation was kept [on them] by a Chief Inspector and a Sergeant of the Liverpool Police Force. As a result evidence . . . clearly showed that the two Constables had been idling and gossiping together at a place where one of them had no right to be . . . [and] that the Acting Sergeant, on his round of inspection, met these two Constables together, failed to note in his book, as was required in the regulations, the place where and the time where he met them, and to see that the Constables then noted in their books the time and place of his visit . . . The two Constables . . . in a further neglect of duty went down a back entry, where they were caught smoking together, and later one of the Constables and the Acting Sergeant falsely concocted a story to disguise these infractions . . . Constable I was charged with offences of disobedience to orders, neglect of duty, and smoking in uniform on duty . . . the light punishment of reduction in one class for six months, the deprivation of fifty-two shillings in pay. Constable II received a fine of 40s. and the loss of his additional good conduct increment under Police Regulations 58 and 61 of 2s. 6d. per week until such period of not less than one year, when he might again satisfy his superiors of his zeal, efficiency and truthfulness . . . The Acting Sergeant was dismissed from the Police Force. (*Police Chronicle*, 1925)

J. V. There used to be a Greek Church in Trinity Road and the bucks used to specialize in knocking the knobs off the railing. The policeman's job was to count the knobs and report that they were all right in the morning. Now if one was missing, there'd be a report; 'Why didn't you do this? Why didn't you lock someone up?' That's the only time you met your Chiefs and that was always a snarling matter. I was once put on a discipline charge because I had to cycle from here to Lark Lane police station on a very windy day and I got there at eleven minutes to six. For being four minutes late for duty, I was warned. It was discipline, discipline.

On the Dock duty, too, temptations were easy, collaboration possible, but sanctions punitive, as a pot-pourri of traffic tumbled through the gate. Risks were nevertheless taken.

K. M. I was on the Dingle Lane gate—Shell Mex place—and I'd been down there a few months. I knew the people from the ship—the crew used to go out at night-time and some of them would come back merry. Never any trouble with them. One night they were coming through, a bit hilarious, and they said, 'Have a drink'. Normally, I wouldn't have one, but this time I did. I don't know what the drink was—brandy or whisky—I had that much, I had it twice, so that the lads had to see me home because I was more or less drunk. Got away with it because the other bobbies saw me home and signed off for me. On East Queen's Dock, there was a very mild chap—bit timid for a policeman. He knew the Customs in the East Queen's and if you wanted a drink, or anything like that, you would go in the locker and have a bit. This chap came out and carried on with the beat. But by that time, he was paralytic and stayed in the outside toilet underneath the overhead railway. Had to take him home in a taxi and we had to book off for him. He'd been going round the beat supping this over-proofed rum from the Customs.

K. M. When I used to work on the dockside, it was a hive of activity, all the horses and the steam-engines parked along the street. It was the dockers who were stealing on the docks. If they saw a case of apples or anything, they would break it open—didn't regard it stealing. Sometimes a bale of cloth went and you wondered how it could get past the Dock gate.

P. C. Thomas Wheeler of Liverpool City Police was fined 40s. by the Liverpool Stipendiary Magistrate on a charge of being unlawfully in possession of two pounds of rice and some oranges, value 1s. 6d. Wheeler said he had been a member of the force for twelve and a half years and had been on duty on the Docks since last August. On that duty he would get to know people pretty well. The oranges were given to him by Mr. Singleton of Houghton's . . . he realised in Supt. Learmont's office that the people he received them from might not have the right to give them. He realised that it was improper for Policemen to accept gifts.

(*Police Chronicle*, 1932)

T. B. Everything on the Dock Estate was owned by the Docks and Harbour Board. A feller Thom—at Langham Street Gate, there used to be a tremendous number of Ellerman boats coming in—oranges and so on—tremendous amount thrown away because they were bad. Thom picked up two oranges from the gutter but someone saw him and they took him to Derby Street police station and he got the sack from the police.

P.C. Alexander Thom was sentenced to two months imprisonment by the Stipendiary Magistrate for stealing four oranges worth threepence from a shed at Liverpool Docks where he was patrolling. He pleaded guilty and said he was thirsty. Mr Fred Pritchard a member of a firm of fruit merchants has written to the Council suggesting that members of the trade petition the Watch Committee to consider Thom's position with a full knowledge of the facts. The handling of fruit on the docks, especially oranges—every case of which is opened to discover how many wasted oranges it contained—is a very happy-go-lucky procedure. Buyers and their representatives will often throw away an orange or an apple or other fruit . . . it is the custom. Many oranges, apparently sound, are thrown out on the quay and if everyone taking one or two of these oranges was arrested for theft, one Police Court would not be enough to deal with the cases . . . Under Police Regulations, Thom's conviction will be followed by dismissal from the Force.   (*Daily Courier*, 1927)

It is not surprising that there is widespread protest against the sentence of two months' imprisonment . . . passed on the Liverpool Constable who admitted that he had taken four oranges, worth threepence, from a shed in the West Canada Dock . . . pilfering by the Police is a different matter from the same offence committed by a street urchin. Even so, the ruin of his career and the disgrace of imprisonment seem, to most people, to be out of all proportion to the crime.   (*Police Review*, 1927)

T. B. You had to see what they were passing through and you had to have a chit and you had to time this chit and sign it and then you went to the hut and put it on the spike. Of course, the result was, anybody watching you timed how long it took to go from the Dock gate to sign in and put it on the spike. If you were more than a reasonable time, they would claim that you were failing to work your beat, or gossiping—things like that.

The Thom case was exceptional and gave rise to something of a public outcry. It did Thom himself little good but it exacerbated the inarticulate anger of other officers at the pettiness of the regulations in the face of the array of temptations.[6]

POLICE CRIME—'WE WEREN'T ALL ANGELS'

There was of course 'real' police crime—whether induced by the pressures of the beat and or by tempting opportunities. Some charges were more heinous than others.

The Liverpool Stipendiary Magistrate dismissed summonses brought against a Liverpool Constable for selling tickets in an unauthorised lottery . . . the Constable had got into financial difficulties owing to a serious illness of his wife and the ill-health of his two children. They had had medical attention since the beginning of the year and he did not know where to turn for a penny. In order to raise money, he decided to raffle his motor-cycle combination. Tickets were printed and he sold them to friends for 1s. each . . . The Constable had been in the Force since 1924 and had an excellent character [and] served in the trenches at the age of fifteen and a half.   (*Police Review*, 1926)

Sixteen men including three Liverpool Police officers were remanded on bail at Liverpool this week accused of conspiring to distribute tickets for the Irish sweepstake.
                                       (*Liverpool Daily Post*, 1939)

James Shelton aged 25, and George Barnes, aged 23, two Liverpool constables, with a taxi-cab driver named Charles Wareing, were accused of breaking into the Co-operative Stores in Wavertree Road and stealing a safe containing £146.

(Liverpool Daily Post, 1925)

Henry Marston (25), a Constable with the Liverpool City Police, and Angus Gray (28), an ex-Constable, were remanded in custody in Liverpool . . . charged with breaking into Beaumont Street Post Office and stealing a safe and contents valued at £500. They were further charged with stealing a motor-cycle combination on which they are said to have carried away the safe. *(Police Review, 1924)*

Constable Mortimer Twamley, 29, Liverpool, was committed for trial on three accusations of stealing £13 in Treasury notes from William Riley, tobacconist . . . Riley alleged that because of certain happenings he hung his jacket behind a door and fitted an electrical device and wires to a wallet in his pocket, connecting it with lights in his bedroom. While in his bedroom, he saw the electric bulbs light up. He rushed downstairs, examined the wallet and found £2 missing. Twamley then came in from the backyard and when accused by Riley, he denied it, offering also to be searched. *(Police Review, 1931)*

. . . the recent prosecution of three ex-Constables for grave offences of shopbreaking and garage-breaking of which they were found guilty at the last Assizes and sentenced to long-term imprisonment. *(Police Review, 1924)*

Discretionary power of prosecution could also be used in deviant ways. The formal rules could be used by the rank and file for their own personal advantage. A shopkeeper who refused to sell constables cigarettes at a discount and complained of the illegal sale of similar goods to the public from their own trading organization, the Police Guild, could find himself summonsed by the same officers for employing children under age (which in turn gave rise to the banning of the Police Guild by the Watch Committee[7]).

More serious crime was possible. The well-worn cliché that the police are only a reflection of the society they serve,[8] can be seen in a different light. Villains as well as angels peopled the Liverpool City Police.

W. S. I operated from the Dog and Gun Police Station. Pettyway comes along with me. 'Look at the sky—there's a fire along there.' So come to Home Farm. When I get there—the whole place is going up and the farmer's in his pyjamas trying to save the rick. Another fire breaks out in the West Derby area, and another one. So the CID gets out to snoop around. So the three of us are in a car—Pettyway and another feller. Pettyway says: 'Whoever's doing this wants their head seeing to.' Six o'clock—off we go to do the usual patrol. CID comes up: 'You can all relax, fellers—we've got him.' 'You've got him—who was he?' 'Pettyway.' Bobby who had been sitting by me. It was him who had been doing it. How they connected it—he was on his way home and there's a telephone box. It's that box that tells the fire brigade that there's a fire. He got three years.

Wearing a police uniform did not sanitize a working man from ungodly ways. Few such blemishes, given the secrecy of organizational practice, came to light. When they did, they would normally meet exemplary retribution.

Laying the Blame

Because of the wide range of sanctions available to senior officers, men on the ground were in an extremely vulnerable situation.[9] The policy was generally to blame the individual, not the organization. Immediate superiors were crucial in mediating the discipline by senior officers, and in the infliction of their own minor punishments. Normally, harsh discipline was personalized as the idiosyncrasies of those superiors. Blaming the organization for its pettiness had major costs. Individual officers might come and go, but the organization was there for ever for the thirty-year man. There was little benefit from carping about the organizational source of the disciplinary impedimenta. The sergeant, the proverbial piggy-in-the-middle, was the ready scapegoat for both juniors and superiors.

D. A. You had sergeants in those days who were holy terrors. If you failed to work your beat and the sergeant went looking for you and couldn't find you, you'd be reported and land before the chief constable. You'd get fined a pound. The discipline was very, very, severe. Mind you, a lot of them had come from the army and from the navy—but I don't think that makes man's nature alter to that effect. Although, if you take a sergeant-major or some corporals even—it's the nature of the man. They seemed to take that kind of man to make him sergeant in the beginning after the Police Strike. There was no Tom, Dick, or Harry business. You had to address him as Sergeant: 'All correct, Sergeant.' He'd give you a visit and put it in his book and you'd do the same.

K. R. At Garston, there was a toilet on the main road and when we were on nights, and there was one officer walking along and I was on the other side—we daren't cross the road. At about 2.30 a.m., he went into the lavatory and I would shout across at him. The sergeant followed him in and found him smoking and put him on a discipline charge—idling his time. That's the type of sergeant you got on the job—Creepers. I was never a Creeper. After I'd been in three years, I got married. Then it was a frightful job because the sergeants were all the same. They wanted to get on but that made me swear if I ever got made Sergeant, I would never treat a man the way I was treated.

Judgements on the sergeants varied according to one's own eventual rank.

T. B. You'd have sergeants who liked to drink and he'd have a constable in his section who knew where to get this drink, but normally amongst the sergeants, you were apart from the constables. You carried the job. The inspector was the inspector. You wouldn't find fraternizing. Sergeants were the backbone of the police. The inspector was remote: 'Yes, Sir, No, Sir'.

Not many sergeants saw much advantage in their position.

A further great grievance that exists in this force in the Division where I am is that the Section Sergeant dare not enter any Station while he is on duty unless he signs the main station book; yet the plain clothes P.C.s and Detective Constables, and even uniform P.C.s can go into the Station as often as they think and there is no order that any of them must sign in and out. But if the Section Sergeant goes in for any necessary purpose, the Inspector comes in, he is reported and gets a severe reprimand from his superiors for idling his time in the Station. When the plain clothes Constables, the Detectives, and even uniform Constables can spend their watch in the Station, the Section Sergeant who does all the work, and who is accountable to the Instruction Book, the backbone of the Force, dare not enter the Station during his hours of duty. What red tape!   (*Police Review*, 1920)

M. B. If you were lucky you might just get told off by the superintendent or you might go up before the chief constable where you could be fined. I know of one case—the chief constable was Wilson. He came from a small force, Plymouth, and didn't realize that big forces were totally different. I remember him telling one man that had been late three times in fifteen years that it was getting to be a habit: 'You'd better look for your previous employment.' And quite a lot of men were emptied off the job for very poor reasons—they had no consideration for the men themselves. There was a large pool of unemployed in those days and it seemed to us that no sooner were you in than they were trying to get you off the job. We had sergeants and inspectors jumping on us for the least little thing and very often trying to get us into trouble, whereas young fellows learning the job, what we needed was assistance.

T. D. We had a CC, Plymouth Bill we called him—and he had a force in Plymouth that wasn't as great in numbers as a division in Liverpool. It went to his head and the superintendents were terrors and they could get rid of a man—give him the sack like slap on their wrist.

The higher the eventual rank, the more likely was blame to be similarly apportioned.

B. T. Some of the inspectors always appeared at the wrong time. I remember when we used to do an evening patrol—6 p.m. to 2 a.m. on Lime Street. There was this particular inspector. He always seemed to be picking on me. I was pretty conscientious. I was talking to this other lad across the road—we were due to go off duty at two and we were just hanging about before making our way down to the station—there was no relief for us on that shift. Weatheralls had a shop there—mackintosh people—with a deep doorway. I was standing there talking to him, and over on the other side of Lime Street, the station side, there was another mackintosh shop and they had ten shilling notes pasted in the window. That was to show off their ten shilling macs. One bright fellow decided to have one of these ten shillings. So we saw this fellow go up to the window and look and then he went and got a stone from the kerb and 'bang' on the window. By the time we were across the road, he had the ten shilling note in his hand. But as we were coming out of the doorway, running across there, sidling round the side was the inspector. He must have known we were in the doorway. Afterwards, he got me and asked what I was doing in the doorway with Symington. I said, 'We were watching the chap steal the ten bob note.' 'You weren't talking were you?' A bit tyrannical that part of it.

The same Inspector had me on another thing. He had a pet theory that if you went flashing your torch about on night duty, any of the burglars would see that the light was going on. Well, you had to flash it in the doorway, and they'd see it in any case. But there was something that took my attention one night, on one of the shop windows, and I was flashing the torch on the window and he comes up. He wanted to know why I was flashing the light. I said I was flashing it to see if the window was all right. So he says: 'You weren't. You were flashing it to look at the display in the window.' 'No, I was checking the window.' And he said: 'Do you want to go forward on a charge on that?' 'Oh, no'—so he ticked me off there and then instead.

Senior officers were so removed from the lowly constable that they were practically out of sight. Rare ones were more flexible and tolerant.

P. S. The superintendent was like God. They could transfer a man two miles away from his house. There was a superintendent called Kinley. When I was on the motor cycles, he used to collar me to take him home for lunch. It was rather pathetic sometimes because he was upset at somebody going down on a discipline charge and getting the sack. He used to tell me it was never intended. When the sergeant visited you, he was supposed to sign your book—you had to keep up to date with everything in it. If there's any alterations, they wanted to know why. Jack Kinley told me about one case. This feller said, 'I didn't alter me beat book', and chief constable said, 'All right, we'll send it over to the Forensic Department.' And this feller caved in then and admitted it.

B. T. Late for duty was another thing. If you were a couple of minutes late, you had to go down and see the superintendent. I was only ever late once and he was an old superintendent—Angus—he wasn't bad. He said, 'What went wrong?' 'My alarm clock didn't go off.' 'Well, next time get two alarm clocks.' He wasn't bad at all making a joke of it.

Over time, constables assumed the same pathological spectacles through which they were seen by the organization. The structure, the disciplinary rules, were immutable. You couldn't budge them. The City Force as an organization was too inflexible to oppose successfully. You had to turn your complaints against the individuals who manned its higher echelons. Blaming individuals for failings endemic to the organization was a necessary survival strategy. You were often surprised that that same assumed frailty might result in a more human, more tolerant superior.

The Final Sanction: 'On Your Way'

Punishments ranged from the formal reprimand to outright dismissal. But there was often little distinction between them in the cause. Sometimes there appeared to be justification enough—even if the manner of the dismissal left something to be desired.

S. H.   There was a lot of us on reserve duty at St George's Hall, about forty or fifty of us, and one bloody bobby sat there with us and they sent for him. It appears that this bloody bobby had been locked up two or three times. They hadn't found out. They sent for him and he never came back. We learnt the next day he had had to hand in his uniform and get off the job as fast as he could.

But normally, dismissal seemed out of all proportion to the alleged fault. It could occur early in your service—or much later.

S. H.   When you join the job, you're on two years' probation. I had a young fellow come up to me one day—he had eighteen months' service. He had tears in his eyes. He says, 'I'm leaving, Frank.' I says, 'What's to do?' He says, 'The superintendent won't recommend me for being a policeman.' He had to go immediately.

H. P.   If your face didn't fit, they could get rid of you within twelve months. There was this bobby, a big chap over six feet, very dour, from the Hebrides —he'd only seen sheep. He came on night duty. There it was in the Chief Constable's Orders: 'services dispensed with, under Regulation 11'. He come to me and said, 'What can I do now?' Inspector comes up and says, 'What are you doing here?'—McLeod, his name was. 'Give me your book, whistle.' (We didn't have warrant cards then.) They took his accoutrements off him. 'Go home. Hand your uniform in tomorrow morning.' That was finish, no redress. His face just didn't fit. In my opinion, they didn't give him a chance.

D. A.   Discipline code was terrible. A young feller rode on the front of a tram, which was the usual thing in those days, if you were signing off duty. Everybody knew the tram drivers and used to hop on the front of the car up to the nearest point of the station and then jump off, and the superintendent was on the car and saw him getting on. He got off with him and he knew he was going to the station to sign off and he asked him, 'Did you pay your fare on the car?' 'No sir, that's the usual thing.' He did him on a discipline charge and he was sacked.

W. S.   Poor old Fraser, he got the sack. He married a girl who was with a firm who repaired old clothes. He saw a bobby in trouble at Old Swan, got off the tram-car to help him, and he got his mac torn. Made a claim for repairs—£3. They checked with the firm and they said they didn't repair it, so he got the sack.

The implications of dismissal were severe. The constable might recover his pension contributions—but that was all. Probably a long way from his home town, he would suffer from the same economic deprivation and social stigmatization experienced by the police strikers in 1919, without the latter's support and solidarity.

DEFENCES: FIGHTING BACK

Of course, not all punishments were taken lying down. A formal, internal appeals procedure was eventually introduced in 1927[10] and, if that failed, as it invariably did, individual strategies could be developed—at a cost. Having the right in the more serious cases to appeal over the head of the chief constable to the Watch Committee had little effect. Local worthies rarely challenged the rectitude of the chief constable. But the major flaw from the constable's point of view was the impossibility of putting a good case to a senior officer who was prosecutor, judge, and jury. Even the rare successful defence might be at a price.

M. B. The Federation helped us but they hadn't any teeth. You were allowed to be defended by a fellow officer who acted as 'your friend'. He would act on your behalf to the chief constable. But that was as far as you could go and often he became in a rather dubious position himself through doing that sort of thing. I remember one fellow Madden, who was very clever. In fact, he would have made an ideal barrister—and he defended quite a lot of men who were indicted for various things—got them away because he was too cute for the superintendent who was dealing with the job. Madden got shifted from that division—you only got shifted if you were in trouble—and he came to the same division as myself. In fact, he was on the same traffic spot as myself and he told me, 'They're after me. They'll get me out.' And I think they did.

Ironically, such tight rule-bound organizations contained their own innate weaknesses, which alert constables could spot.

T. D. One time we had an acting sergeant. I'd been going round all morning and never seen him. About half an hour before I was due to go off, he made my half-hour point. But I'd disappeared because I'd a man shouting 'fruit and vegetables' (in those days, you had to have your name and address on your cart). I thought, 'I'll go and see what's doing.' Now he wanted to know why I wasn't at the point. So when I went inside the station, I told him where I was. But I had made a mistake and not put the fellow's name and address in my book. 'You should have done—don't do it again,' he said. 'I don't believe that there was a hand-cart. While you were missing, I had to deal with a dog that had been run over.' (That was a ruddy lie). 'Don't do it again.' I says to myself, 'I'm not having this.' The following morning, he was on again. So I put everything in my book, such-and-such-a-thing, such-and-such-a-thing. So I went on until just after refreshment time: Spoke to Mr so-and-so—lots of things in my book. Then he says when I get back, 'What's all this?' 'You're not making me out to be a liar.' 'Rub it out.' 'Not rubbing anything out—you know as well as I do, you're not allowed to rub anything out.' 'Don't be like that.' 'From now on, when you're acting sergeant, everything's going to go down in my book. Once you doubt my word, that's it.'

As with the pre-existing right to appeal to the Victorian Watch Committee,[11] over the head of the chief officer (local worthies rarely asserted any independence from the chief), there was little chance of overturning the verdict. The Federation representative could suffer unofficial penalties for any such assistance. Instead, sanctions could sometimes be avoided by using the organization's rules against a superior—'working to rule' has a long and honourable tradition in labour history, especially where industrial action is prohibited.[12]

REWARDS: THE CARROTS

All organizations work on a carrot-and-stick policy. Punishment and rewards go hand in hand.[13] Police forces are no exception. In the words of the chief constable some years after the post-Strike intake: 'There is much more stability amongst the Constables due to rising years of service, too valuable to be risked.'[14] The body of penal regulations was counterbalanced by some rewards. The basic promise of the organization was pay. Police earnings in the 1920s were substantial by comparison with most other occupations to which a working man could aspire. Few jobs today offer pensioned retirement after thirty years. Promotion was a further carrot, though like the former hedged round with qualifications and caveats. Finally, there were occasional commendations, whether verbal or in the form of small sums of cash, from philanthropic organizations.

A Good Wage

Within the financial horizons of a working-class man after the Great War, police pay, including allowances, small increments, and pension, was both tempting and binding.

H. P. You put up with the discipline because of the unemployment. In B Division, the discipline was about the worst in the force—the thing was that it was not a bad pay-packet plus there was the pension at the end—a big item. We had to go ten years before we got our first increment of 2*s.* 6*d.* It depended on whether your face fitted—it wasn't automatic. At twelve years there was another 2*s.* 6*d.* My first week's pay was £2. 17*s.* 6*d.* But the average pay was still below the police plus there was job security—there weren't a lot of jobs paying pensions then.

T. B. In those days, a bobby was a good catch for a woman—in a regular job and a good wage—average working man's wage was around a pound to thirty shillings. During the greater part of the time, at the beginning, you had to put up with it because the alternative was ten bob a week unemployment. A policeman's wage with ten years' service was on £4. 10*s.* plus his lodging allowance—you were well on the way to the top of the money league. If you passed for Sergeant, you got two ten-shilling special allowances, and when I got made Sergeant, I was on a bike allowance of seven shillings a week.

The pension was the ultimate, binding, financial carrot. Once you had served a few years, you might come to detest the job, but you committed yourself to the future.

P. H. If you went at 25 years' service, you got half pension. If you were getting £8, you'd go at £4. When you'd done your thirty years, you'd go off at two-thirds pension. I had no prospects, so I decided to do my thirty. Besides, you always knew that there were three or four thousand willing to take your job on if you didn't like it.

A. M. You were tied down by your pension. You had something that very few other people had and this to a large extent tied you down.

It didn't help when Westminster enforced successive cuts in pay as part of the public-services' sacrifice in relation to the national economic crisis of 1931 and 1932.[15]

Constable Mooney joined the Force,
A fine upstanding man, of course;
Nor cared a jot as long he tripped
On his first day's duty how much he chipped.

The very first week upon his beat
And a dog almost cleared the street.
On the Super's report to the Chief was written
'Constable Mooney was badly bitten.'

On Saturday night loud sounds of strife,
Drunken navvy ill-treating his wife.
Next day a Policeman's face all patched,
'Cos the woman turned round and Mooney is scratched.

But a disturbance down the road,
Down that way Mooney quickly strode,
Fierce, sharp tussle. Handcuffs clicked,
But Mooney's shins severely kicked.

Runaway horses, bairns leaving school,
Bystanders breathe 'The plucky old fool.'
And Mooney's grinning—but what's the joke,
As they help him away with his forearm broke.

Armed bandits. High-powered car.
Telephone messages flung out far.
Mooney ne'er moans about his lot
As he lies in hospital next day, shot.

P.C. Mooney is still in the Force—
Not quite so upstanding now, of course—
A fine, old Policeman, still smiling, but
Would you believe it: his pay has been cut!

(*Police Review*, 1931)

There was some public criticism of police pay—and of perks such as the housing allowance, resentment that crystallized during that austerity period in the early 1930s.

Having seen the various statistics covering police forces throughout England, I find that the Liverpool Police Force costs more than any other . . . The country is crying out for economy; why not an enquiry into the Liverpool Police Force?   (*Liverpool Echo*, 1931)

. . . the practice of paying allowances for housing and rent allowances, in the case of married members of the force. Will city fathers, in the name of economy, explain why those practices should be maintained?   (*Liverpool Echo*, 1931)

Is the city over-policed? . . . Manchester manages with one constable for every 524 inhabitants, in Liverpool a constable has only 467 to look after.

(*Liverpool Daily Post*, 1931)

There were criticisms over police costs that spread beyond the question of police pay:

it will be interesting to know what the Police Band costs, which the ratepayers never hear, and what did the rodeo, performed by the Mounted Section, cost the long-suffering ratepayers?   (*Evening Express*, 1931)

. . . city council proposal to disband the mounted police 'being mainly ornamental rather than useful.'   (*Liverpool Echo*, 1932)

The vast majority of officers learned to grin and bear it. As they grew older, pay might increase only gradually, but the pension carrot grew. Especially in the early 1930s, notwithstanding the pay-cuts, police officers in the city had a job secure from redundancy —which was more than you could say for most of those they policed. Similarly, promotion continued as a further inducement for some.

The Lure of Promotion

The promotion reward was like a game of snakes and ladders. There were few opportunities to rise quickly. If you caught a sponsor's eye (Liverpool had its own version of the Trenchard system of accelerated middle-class promotion[16]), or, in the view of many officers, had the right 'connections', there were possibilities. Some took the arduous climb, a square-by-square approach, passing the hurdles of Sergeant's and Inspector's examinations, serving time on a variety of specialist duties, and beat supervision.

EXCERPTS from the Liverpool Examination Papers, 1927

CONSTABLE TO SERGEANT

Time allowed, 1 hour. Answer 6 questions only.

- Define the following geographical terms, and give an example of each—Estuary, Straits, Volcano, Isthmus, Watershed.
- Name the County Town of the following counties and the river each is drained by:— Norfolk, Hampshire, Buckinghamshire, Glamorganshire, Brecknockshire.
- Name the different classes of crops in England. Where do you generally find land suitable for the grazing of cattle?
- Name five lakes in England and state where they are situated. Where does each of the following towns obtain its water supply?:– Liverpool, Birkenhead, Manchester?

SERGEANT TO INSPECTOR

English and General Intelligence

- Show by inflexion, each of the proper nouns as adjectives:– Spain, Ceylon, Portugal, Denmark, Switzerland.
- Explain the meaning of the following by embodying each in a sentence:– Course, source, recourse, discourse, concourse.
- Name five different fashions for men's civilian head-gear and give a brief description of each.

Snakes and Ladders

Careers progressed square by square and there were slippery patches too. Examinations aside—there were many ways in which the unlucky, rather than the unwary, could slither down.

A. T. The worst part of the job was after passing the Sergeant's exam and waiting for twelve to thirteen years to get promoted—you'd have the Chief Constable's Orders come out and you'd see people who had passed years after you being promoted and you'd think that I'll do my thirty years like this.

M. B. I am quite candidly of the opinion that I would have left the police out of a feeling of resentment because I was overlooked time and time again for inferior men. I say that with every degree of confidence. I was just a stranger up here in Liverpool, coming from Scotland and I didn't have anybody backing me, which a lot of people do—somebody pulling strings for them. I was overlooked repeatedly, to such an extent that I became completely disgusted.

It used to be said with a considerable amount of justification that you could get as far as Inspector on your own bat but after that 'No', you needed somebody pushing you—city councillor, anything. I came across many, many instances of that sort of thing. As an inspector, there was one particular PC that I detested because he was a dodger in my opinion and gutless, and when he put reports in, I would repeatedly scrub across it: 'No further action'. Superintendent said to me one day, 'You don't like this fellow very well.' 'I do not. I detest him.' I threatened to put him on a discipline charge because whenever the drunks were turning out, you'd find him in the station writing some trivial bike without a light. So the superintendent said: 'You know who he is? He's so-and-so's nephew.' His aunt was a lady barrister and a member of the council, a JP. So this individual, who I wouldn't have given three stripes across, eventually became a Chief Inspector. That sort of thing used to happen to an enormous degree.

Such claims of sponsored promotion were obviously difficult to substantiate. However, in the early 1920s there were evident short-cuts. The expansion of the police administrative staff guaranteed a faster route to the top for those who were drafted in as clerks. Chief Constable Caldwell is supposed to have never actually served on the beat—being recruited directly into the administrative apparatus and rising quickly within it.[17] *Graduate entry with resultant opportunities for promotion was then—as now—an especially sore point.*

M. B. I never forget being called by a superintendent, who said: 'Sergeant Bullock, you're acting inspector over the weekend. Sergeant so-and-so has just passed the Inspector's exams and I'd like you to take him with you. Give him an idea of the inspector's duties.' So this particular sergeant who had been a PC when I had been an acting sergeant, sat alongside me. We went along to the various stations. He came with me. He saw the work that I examined and dealt with, and on the Tuesday, I was saluting him as an inspector.

That's not an isolated incident. I was dragged out of my bed one morning when I was in A Division, and at that time unless you passed your life-saving exams in the water, you couldn't be considered for promotion. I got there—the message had come up via the landlady. 'You've got to be at X Baths.' I said: 'Not me, I've passed all my exams,' and off she went. PC came back later on. 'Bang, bang, bang' on the door. 'You've got to be there and you've got to sign this to show that you're aware of it.' So when I got there, it's the swimming coach there and a uniformed inspector and a particular individual who came from Cambridge University (quite a few of them came into the force at that time—in 1932). Inspector said: 'The superintendent has spoken to me—you're the best life-saver in the division. Now this individual has passed his exam and it is up to you to get him through.' Sure enough, I dived in the water, swam up the other end, and he came after me. He damned near drowned me. He eventually let go of me and I had to go the bottom of the baths and bring him to the surface, take him to the side and get him breathing again, and I was considered a failure for that.

The man was to be got through this particular exam because he was from Cambridge. In those days, I think the Home Office and the Foreign Office were full up and we were getting people from universities and some of them were pretty useless, heads full of all sorts of knowledge but no common sense. I know another one—a friend of mine said: 'There's a young PC lodging with me and he's got all sorts of new ideas. He's going to be a sergeant in five years, and inspector in seven, chief inspector in eight years—you'd better come and talk to him.' So I went round. Sure enough, he told me that's what they planned for him. He was a la-di-dah Cambridge graduate. He came to A Division and got himself into a lot of trouble through damn stupidity. Head full of academic knowledge but nothing else—and before anybody could bat an eyelid, he applied to sit an exam in London, and the next thing he was in the Metropolitan Police. And he did become a chief inspector in eight years.

> Now they're shouting for recruits
> To wear regulation boots;
> To patrol the dirty streets on town beats
> So that the Hendon 'nobs' can get the 'cushy' jobs.
> And snore till ten in the morning.
>
> (*Police Review*, 1936)

M. B. It's all very well this business of collegiate training—you've haven't got the knowledge of working on the beat. In the school, I was told in the First Aid that you could always tell a fractured femur (which happened with elderly women as a rule). The foot is always turned out. Within a very short time, I dealt with three fractured femurs in Church Street—I never saw one with a foot turned out. It's the practical knowledge that is far more important than the academic.

Some years earlier, the Liverpool Watch Committee had tried unsuccessfully to ban police officers from membership of rival Protestant and Catholic quasi-political organizations.[18] *Such old-boy networks were one way of jumping the promotion queue, of obtaining sponsorship.*[19]

A. T. I passed for Sergeant seventeen years before I got made up. They had a very large number of Scots sergeants and they all seemed to be very close. In fact, one chap, Jack Bruce the name was (he used to do traffic duty on Scotland Road. He used to stand there playing his imaginary pipes. His daughter was a champion at the Highland Fling). Jack said to me, 'Aren't you in the Bobby Burns Club?' I said, 'No.' 'Well, come down and I'll introduce you and put you forward' —because he was something well-to-do there. I thought that that was an opportunity to get promotion. Now I'd always said to myself, 'I'll never join the Masonic Lodge,' and therefore I wouldn't join the Bobby Burns Club. I might have suffered—seventeen years waiting for promotion, for some of them were made sergeants very soon.

The chances of promotion in Liverpool depend upon the candidate's relation to his Super—'. . . matters have gone from bad to worse . . . Today, service, seniority, and experience do not appear to be considered at all, your religion or creed appear to be an important factor in regulating your progress in the Service . . .' We deleted the paragraph in the letter in which particular reference is made to the form of religion specially favoured.

(Editorial, *Police Review*, 1932)

Accelerated promotions had first given rise to major complaints in the reorganization after the Police Strike, when many younger and inexperienced officers were made sergeants.[20] The bitterness left by the scheme for accelerated promotion for graduates left its mark. There have been recurring attempts by the police service since World War II to develop alternative means of entry and promotion to the traditional progression from the ranks,[21] which have always been met by by bitter reference to the schemes of the 1930s.

Narking as a Factor in Promotion

There was a stark personal conflict in the struggle for promotion. Where there were more Indians than positions as Chiefs, when, for example, many constables had passed the Sergeant's exam, personal animosity could be severe.

A. T. With the strike having taken place, everyone was jockeying, everyone that had sat for Sergeant and passed their exams, the only way they could see to get promotion was to report another man.

A. M. Three policemen on the evening patrol—lots of publicans used to leave bottles of beer on the doorstep for policemen and one of these policemen, he liked his booze. The other two were good as well—they'd both passed for Sergeant, stable, fine fellers. And some sneaky feller who was in the promotion stakes as well, he found this out and passed the word on and they laid a trap for three fellers, one night after twelve. Two of them disappeared without trace as fast as they could. But the old bobby—he'd downed his pint of beer—he got taken before the chief constable and he got a serious fine, £1. But the two acting sergeants got caught. They never made Sergeant. And two more likely fellers that you'd make Sergeant, I hadn't come across.

> I see that you're mentioned in Orders,
> That you've caught 'Spike' Smith and his mate,
> I've heard that they're the midnight marauders,
> Who've caused so much trouble of late.
> A fairly good case—were you working
> As laid down, correctly your beat?
> Or were you, as usual, shirking
> And resting your—well—er, flat feet?
>
> You watched them! Now tell me another,
> I'll bet you'd 'put up' in a door,
> And you heard 'Spike' Smith and the other
> Before they had noticed your snore
> Don't go—I don't mean to be nasty,

Hang on, I'm coming your way.
Your temper, old man's, getting hasty,
Don't take it like that, what I say.

Don't think for a minute I'm jealous.
How could I be jealous of you?
For you must admit I'm more zealous,
A far better policeman than you.
For I've no end of good cases,
I've had in 'Knife' Jones twice before,
I caught him with picklocks and braces,
Just breaking in 'Lewis's' Store.

I caught him by cute observation;
There's none that could not but agree
That anybody else in the station
Is half such a policeman as me.
I did not cry out for assistance,
I carried the 'job' through alone,
And 'Knife' did not offer any resistance:
He knew I could well hold my own.

Of course, you know, 'Knife' is a rough'n,
The roughest, I think, of the rough,
I daresay he'd heard I'm a tough'un,
He came along quiet enough—
Hang on, eh, which way are you walking?
Alright, it's your best way, I see,
And confidentially talking,
The Chief thinks the world about me.

I had a good case one December—
I think then you hadn't joined us
The snow was that deep, I remember,
Hold on mate, that isn't your bus,
I'm coming, don't push, wait a minute,
This tale on the way I can tell . . .

(*Police Review*, 1932)

A. T. The system then was, there was a number of sergeants who had been in the army. There was a number of men who had passed for Sergeant's rank, and the only way they could get it was to report another policeman so they could go to the chief constable on a discipline charge.

P. S. You'd get a feller that was friendly with the bosses. He'd tell over you and the next thing you know, you were on a fizzer form. You'd get a case where there were two acting sergeants and one would want to get ahead of the other—he'd run the other down to the inspector.

.   .   .   .   .

Six feet in height, plus inches three,
With limbs as strong as any tree
To be a Policeman was his hope.
Spurred only by that insidious dope
    'Promotion'.

.   .   .   .   .

Snared in promotion's sinuous coil
He burned, too much, the midnight oil.
Result he cracked, and almost died
But in delirium still he cried—
    'Promotion'.

And thus he finished. Broken nerves,
Marked 'Unfit for further service'
—Plain Clothes for Life, they said goodbye,
No longer does that poor lad cry
    'Promotion'.

(*Police Review*, 1937)

Colleague solidarity counted for little when there was a chance for one of the few organizational carrots—that of promotion. Apart from that possibility and the final pension, there were only a few other possibilities of organizational reward.

A PAT ON THE BACK

Beat work and manning the Dock gates produced few opportunities for praise. Keeping the locals quiet on the street and patient watch on the gates, unlike Plain Clothes and CID work, offered no glamour and caught no superior's eye.[22] Valorous actions might sometimes result in a small award from a philanthropic organization, but generally received minimal recognition.[23]

J. V. One night, I was on duty at the Herculaneum Dock when the high winds were blowing in November (half the windows in Grafton Street were blown in). There was a stack of timber being unloaded from the Dock and the wind threw that all over the place. On the west side, where we were, a lightship was being reconditioned. It was about two or three in the morning. She bust her moorings and she belted into the coal-tips, ready for loading. We dashed along. There were two dry docks and if she had veered over, she'd have gone into the oil storage area. So I climbed aboard with a flashlight, trying to find a rope. Eventually, I found a rope and threw it to my pal and they made it fast. All the police knew of that—was what I put in my book—not a word of praise. I did have three commendations over the thirty years—three ten bobs!

Public commendations and small gratuities were so minor in character, and so random in distribution, that they contributed little to the City Police's power of inducement.

Charles Peace, a Victorian villain, once commented that the dangerous constable was the one who 'neglects his duty to go courting the servant, or nips up the entry to get a surreptitious drink. You never know where you may meet up with him.' However, you were always aware of the location of the conscientious, beat-grinding constable. Discipline in the City Police had little to do with questions of efficiency. Instead it had different functions.

Tradition, the military-style organization inherited from the New Police, was the one imperative for the Panopticon discipline. In the aftermath of the Police Strike, senior officers were doubly concerned to prevent the kind of rank-and-file interaction that might lead to common cause against their superiors.

The disciplinary image was presented to a larger audience. 'Peacekeeping', that euphemism for controlling the city street, depended in part on fear. Instilling trepidation by a mass display when the Inspector of Constabulary visited, like the uniform paraphernalia of the beat constable, saved on the use of physical force.

Such an imposition created its own problems. Deviance, the rule-breaking activities of the beat constable, was often produced by that very authoritarianism. Survival, remaining relatively human, required that officers find some relief through scrounges. In turn, those strategies of survival justified further discipline, strictures rationalized by the organization as a result of the assumed individual pathology of the lower ranks. It was the person that was fallible, not the organization.

The other side of control consisted almost entirely of the cash nexus—the economic benefits. Wage, pension, and housing were important considerations for working men with a skill irrelevant to civilian occupations. For many, aspiration to higher things through promotion was tied up with the idea of a larger wage-packet. Such a concentration on the economic principle underlying the police occupation inevitably gave rise to backbiting and to justifiable criticisms of those who appeared to have obtained their rewards through subterfuges.

Carrots and sticks are relative. Not merely donkeys chase after carrots, urged by a hefty stick, when the alternative is no job and no pension. Despite the tedium and the alienation of beat work, the lack of praise, and the inexorable discipline, most officers lasted out their time. A passive fatalism at the capriciousness and heavy-handedness of authority prevailed amongst the thirty-year men. They imbibed of necessity the belief in order and stability and, inevitably and as was intended, projected the same values on to the street people.

4

Controlling the Street

A year ago in Liverpool, a boy was caught upon a Sunday evening in the act of stealing a handkerchief out of somebody's pocket and was arrested. His father objected that the police had arrested him unlawfully, because the law lays it down that no-one is allowed to do on Sunday the work by which he earns a living, and the police were therefore not allowed to arrest anybody on a Sunday. The judge agreed to this, but continued to question the youngster, who admitted to be a professional pickpocket. He was fined five shillings because he had pursued his trade on a Sunday.

(Frederick Engels, 'The Position of England', in *Articles on Britain*)

'This boy,' says the Constable, 'although he's repeatedly told to, won't move on . . .'
'But where?' cries the boy . . .
'My instructions don't go to that,' replies the Constable. 'My instructions are that this boy is to move on.'

(Charles Dickens, *Bleak House*)

THERE is a curious idea, a remnant of Victorian broadsheet titillation, echoed today by the popular press and in the pontifications of chief police officers, that police work is about 'crime-fighting'.[1] Patently this is nonsense. Police work is only marginally involved in crime. The blanket mandate of Victorian 'preventive' policing justified a multitude of duties. Acting as a walking/talking A–Z, directing traffic, dealing with accident victims and domestic disputes are several of the myriad activities that absorb police personnel. Few have anything to do with popular images of 'crime'. More importantly, historically the key feature of police work has been about maintaining a particular form of social order on the street. From chasing street-corner kids to opening flood-drains, Victorian police work centred on the control of the street, independently of a recognizable image of criminality. When Jack London described the 'move-on' confrontations that he experienced with the police in both the Metropolitan capital and in Chicago, he was documenting the normal encounter between the residents of the streets and the patrolling officer.[2]

Between 1860 and 1930, some 5 per cent (often characterized by the common denominator of illiteracy) of the city's population appeared annually in court, almost entirely in relation to minor street incidents—from 'suspected persons' to the moral iniquity of riding a pedal cycle without lights.[3] Such judicial records, of course, do not enumerate the sundry street harassments such as that noted by one Liverpudlian in the 1920s: 'Everyday, you'd see twenty or thirty men standing on street corners and sitting on doorsteps. Then suddenly one of them would call out 'Aye, aye, lads . . . here's the cops' and they'd all move. The police would walk in single file on the edge of the pavement and if they caught the men hanging around, they'd book them.'[4]

As early as the thirteenth century, powers to control the street had been central to the police mandate.[5] In the first published street legislation, during the reign of Henry III, the new halberds were formally required to 'keep in order the unruly'. During the sixteenth century, a series of proclamations targeted the major object of early police work—the 'suspectid person' and 'any maner of beggers or vacabond or eny evill disposed person' who were to be driven from the streets. Being the wrong class, in the wrong place, at the wrong time—in a foreshadowing of later night-beat practices—meant trouble: 'not any suspectid personne nor persons after nyne of the clocke shall not walke, but rest an kepe they theyr hoostes houssies, uppon payne of imprisonment'. The early and continuing police function was to control particular social groups—rural migrants and the growing urban poor. In the early eighteenth century, some sixty Watchmen were appointed to patrol the town with the major function of apprehending 'all night-walkers and all disorderly persons'.

The commissioners' Instructions to the Watch in 1817 were similar: 'You are to apprehend all night-walkers, rogues, vagabonds, and other disorderly persons, disturbing the public . . . you must be very circumspect . . . and not wantonly or inconsiderately apprehend persons of a different description.' In the Instructions to the Night Watch, 1834, the priorities of police work in the city were reaffirmed: '. . . the good order of the streets, secondly, for the safety of the persons of the inhabitants and, thirdly, for the security of property'.

With the advent of the New Police in the city in 1836, new legislation reformulated old practices and the continuing target. The Liverpool Improvement Act 1842, provided the legal mandate—the arrest of all 'loose, idle, or disorderly persons' (Section 276) and stop-and-search powers on the River Mersey and on the city streets (Section 278). The Instruction Book issued to new constables in 1878 turned legal power into street practice:

. . . watching vigilantly the movements of all suspicious persons who pass through his beat . . . If it be at an untimely hour, or if they fail to assign a proper reason for being in a place, he is to arrest them . . . showing bad characters that they are known and watched by him . . . their habits will point them out without further ado . . . For the purpose of seeing whether his suspicions are well-founded, he may . . . stop any person carrying goods which he suspects to have been stolen, he may also examine the person and detain him.

Successive Instruction Books reinforced the message. Street control was the primary duty. The passing of the Liverpool Corporation Act 1921 set the stage for inter-war policing. The 'suss' provision was spelt out (Section 314) and a municipal 'frequenting' charge underpinned the stop-and-search power of the 1824 Vagrancy Act. Together, by-laws governing every aspect of street life —from the suppression of nuisances to the licensing of pedlars, statutes on betting and gaming, prostitution, street obstruction, drunkenness, begging, and unlawful possession—equipped the Liverpool City Police with a vast array of legal authority. Social control of the streets, not crime control, was the major historically derived police function when these officers were recruited through the Everton Police Training School.

A BATTERY OF LEGAL POWERS

For the new constable, the Instruction Book, with its sundry detail of by-laws and enabling statutes, was the bible that informed street practice. Above all else, you knew THE LAW *with all its tortuous semantics, its convoluted clauses—and hazards for clumsy implementation. Some power was always available—if only through the mythical Ways and Means Act—although it might have to be handled with kid gloves. Police powers were permissive in dealing with the lower classes. English common law, in statute and in practice, allowed the dominant party to have* his *way normally without resort to violence or to dubious devices.*[6]

A. M. Everything we did, we could find justification for. We could always find something in the law to help us. You had to know your Instruction Book very well, because if you locked someone up and they got away with it, next day in court, there was a chance that you might be deemed excessive in your law and of course then you were on your own. You may have locked someone up and made a mistake. And of course some points of law are very involved.

For example, all through my service, I had in my mind the difference between 'false pretences' and 'stealing by trick'. If someone said, 'just taking £5 off you,' and said they 'knew me son' and all that rigmarole and 'so I gave them £5', then your knowledge of the law came out immediately. You say 'false pretences' —there's no power to arrest unless you are on the spot and see it happen or you are in immediate pursuit. Now 'stealing by trick', you've got all the powers that go under the Larceny Act. You could lock anybody up that fell under that power —even if it happened a week ago. They were a kind of enabling powers—you could set up circumstances that would fit either.

It was up to you to see that you were justified. For example, somebody would go into a restaurant in Lime Street—we got quite a few of those. They'd say, 'I can't pay, I've got no money.' Well, the policeman, if he was any good at all, would say, 'Well, did you get a bill?' 'Yes, but I can't pay for it,' the price of the meal. 'I'll lock you up for stealing this.' But if he had no bill and or didn't pick it up, you'd tell the proprietor that he must take his own proceedings—he's swindled you out of the price of a meal and it's a civil action.

Experience taught you how to exploit the law, while steering clear of its pitfalls when faced with high authority

H. P. I remember a policeman arresting someone under the 'being a suspected person/loitering with intent' power—who sued him. You'd see fellows in the middle of the night, especially if they were carrying something. For example, we used to get a lot of people from the printers but you knew them. But if you got somebody strange, you'd say, 'Would you mind opening your case?' Never any argument—well, there were arguments but you knew the answers to them. A policeman had suspected them for loitering about, they wouldn't give a reasonable explanation or account of themselves. Search them, take them inside, lock them up—be a 'suspected person loitering with intent to carry out a felony'. Until some clever solicitor come along and he puts a new interpretation of the Act: 'What is a suspected person?' Not that you suspect him because you don't like the look of him walking the streets—he's got to be a suspected person. A common prostitute —you couldn't call any woman a common prostitute because they were on the game with some chap. You had to be sure that she had convictions as a prostitute—first loitering and then prostitution and then finer points came up over suspected persons. Then the Orders came out   they took action against the policeman over this and the police got into trouble. But you've got to prove that they are a suspected person—they had to belong to a particular class of person to be classed as a suspected person. Then you had got to have good grounds to believe that they were going to commit a felony. But we got away with them. You had to learn them off by heart.

The Court of Appeal . . . dismissed an appeal from two Liverpool police constables against the awarding of £15 each as damages to Edwin Ledwith and Christopher Crothers, on the grounds that they were wrongly arrested by the appellants. Ledwith and Crothers were described as window cleaners, and it was alleged that while one of them was inside a telephone box and the other was outside, P.C.s Roberts and Pearce arrested them and took them to the Bridewell. They were detained over two hours and eventually released. The Policemen submitted that . . . under the Vagrancy Act and the Liverpool Corporation Act, 1921, enough suspicion was aroused in their minds by the actions of the two men to justify arrest. Lord Justice Greer said the decision of the Court involved . . . an investigation into the history of the words 'idle and disorderly persons'.

(*Police Review*, 1936)

The combination of three different 'suss' powers had awesome implications for the street dweller.[7] (A century earlier, one unforunate individual had been imprisoned twelve times in a year—one month at a time—under the local Act.[8]) The powers were occasionally complicated to use and could sometimes penalize their user.

M. B. 'Suss' power was used quite a lot—but it fell into disfavour later on. It was looked on as not advisable to deal with it under the Liverpool Corporation Act. The record might come into it but it was largely their attitude. If they were going along trying to open shop doors, they could go in as a suspected person loitering but it wasn't looked upon very favourably by the courts. To prove that you suspected that they were going to commit a crime isn't so easy. Very hard to get the evidence of frequenting. If you knew him to be a criminal, you suspected him of being up to no good. You had to be very careful in those days. If the courts did throw out a case that you'd dealt with, you stood a chance of being sued over it. So you had to be pretty sure of your ground. Unless the Watch Committee took a favourable view and said, 'Yes, we'll back you,' you were on your own and stood a chance of having to pay damages. In London, it was different. They had a fund for dealing with that sort of thing and that's why you saw many of those cases there.

£100 DAMAGES AGAINST CONSTABLE

The reserved judgement of Sir W. F. Taylor K. C. . . . in which a dock labourer claimed damages from P. S. Kerr and P. C. Neame, members of the Liverpool Force, for alleged assault and battery and wrongful arrest and false imprisonment.

The Judge found in favour of Sergt. Kerr . . . but for the plaintiff against P.C. Neame for wrongful arrest and false imprisonment, assessing the damages at £100 with costs . . . it was alleged the plaintiff was struck by both police officers and severely handled in the street and in the Bridewell, with the result that he received an injury to his right eye which necessitated its removal in hospital . . . 'The arrest . . .' concluded the judge, 'has not been justified, and the plaintiff is entitled to succeed in this part of the case. I exclude from the question of compensation the element of injury to the eye, which I feel was accidental and not due to any negligence.' (*Police Review*, 1926)

DAMAGES FOR FALSE IMPRISONMENT

A verdict was given against a Liverpool Constable by a jury . . . in a case in which Mrs Jane Roche, wife of a bookmaker, claimed damages from Sergt. John Borrows (who was dismissed for the malicious prosecution claim) and Constable Ernest David Laurie of the Liverpool Police . . . Mr Patrick Roche, a licensed bookmaker carried on a credit betting business in Houghton Street. On 6th August, when Mrs Roche was alone in the house, Constable Laurie entered, followed by Sergt. Borrows and three Constables. A search warrant was read. The police searched the house for two hours, and there betting slips were found. They then searched Mrs Roche and, having found nothing, took her into custody, and conveyed her by tram to the Police Station, where she was released on bail. The charge against her of having assisted in conducting a betting business at her house was dismissed by the Stipendiary Magistrate on 20th August.

. . . Constable Laurie gave evidence that on 5th August he entered at the back door of 149 Chatham Street, that he received from her 1*s*. 9*d*., and that she received from him a betting slip. On 5th August, Mrs Roche was on her way to Liverpool from Scotland . . . The jury . . . found that Constable Laurie was not actuated by malice or direct motive, but had actually been over-zealous; that he had no reasonable and probable ground for believing that Roche's house was used for betting, and that he did not honestly believe that he made bets with plaintiff. (*Police Chronicle*, 1932)

For false imprisonment, Mrs Gertrude Anderson of Liverpool, has been awarded £200 damages against Det. Sergt. Peter Woodhouse of the Liverpool Police . . . she told the police that she did not think her husband was carrying out a strictly honest business. Eventually she took some goods her husband had left at her lodgings to the Police Station. As she was leaving work, she was taken to the Police Station, where without being cautioned, she was cross-examined by Sergt. Woodhouse. She was kept in a cell from 2 p.m. until 8.30 p.m. when she was charged with unlawful possession of a pair of hairbrushes. No evidence was offered against her and she was discharged after several remands. *(Police Reivew, 1932)*

a special jury at Liverpool awarded Herbert Waring £25 against a Liverpool City Constable for assault and false imprisonment. The Constable was walking along a busy thoroughfare when a crowd assembled owing to the breakdown of a motor car. Waring was a member of the crowd and alleged that the Constable struck him, and when he refused his name and address, took·him into custody on a charge of obstructing the traffic. The next day Magistrates dismissed the informations against Waring. *(Police Review, 1923)*

However, there were ways of avoiding court hazards while still underlining police power.

D. A. Cautions were used a lot. They were always legal in the police force. If he didn't want to go to court for a very minor offence, then you could caution him. It wouldn't go on his criminal record. It would be retained in police files but not in the criminal files—the superintendent would issue the caution

Legal powers were reinforced by experience.

K. R. You might be in Park Lane and a fellow's walking towards you with a suitcase. He might be a shopbreaker. 'What's in your case?' 'I've just come off the Isle of Man boat.' 'What time did she dock? Where did she dock?' One or two questions to which you knew the answers and if you were satisfied: 'Nice knowing you. Bye.'

Law, however, legal procedure, could be tortuous. In particular, there was a gulf between police practice in the provinces and in the capital.

A. R. There was a vast difference in the provincial cities. For instance, if a man came into the station and said, 'The man next door has stolen a bottle of milk from my doorstep,' in the Met., they would say: 'This man has made an accusation. He's entitled to have a hearing in court so that the matter can be dealt with.' But here, we wouldn't do that. If we found there was no basis in our opinion, we would scrub it.

In earlier years, kids trundling hoops or playing pitch-and-toss had been a target. By the 1920s, it was street football.[9]

T. D. The first time I saw a football was when a caseball hit a horse in the face,[10] and the horse reared up. So I did something. Chased them, got one, took him in, and told him he would be summonsed for playing football in the street. He was just cautioned by the superintendent. If kids were playing football in the street, they had to accept your authority and get out of the way.

Ayers cites one such constable: 'He was known as Hitler because of his moustache and being very cruel to kids playing football in the street. It was nothing for him to take the ball off them and stick the knife in it to burst it.'[11] But in the folklore of Liverpool Police it was the 'bucks' who had always been the primary object of street powers.

P. E. 'Bucks' was the ordinary police talk for the working man or yobbo—the unruly kind of person that hung round street corners. Young fellers about fourteen to twenty—hanging round the corners, making a noise, and upsetting the people in the houses. There was Razor McGloshan's gang of bucks in Crown Street. All the young men were bucks—a young buck in the old days used to be a gentleman. Bucks and buckesses—below the par. I only took the term up because it was general conversation in the police force. You could assume that the bucks would present themselves for locking up. Drunk and disorderly, playing football in the street—they were all bucks.

English law is commonly portrayed as adversarial, embodying a series of safeguards to prevent an accused from being wrongly convicted. Innocence is presumed until guilt has been established by formal trial. In real practice, law is very different for the majority of people, then and now, who appear before the Magistrates' Court.[12] (The old, more correct name, Police Court, is still emblazoned above the door of the city's main court-room.) Being the wrong age, being in the wrong place at the wrong time, or being domiciled in a particular district reverse the assumptions of due process. The suspect has little opportunity for demonstrating his or her innocence against any one of a medley of permissive street powers. Although the courts might occasionally—usually for those with means—award damages against wrongful arrest and detention, the police in effect only arrested 'guilty' people. Street kids—and their elders, the Liverpool 'bucks'—were of course inevitably guilty of whatever charge the patrolling constable thought appropriate.

DISCRETION

Street power was permissive. The irony of police work is that the lowest of the low—the street constable, unlike in other 'professional' occupations, is the one who can exercise the maximum discretion at work.[13] He could always pick and choose over whom to arrest and on whom to give the Nelson touch.

T. D. You used your discretion all the time. Not arrest if you didn't have to. You'd see two fellows fighting in the street—you'd pull them up and send them on their way. You'd see a drunk, and if he wasn't incapable, send him on his way. You'd take in an incapable because if he fell in the roadway, he might get run over. If he was incapable and vomiting and so on, you'd take him in for his own consideration. If they were drunk and disorderly and so on, they only had themselves to blame. You'd try to get rid of them, tell them to go away—until eventually you had to do something—couldn't ignore it.

A. T. You didn't have to lock drunks up. I used to take them home on quite a number of occasions if I'd known that they lived in the immediate vicinity. Take them home, get rid of them. It's no criterion to arrest a man for being drunk. You get no medals for that. If a policeman felt like having a lock-up, he'd book them for obstruction. No medals for having a lock-up if you were on nights. You'd get off at six o'clock in the morning and you'd have to be in court at ten o'clock. No gains at all from locking somebody up.

W. S. I've let plenty of people go. I used to think, 'What would you do if you were in his position?' And if they were very poor, what satisfaction would you get from locking them up? Two fellers fighting outside a pub, so grabbed them both. They were older than me. I was going to chase them. Got their names and addresses. One feller said he was from Great Homer Street. Then we sent up to the Division—'Will you check on this address?'—comes back, 'Not known'. No—I wouldn't take them in for fighting.

Discretion could also be tempered by an appreciation of the odds.

K. M. One time there was a big crowd in the street and two men fighting—about six-deep, the crowd. I went in there, shouldered my way through the crowd. This fight was going on in the middle of the road. When I got on the edge of the road I said to them, 'Who's winning?' They were slogging away and pretty well worn-out. So I went over and said, 'That's all . . . break to your corners'—took it as a joke. By that time, their wives had come out of the crowd and got hold of them, and were taking them away.

Law enforcement is often opposite to the requirements of peacekeeping.[14] Whatever the strictures from his commanders and from the virtuous, local middle class, and newspapers on enforcing the law, a constable with his wits about him recognized the expediency of a 'live-and-let-live' policy.

THE PRESSURE TO ARREST

Police forces have always had problems with measuring 'efficiency'. How do you measure the effectiveness of police work?[15] Inevitably, superior officers fall back on the 'arrest rate'. The more arrests on the street, independently of any concern with 'keeping the peace', the more efficient the police constable.[16] The Police Union, as always, articulated a pragmatic cynicism about the pressures for arrests.

Each policeman is supplied with a police court attendance card, on which is recorded the date of all attendances at police court in connection with charges or summonses, and each entry has to be initialled by the officer in charge of the station. When the card is full, it is handed in to the station in exchange for a new one; the old card is kept for reference. Innumerable cases have occurred in which young and zealous sub-divisional inspectors have used the police court attendance card of a constable as the only evidence worth having of the constable's efficiency in the performance of his duty. When the process of 'waking things up a bit' commences, reputations, and records of attendances at police court, are made and broken every day. In one area, there was a wholesale slaughter of the innocents. Policemen of twenty to twenty-five years' service were harassed from pillar to post in the hunt for improved returns of charges and summonses. One after the other was called to report why he had not been to the police court for a long period, and threatened that if he did not do more work in the future he would lose pay. Men were designated by superior officers as being lazy, inefficient, absolutely worthless, and whose only object in life was to go to the pay table on Wednesdays to receive their pay. The following dialogue can be taken as representative of what frequently takes place:-

OFFICER. I have sent for you this morning, Jones, because I find on looking up your record of attendances at police court that you have had neither a charge nor a summons during the last three years. What explanation have you to give?

P.C. Well, Sir, I have always done my duty. I have never had occasion to effect an arrest nor to summons any person.

OFFICER. All rubbish! What do you think you are paid for? I never leave the station unless I witness some person or persons committing or about to commit some offences, minor or otherwise. I could have summonses every day if I chose. Do you mean to tell me that you never see any case of obstruction, street shouting, begging, carts and cycles with no lights, no offences against the motor car laws, or in other words, that everybody—men, women, and children—know the laws so well that they can avoid the many pit-falls? You'll have to find another excuse.

P.C. Well, Sir, I have always endeavoured to keep my beat clean, and I have seen people committing perhaps but technical offences, but I have not thought them sufficiently serious to caution them. I have cautioned a lot of people, and the caution always seems to be effective.

OFFICER. In the future, every time you caution a person, enter the particulars in your notebook, and see he doesn't get a second caution, and also remember that it is not necessary to caution a person before summonsing or arresting him, as the case may be.

P.C. All right, Sir, but I always thought that it was more creditable to prevent crime and keep one's beat clean and free from nuisances or offences than to have charges or summonses of a trivial character. I have always done my duty, as my record will show. It is a clean record.

OFFICER. Oh, yes! You've got a clean record all right, but a man who never does anything never gets into trouble, so that's no argument.

P.C. Well, Sir, if I have neglected my duty in the past, why haven't my superior officers done their duty and made a defaulter of me. I have never been a defaulter.

OFFICER. You soon will be if I have any of your insolence. Don't you dare to be insolent to me again. Do you know you were on the verge of rank insubordination? Go back to your duty, and remember what you're paid for. Let us see the result on the Police Court attendance card, and when you do get a charge or a summons, I will send one of the young constables with you to show you the way to the Police Court, for I expect you have forgotten it. Right turn, quick march!

One can imagine the feelings of a P.C. after such an interview, but worse still is the evil effect aimed at. This particular P.C. may be a very strong-minded man and be determined to withstand the pressure being brought upon him. In course of time he finds that he is the pet antipathy of his superior officers, that he is made a butt for the amusement of other men on parade, and that if there is any unpleasant work or unpopular beat or point going vacant it falls to his lot to fill it. His Sunday duties are arranged to his disadvantage, and the example of one or two others, is not, likely to be lost on his brother officers at the station.

(Bull's Eye, 1921)

Folk wisdom on policing recognizes the infinite possibilities in law enforcement. Implementing every law on every occasion implies unlimited police resources. But where constables under common law can be creative in their construction of nebulous charges—such as that of 'obstruction', there can be no end to the opportunities for street summonses and arrests. The sane constable rapidly learnt to withstand the pressure from his seniors to work by the book.

Cutting Corners

Legal procedures were the preserve of the Instruction Book and of the advocates in court. On the street, expediency and common sense taught a different style.[17]

G. E. There's no question of cautioning—by saying, 'I caution you and you have no need to say anything . . .' You just say, 'Come on'—speak to them in their own language and they'll understand you. Somebody would give you a squeak as to who it was.

There was some street detritus which required more imagination than most. Police folklore tells of one officer who, having found a dead body on the street at the end of his duty, shifted it on to the next beat. Two days later, the body was still appearing on different beats.

T. B. Bloody pest was stray animals, stray dogs—people would come up and say they'd found a stray, and you'd have to take it off them, take their name and address. You carried a cord around in your pocket and you'd take the dog to Wavertree Pinfold. It got to be a bloody bind. One day outside Aigburth Huts, waiting to go off at 3 p.m. on the afternoon shift, two of us on a bike job. The lady came up—she was a member of the RSPCA—comes up with this dog on a piece of string. Lucky Ted got it. 'Right-ho'—and he knew the situation as well as I did. 'What is your name, madam?' Then a tram came down and off she trots. Of course, as soon as her back is turned, we give the dog a kick and it shoots off. The next day, there's an advert in the paper—that she'd found a black and white dog and handed it in to the police at Aigburth. People enquired but there was no trace of it. So there was a right hoo-ha. Everybody was questioned about it. I said to Ted: 'We'll say that when she went for the tram, the dog run after her.' So he writes it down and everybody writes bits about what's happened, and thus eventually a few questions were asked and reply came from the Super. 'The matter is now closed. The only one that seems to have used his sense in this situation was the dog.'

Not every incident on the street contained the potential for legal action. The officer's historical role as a street cleaner occasionally required a measure of dexterity and imagination.

Instant Justice

In any case the law was often viewed as a last resort, a clumsy, time-consuming, bureaucratic impediment that hindered order-maintenance on the street. Its procedures often seemed too specific to be worth the candle of locking someone up.

B. T. In those days, they had nowt to do on the Sunday night. It used to be the girls' parade. They would all walk down Dale Street, down to the Pier Head, and all the girls would be out. They'd get a bit cheeky sometimes and have to be checked. Now and again, you'd get one start fighting. You might give them a clip round the ear. If you were too soft with them, they wouldn't move.

S. H. Patrolling up Prescot Road during the war, if I saw a light on, I used to shout, 'Put that bloody light out,' and if nobody put the light out, we used to let fly with a brick. They come down then and says, 'Who's broken my window?' and I used to say: 'Yes, I broke the bloody window—go in the station and tell them you wouldn't put the light out,' and they got a summons on top of it.

Arrest, too, could involve both formal and informal procedures. There was a formal process for dealing with the arrested.

T. D. Drunk-in-charge would stand out—slumped in the car, head out and sick all over the car. You could see yourself that he was drunk. Took him to the station and routine happened—they had to call the bridewell surgeon and the drunk could call his own doctor, fixing bail and so on.

But situations were also encountered that had not been foreseen by the Instruction Book.

W. S. The Black Maria used to call at different stations at two in the morning and take the prisoners from there to Cheapside. One night at Rose Hill, there was a feller kept making a bloody nuisance of himself—kept kicking the cell door. Sergeant says, 'Go and take his bloody shoes off.' Took his shoes off and Jock come with the Black Maria in the morning. 'Put your shoes on!' Put them on? He wouldn't put them on. Sergeant says, 'Go down and bring Sweeney and two bloody big fellers.' I used to laugh at their antics. It was a wet morning so they just took him to the corner and ran him to the corner of Richmond Row in his bare feet—brought him back—'Put your shoes on!'

Where the law or the Instruction Book was hidebound, a little imagination was a useful supplement.

MOVING ON: LEGAL AND PHYSICAL COERCION

Few confrontations resulted in arrests. Threat was usually sufficient in cowing the street people.[18] *Most memories of both police and public were of 'moving on'.*

T. D. We were pretty heavy on individuals in the street. We never allowed two or three to gather on the corner. We just moved them on. We used to chase them. Some we chased but it was only a matter of chasing them out of the way.

H. P. You got plenty of violence when the pubs let out—but you were on your own. The only times you were allowed to double up—that's two beats together —down Scotland Road, say, where two would be allowed together, until they'd cleared the street after the pubs had been let out. Normally, when the pubs let out—pubs on every corner, just drinking dens, they used to let out and they'd all be full of drink just yapping and talking. But we used to move them on immediately. We didn't give them a chance to cause trouble. If they started to cause trouble, we just asked them to move on and they appreciated it. They accepted it. You'd give them a quarter of an hour letting them say their good-nights—then you'd start moving them on, not aggressive. They'd all see sense. Sometimes, some of them would try and be clever and just step off the pavement. They were never allowed to be naughty. It was a good game between them and us. We bore them no malice.

A. M. The worst part of the job was chasing fellers off the corners, a crowd of drunks, especially when you were the only policeman. One of them might dare to do something but if you used your head—you learn in time—you'd be all right.

The stick and the fist backed up the array of legal powers.

T. B. By yourself normally on the beat but on Saturday night till midnight, you had to go in pairs, like in Gerrard Street, where they didn't like a bobby. It would cause a fight if you went up there. We had fellows who had come straight out of the First World War, afraid of nothing. One fellow called Birtles, who worked with me—he never looked at you straight, a fisherman from Grimsby. I used to come up Chisenhall Street on my beat and I could tell when Birtles turned the corner. The fellows went like that off the corners—never asked to move. They just knew.

Folk memory, rumour, and first-hand experience combined to warn the street people that obduracy in the face of police pressure offered little profit.

'The State' on the Street

Moving on was a ritual, rarely leading to either conflict or arrest. It was important in that it signified the gulf between the police and the policed.[19] *Police practices brought an appreciation of the omnibus power of the 'state' home to the nooks and crannies of the cobbled streets of the English city. The rite of the move-on constantly reaffirmed relative social status.*

A. M. 'Bucks' were always chased when a policeman came along. In fact, they were so well drilled that when I went to C Division—Essex Street—you'd wait on the corner of a back street and there'd be a crowd of fellers there and within no time, before you could get near them, they'd all have disappeared. But the older men—forty and upwards—they got off the side walk and paced up and down the road—deferential. They were afraid in that some time or another, some of the fellers on the corner had been locked up for obstruction. I'd walk up to the corner of Mill Street—a very scruffy street, and there was a gang of fellers standing on the corner and some of them were sitting on the pub sill and others standing around. There was a bobby on the beat facing me, waiting for me to come to him, and when I got there, the lads are still sitting there. So I said, 'Come with me.' I walked up to these fellers, a few paces, and just stood in front of them, looked at them—they knew what was wanted—'Clear off!'

It was a ritual acknowledged by both sides. Pat Ayers quotes one of those same street people: 'Just say you were standing on the corner, now if you had seen a policeman coming over the bridge . . . you automatically moved. You didn't wait for him to come down. He'd say to you 'Move'. And you just walked through the street and he'd carry on by. And by the time he got to the next corner, we'd be back on the corner.'[20]

T. D. There were always twenty or thirty or so bucks hanging around the corner on Nichols Street, and if they saw you coming, they'd all move. It was no use snarling at them. They'd just move without it.

Authority was not to be challenged; the personal status of the constable as well as the symbolic power of the state was not to be affronted.

P. P. I used to go down a street and perhaps a week previously I had locked that fellow up and I used to walk past him and if they said anything to me I'd say, 'Shut up and get inside.' Or as long as they said nothing, I'd say nothing; or if they started talking, I'd say, 'Listen, inside you or get about your business.' Course if they started cutting up rough, then I'd cut up rough but as long as they didn't interfere with me, I didn't interfere with them.'

But rituals, of their nature, lead to boredom, and minor rebellion by the beat constable.

A. T. I used to go round and there'd be crowds of people standing at the corners by the pub, leaning against it. If I got a new beat, I'd go round the beat and say, 'Get to the kerb!' and they'd move to the kerb reluctantly. As soon as I had gone they were back. So I got fed up with this. So I used to say to each crowd: 'Look, when you see me or see my inspector, move to the kerb and stay there. What you do after I've gone, I couldn't care less.' That was how I used to treat them. I didn't use to curse or swear at them. They used to do that: the chief inspector walking down on a Saturday morning in full regalia and one of these fellows would nod and they'd always walk to the corner, and the Chief wouldn't say anything about it because they were on the corner and not causing any obstruction.

Justifications for the move-ons, too, had become ritualized. The Victorian Watch Committee had soon learnt that its mail-bag consisted mainly of complaints about kids and their elders 'doing nothing' on the street.[21] Working-class leisure offended the susceptibilities of their betters.

B. T. We had to make sure—it was the strictness on our part—that gangs weren't allowed to gather on the corner. There was always complaints coming in from the people who lived in the area about the gangs making a noise on the corner. So you just got rid of them. What actually happened was that they would disappear before you got there. They might come back after you had gone. But they wouldn't stand there. If they did, if one was half-drunk, it always ended up with him being pitched in—becoming disorderly and arrested.

Moving on was a prophylactic, a social cleansing function, keeping one's beat clean.

K. R. I've moved on people sleeping rough—perhaps take him a hundred yards from the shop wherever he was—'On your way.' If they were drunk and disorderly and so on, they only had themselves to blame. You'd try to get rid of them, tell them to go away—until eventually you had to do something—couldn't ignore it.

A. M. Drunks could be a messy business. A lot were passive. 'Come on, you're being locked up.' 'I'm not drunk.' You might get a real bad one and then you had a rough time but mostly they gave way and very often, if you got a drunk, another policeman saw you were having some difficulty. He'd help. I've locked up as many as two to three in one evening—not all that common. Perhaps one a week when you are on afternoons. Main reason for locking up drunks was keeping the streets clean. A lot of these drunks were stopping women—thinking that any woman on Lime Street was a prostitute. That in the main was true but not always of course. A drunk, if he's a man of any physique at all, is ready to pick a fight with anyone—bump into people and so on—and with policemen then, it was a matter of pride—'Drunk on your beat—look at that man loafing on your beat.'

Occasionally, inhibitions released by drink or instant rebellion against the ritual of subservience would flare into sudden challenge to the constable's authority.

A. M. I went into Lime Street one night at ten o'clock and found a crowd of lads on the corner of Skelhorne Street coming out of the pub. I said to them, 'Come along. Move along, please.' They all looked at me and suddenly, horror struck me: the two or three policemen normally along there had disappeared—had taken a prisoner along to the station—and there wasn't another policeman within half a mile. I just stood there solid as a rock and this feller looked at me as if to say, 'For two pins . . .' But then the older men in the crowd persuaded them to move along.

B. A. I've had a few scuffles—all the men have. But if it was a case of 'I'm going to get you' your dignity wouldn't allow you to let them get the better of you. You'd manage somehow. But if he got away, that was just too bad for you.

P. H. I've been on the street when helmets have gone flying. But our motto was: 'Get your man.' Didn't matter if he was guilty or innocent, if you wanted him you got him. Many a time a fellow would get away with a caution. I never went looking for trouble—it normally came to me.'

In any case, for the locals, a fight with a copper could provide a welcome break in the street corner tedium.

K. R. I've been in rough houses—they wouldn't come out to help us but they'd form a ring and let you fight—they wouldn't just all join in to back somebody up.

Cleaning the beat meant fitting each new situation into past patterns, trying to handle them according to traditional recipes.[22] Each encounter might be new but there were adaptable, tried, and trusted tactics, an array of legal and police craft tools.

CONTROLLING KIDS ON THE STREET

Children were the normal target of street policing. In a historically sanctified relationship, street kids and the police were in casual, intermittent, hostile confrontation.[23] As an object of street policing, they posed special problems. There was considerable pressure for actions against them from a sanctimonious middle class, some of whose members held extraordinary delusions. The due process of law could be a bit of an ass when you arrested someone under age.

the Rev. Eric Treacy of Edge Hill, Liverpool, strongly criticised the Juvenile Court system and urged that the Police should carry canes. Advocating a greater use of the birch he said 'Young offenders are leaving the juvenile courts laughing at the Magistrates and the Police. I think Policemen should carry small canes, which I think would probably be very effective. We must face the problem of flabby parentage.   (*Police Review*, 1937)

One of the many ways in which grown-ups take a mean advantage of the innocence of childhood is by creating bogies as aids to authority. Among the bogies foolishly trotted out for this purpose is the imaginary policeman . . . Not long ago we reported a case where a child died of fright caused by the approach of a Police Officer in Uniform.

(*Police Review*, 1937)

Can't the Watch Committee . . . rid the police of the hooligan element . . . gangs of young and hefty idlers squat on the pavement or lurk in subways to annoy passers-by, to play tricks on defenceless shop assistants, or to gamble in the face of the public.

(*Liverpool Echo*, 1919)

The time has gone when a poor ragged child would take to flight at the sight of a policeman.   (*Police Chronicle*, 1920)

A. T. Kids used to jeer and pull their tongues out. Occasionally, you'd come across a child, mostly down by the canal. I got one down there once for some reason. I asked him what his name was and he said, 'Tommy Jones' or something, and I said, 'Who lives next door?' and he gave me another name, and I said, 'Oh, no she doesn't.' He said, 'She does' 'All right, I'll take you home.' And I walked all the way up Great Homer Street. But he didn't live at that address and eventually he took me to his own home. What I used to do with a youngster was to knock at the door and his mother would say, 'Oh, God, what have you done?' I'd say, 'Is his father in?' 'Yes, sir.' 'Can I see him a minute?' I'd tell the father what he'd done and what I brought him home for. I'd say, 'Can I leave it to you to deal with him?' 'Yes'—he'd give him a clip round the earhole. You always took children home and let the parents deal with them. Normal to call you 'Sir'—very respectful the parents.

W. R. The kids were all scared of bobbies in those days. We wouldn't let them meet on the corners because the people in the houses on the corners always used to complain of the row that they made—used to chase them.

W. P. With kids, I used to carry my gloves in my hand and without any fingers in, and I used to catch them with the gloves if they were cheeky, and if they got cheekier still, I used to take them home for a belt. Not much you could charge them with. You couldn't say, 'He made faces at me and swore at me.' Mind you, then a child was responsible at seven years of age.

P. E. When we were at Old Swan and had to go to Fairfield, we used to pass the end of one of the little streets there. The kids used to be standing there one time—well, we hit them a few times with the cape and it had a bottle in it. They didn't stand there any longer. Or we cuffed them under their chin—and after about half a dozen times, they never stopped there again. They hopped it.

There was some ambivalence about kids. Beats varying by social class might mean a different perception. Or memory might take on a rose-coloured tinge—as with one officer who had commonly thumped prostitutes:

S. H. The kids—many a time you would go about with a dozen bloody sweets in your pocket. When the mothers were taking the kids across the road, you had to hold the traffic up. I used to go with half a ton of sweets in my back pocket. I used to say to the wife: 'Look at this bloody lot. If I don't take them, I'll offend the bloody kiddies.'

It was possible to have a rather different relationship with kids. For thirty years a charity, financed in part from police pay, had helped supplement the clothing of the city poor.[24]

P. H. Police Aided Clothing Association—chipped in a few bob from your wages. You'd be walking the beat and you'd see some kid with his backside hanging out of his trousers. Call him over. Get his address. Take him home. 'Form

150'—went through channels and then rubber-stamped and approved. Take the kid to the big stores and they'd be rigged out from top to bottom—all stamped PACA.

W. S. When we were on nights, we used to give two hours free, seven to nine, with collecting boxes. When you were on days, you had a bunch of forms. You could get stopped by women, saying: 'Can I have the police clothes?' You would mark down how many children she had and her circumstances. Then she would be sent for. In the parade room were all the clothes, and the mothers were stripping all the kids naked and fitting them out—the place stunk with corduroy trousers.

Larking about in the street reflected the relative freedom that a world without walls gave the children of the city's urban poor. It was a partial escape from the cramped authority of the home. Street autonomy might readily be restricted by the patrolling constable. A feud would often develop in which the uniformed officer was 'taunted from a safe distance with nicknames and insults such as "beetlecrusher", "narker", or "copper-copper wax-ass"'[25] In turn, the police officer came to view all kids as trouble—to be chased. The ritual of insult–chase– insult–chase was a characteristic of the life of Liverpool street kids from the onset of the New Police to the present day.[26] The palliative of the PACA was given more importance as a piece of social engineering than its reception by the street kids warranted.

RESPECT OR FEAR?

Social order on the street had the characteristics of a truce, a lull in which warring parties tacitly held back from strife.[27] It was a fragile relationship, interpreted in contrary ways by different constables. To some, street tranquillity signified popularity, deference, and respect, a 'thank you' for the service practices of the patrol officer. Another might recognize that genuflection as one of fear.

T. D. There was no abuse from children. None at all. I think children had a considerable amount of respect for the police in those days. They either called you 'officer' or 'sir'. The women particularly addressed you as 'sir'.

W. S. Did seven years down Scotland Road. You got respect. You got abuse from a drunk—well, you dealt with him depending on how far he went before you decided to lock him up. But you did get respect from people. You used to help them, if you could. Next to nothing in the way of violence. The worst place was Great Homer Street. There was a pub on every corner and policemen who drank knew every one round the division. Few fights—occasionally, you'd get a man who'd been gashed in the face with a bottle, that had been drunk in the bar and you'd be called in and you'd take him to hospital.

Ritualized obedience, and the constable's streetwise judgement, could in any case often limit if not prevent street conflict. At the end of the day, there was no ambivalence about the key to the officer's authority.

J. V. The police weren't popular around the Bogs in Garston, when I was being shown around there with Jim Bealey, when a brick came flying over. If there'd been any more trouble, we would just have drawn our staffs and knocked all hell out of them.

B. A. One time, when I was coming down Commercial Road, there was a crowd gathered at the bottom of Regent Street—you accepted the fact that you had to deal with it—and this crowd had been watching a couple fighting. I had my cape over my shoulder and a milk bottle. They co-operated by going off to fight somewhere else.

In the cameos of street life, certain characters appeared larger than life, as the source of ritualized conflict. Mary Jane Worty appears in several accounts as a 'street character', an individual who summed up in her behaviour all the contradictoriness of street life, deference combined with challenge.[28]

M. B. There were all sorts of people in the old Chinatown area. We often got into trouble with foreign seamen that came there and they started making up to the Chinamen's wives. In consequence, trouble started, and arrests were made for drunkenness and there was one woman there, she was a very big woman, at least six foot or more, and she wore a man's jersey and a man's cap. If there was any trouble where a young policeman was concerned, she would get going with a whistle and summon assistance. She was always on our side. A great big strong woman.

There was another woman—Mary Jane Worty. She was a barrow woman and these barrow women were as strong as horses. They were out selling fruit or whatever and they were immensely strong women. Mary Worty had a habit of getting drunk and then getting into fights and her face was criss-crossed with cuts and she would get in the window of her bedroom, start giving the history of people all the way down and then they'd all get out in crowds. They'd be throwing bottles and stones at her. Somebody would come rushing down to the station: 'Mary Worty's out.' And the Sergeant would come 'You, you, and you—up the street—right away.' So up we'd go and we'd have to keep the crowd back and the object was to wait for Mary to come out for some more beer which was the pub across the road, and when she did, grab her. It usually took four policemen to control her. She put one policeman in hospital.

She had a daughter, Rosemary Worty, who looked up to me because I locked her up one night. (Very often this happens to those people. They come into contact, and they accept you as one of themselves, even as a friend, though you've locked them up.) Years later, when I was an inspector, a horrible apparition—she was a prostitute—stopped me. This person stepped out in front of me and she said, 'You don't remember me, do you, sir?' So I said 'No.' 'I'm Rosemary Worty'—so much to my horror! I said, 'How's your mother?' 'Oh, she's gone away from Upper Pitt Street. She's not well at all. She misses all her old friends.' And she had battered half of them.

On one particular occasion, when I left the force, I went to the Magistrate's Clerk's Department. I was talking to a woman and she was saying that young people weren't the same in her day. She said, 'I was born in Upper Pitt Street and I remember the hard times we had.' So I said, 'I was a PC in that area.' 'Do you remember Mary Jane Worty?' 'I certainly do!' 'Well, I remember one day, there was an awful row and a crowd gathered and Mary Jane Worty said: "I'll come down as long as that young PC there takes me into Argyle Street Bridewell." She came down and this young PC walked her into the bridewell.' I said, 'I'll tell you something. I was that young PC.' She came with me for no reason at all, whereas it would have taken quite a few other PCs to shift her. I had a similar experience in the Byrom Street. There was another woman who was a real fighter and she came in with me as quietly as can be—perhaps because I looked so young.

Given the major schisms within the lower class of the street—encompassing both the collective solidarity of a community in relation to outsiders and the entrepreneurship by which individuals ensured their personal survival, and the schisms of age and gender[29]—police relations with that public were inevitably confusing and paradoxical. Within the minutiae of the constable's experience, policing the street daily met consent and at the other pole, antagonism.

THE STICK AND THE FIST

But there could be more serious explosions. Apparently random violence in certain streets enlivened the working day—but sometimes left physical scars. Or, more expected, there might be a scuffle during an arrest.[30]

S. H. Used the truncheon many a time, especially on Lime Street. Used to hit them on the arm, never on the head. Take the strength out their arm. Always used to draw my truncheon if I went into a place where I thought there was a burglar but never actually used it to hit them. You'd use your hands in a scuffle outside a pub. What I used to do was to get hold of them behind their hand. They'd be on their back in no time.

> One day to the 'Old Bug and Glue-Pot' I hurried,
> By request of the potman who was looking most worried.
> A man who refused to pay for his beer,
> Was drunk, and so I told him to 'clear.'
> 'Do you know who I am? I'm Basher Brown,
> I could eat men like you for a dud half-a-crown.'
> My ju-jitsu training was needed already,
> Yet my knees appeared to be rather unsteady.
> How it all happened I now don't quite know,
> Except that my nose stopped a terrible blow;

Several more in the ribs, and a thump on the jaw—
Then I peaceful slept on that public house floor.

(*Police Review*, 1933)

W. S. Rose Hill Police Station on a Saturday night was packed with prisoners. All our stuff was hard stuff, fighting and drunks. We had an old inspector, a Manxman, he used to laugh when he saw them coming in with the blood pouring down their heads, fighting and everything. I got told to take care of a young Scotch bobby, not far from my own home. 'Will you take Mowat with you, Jock? There's a feller putting through a plate glass window in a pub in Crosshall Street.' I says, 'We can't have that—we'll have to get the feller.' We get hold of him, got him to Byrom Street. The usual crowd come. Getting near Richmond Row going up to Rose Hill Police Station, and a big feller comes to Mowat's side appealing to him to let his mate go. So I whispered to Mowat to collar the other feller. Bloody good job he didn't though—James Molloy, a ship's fireman. We get up and Molloy gets hold of Mowat again and Mowat swings round battering him right across the road. Could he fight, Mowat! Flattens Molloy and lays him out. Mowat isn't half going for him. Somebody runs out of the crowd and hits Mowat on the back of the neck. Mowat goes mad then. As soon as Molloy saw that, he got Mowat and split his nose. Mowat goes mad, loses his cap. I blow my whistle. He's got Molloy there on the ground. He didn't half go into him with his stick. Fellers come running, bobbies come running and it was a right old dust-up. That was the only time I'd seen a stick being used. It was all due to that person running out of the crowd.

It seems likely the use of violence by police officers is much understated in this account. There is some evidence that the history of policing in England and Wales contains much more resort to the stick and fist than is recognized in the orthodox accounts.[31] The stick, in particular, backed up by the practical invisibility of the night beat, was a useful device to save on unpaid overtime. The inducements for the Victorian police officer to use that strategy were not that different from those of night-beat patrolling between the wars.

The policeman could employ a good deal of violence on his beat to avoid the need for tiresome court appearances. After an eight hour [night] patrol, it was only to be expected that the policeman would prefer resting to hanging around the courts waiting to bring petty offenders to book. A simple push might suffice to move on a street seller or a drunk. A degree of violence might also be sufficient to control certain types of behaviour for which conviction was difficult or unlikely.

The stick itself (Emsley, 'Police Violence', 129), was a last resort. You never used it where a fist would do or a belt would do. But there were occasions.

W. S. I tried to avoid using the stick. Ran up against it once. We had a bit of a rough do. I was on Fontenoy Street. Coming down was Tony Butcher—he was a good boxer. He and his brother sold ice-cream. 'Do you want an ice-cream, Jock?' So I got down an entry, eating it. When I come out, there's a gang on the corner of

Scotland Road. They took to their heels and ran up the road. So people looked at me and I ran after them. Turned on me. Had to draw the stick—it was the only way to save myself.

Or there could be a spontaneous mass eruption.

K. R. There was one occasion when we took about ten in. There was an Argentine sailing ship in the river and the sailors came ashore, and then made their way to a dance-hall in Great George Street, where our Liverpool lads were foxtrotting and waltzing. The Argentinian sailors taught our girls to do the tango and South American dances. The Liverpool lads got the brush-off and were annoyed. Went up there the following day and they came back armed with all sorts of things —knives and cudgels—and they went up there and a real fight developed. I'm 200 yards away on my beat. When I call in at the station, the sergeant says, 'Great George Street—riot on'. I'd only got half way and I heard the row going on, so I cut across and met them. They were being chased downwards. There was I alone by myself. The Liverpool lads were chasing the sailors downhill. One of the sailors hit me with a piece of gun cable, heavy, wire-armoured cable with a knot on one end. He hit me round the back and the knot on the chest. I was gasping for breath. By then, bobbies were coming from everywhere—and we filled the bridewell with sailors. Charged with 'riotous and tumultuous assembling to the terror of His Majesty's subjects'. Chief Inspector of CID took charge and charged them all and then diplomacy came in and they went to court, discharged, back on the ship, and away.

Then there were occasions that could be predicted long in advance. The annual rituals of Orange and Hibernian celebrations were of course occasions when clashes were inevitable.[32]

T. D. Orange Lodges had their processions—be an occasional explosion when someone tried to dodge between you and they decided that once the procession started, nobody must cross the bows.

S. S. The only bit of crowd trouble we had was the Catholics on the north side of the division and the Orangemen on the south side; when the 12th of July was approaching there used to be a bit of trouble. They used to meet in Bold Street and stone each other. We just chased them off. Then there was trouble in Netherfield Road, round where the Orange bands were. There'd been some trouble up there between the Catholics and the Protestants and we were ordered to put a line across the road and were ordered to take out our truncheons.

on the night of March 3rd, he [Detective Sergeant Kelly] and another officer named Bardely saw Underhill pushing a hand-cart on Duke Street, Liverpool. Underhill stopped in front of a lock-up on Dale Street, opened the door and then began carrying out large cardboard cartons which he placed on the hand-cart . . . Bardely intercepted him before he had gone many yards . . . Underhill whipped out a jemmy from his pocket and began striking left and right. 'We closed with him and the jemmy having been knocked away, he started fighting and kicking. In a struggle on the ground, my raincoat was torn from top to bottom and Bardely exclaimed 'He's biting my little finger off.' I got my hand on his jaw and forced it open. Underhill then turned on me and bit me on the back of the hand. A man in the crowd that was watching, kicked Underhill on the head and this caused him to release his hold.   (*News of the World*, 1931)

It wasn't always the humble constable who resorted to the fist or stick.

W. S. We had a chap with us called Bob Freeborough, a Super.—family were all boxers. He used to go along Great Homer Street and used to get the fellers lined up—challenge anybody. 'If you beat me, you can go. If you don't you're right away into Rose Hill Station.'

Some officers, used to patrolling the 'bobby-bashing streets', were much more prone to start with the truncheon. It was taken for granted that where the 'bucks' predominated, the stick was the first resort, and the law an afterthought.

T. B. Some fellows had a hell of a time, in the rough quarter. But they don't mind. Round the Docks and St Anne's Street, batting dockers and labourers. There was some people in Reading Street off Lambeth Road. There's a public house on the corner called the Lighthouse. Next to it, there's a street, Regent Street, with balconies. Sergeant and I used to go up there every night. There was always a free fight in one house or another. We used to get mixed up with the fight. Throw them down the bloody banisters and then lock them up. Hill Street used to be a problem, with bucks and bobby-beating. Used to waylay the bobbies in Hill Street. They'd think nothing of going into them. Essex Street was a tough quarter because you had bobby-beaters there.

Indeed, some senior officers taught the new recruits to use the stick in a manner appropriate for the bucks.

G. E. Policemen in those days, particularly like me who had been away to sea, were a bit rough. We didn't carry batons for ornaments. We used them. You had to do it. I remember when after a few months in uniform duty, walking the beat, I was on West End Road, next to the Olympic Theatre, where there had been a building site and there was Collins World Fair there. A great place for young fellers to go after they come out of the pub and there was always trouble there. There'd be fighting amongst themselves. There'd be twenty or thirty fellers fighting in the grounds. Well, you don't argue with a drunken man when he's fighting—baton, 'Clonk!' I used to teach the young coppers afterwards. They were afraid to hit a man on the skull. You should hit him on the head, see some blood running—wouldn't stun him at all. The old coppers who I knew—they used to hit hard enough to stun them, as hard as a butcher hits a cow before he kills it. I knew about that and they hit them, they'd go down and stay down. Mind you, it meant that the bridewell sergeant had to make sure that the surgeon was on duty to sew their heads up, a few stitches, 'cos you had to sew their heads up. You had to split the skull. It was rough but people were used to that type of thing.

standing terrified by the door, I saw an officer lean forward on his horse and hit a neighbour with his truncheon above the eyes, heard the blow like the thump of wood on a swede turnip. The man ran crouching, hands on his face, into a wall and collapsed. My mother grabbed me, screamed after the charging police, fled into the shop and slammed the door. For half a lifetime afterwards the same man stayed amongst us, but did little work after. Something about him seemed absent. 'They knocked him silly', old people said, 'in the dockers' strike.'　　　　　　　　　　　　　　　　(R. Roberts, *The Classic Slum*, 94)

T. B.　I was at Lawrence Road, and on Saturday night, there used to be bedlam outside the Pavilion Theatre and there were fights between drunks. It was the Irish Protestants and Catholics—they used to knock hell out of each other. You had to be careful around that part of the world. There was like big tenement places. There would be all sorts of things rattling down on you—railings and chamber pots and lavatory pots. They'd turn on you together. So a sergeant named Jimmy Barlow—he took us all down. We lined up across the street and he said: 'You keep in line and if you knock anyone down, leave him and keep going.' Line with the rest, and if there's anybody on the floor, you step over them. Don't give them a thump. Stay together!' And we walked down clubbing right and left, and we cleared the streets and those that fell to the floor were carried off by those who had hidden behind when we went past. That happened a few times. Nobody seems to remember them now.

For some, the fist was an alternative to the stick, especially where a conflict with a buck had taken on the form of a personal feud.

W. S.　We had a bobby, Basil Rose, afraid of nothing. He says, 'I'll fix bloody Sweeney.' He does the worst thing he could have done. He sees Sweeney in broad daylight in a pub on Gerrard Street, 'I want you out here, Sweeney.' All the tram-cars and traffic was held up while Basil battered him all over Byrom Street. Put him in hospital for two months. But Basil got summonsed for wounding—an inspector in a tram-car had seen it and went and gave evidence against him. Basil got the sack and next we heard Basil was trying to capture Rommel with Lord Lovatt's son. I think he got killed at El Alamein.

Basil Rose, a Constable in the Liverpool Police, was indicted to the Quarter Session for unlawful wounding. Rose, giving evidence, said Sweeney had been refused a drink at three pubs and left a fourth. When he told him he would be arrested for being drunk, Sweeney butted him in his left eye and brought his knee up to his groin. They both fell to the ground and Sweeney kicked and struggled. There was a hostile crowd and to save himself and prevent Sweeney from escaping, Rose hit him twice with his baton. He also struck him when Sweeney tried to escape on the way to the Bridewell. Rose was found guilty of common assault and fined £10.　　　　　　　　　　　　　(*Police Review*, 1937)

Occasionally, the constable could enjoy the privileges of a spectator. The Sweeney family sometimes played a folk-devil role.

W. S. They terrorized Scotland Road. In Scotland Place, there was an ice-cream shop called Capaldi's and Tony Butcher was there with his girlfriend on a Saturday night. Sweeney came in and assaulted him. Tony Butcher says: 'I'll see you in Linehall Street.' We get tipped off. 'Right, what time's the big occasion?' So three of us went around. I was smoking a pipe, sat down on a doorstep. Sweeney and Tony Butcher came in—all the crowd was there. We were on the doorsteps, the bobbies having a smoke. They came up and fought for half an hour till they was both flat on their backs, on the waste land there. Then we all packed up. It was good fun, that.

In a rough-house, there were some constables who, even their colleagues recognized, could go over the top.

W. S. Saturday nights, there were battles everywhere. We had a mobile reserve at St Anne's Street. They had a blue van, and ropes, and lamps—six policemen and a sergeant —did for a week in turn. We got a call to a pub—near the Dock Road. There was a big Irish bobby, and the sergeant in the station said: 'Watch that fellow! You're unlucky to get with him. He's brutal—Birtles.' We came to the pub. We all piled out at the back. Birtles gets there before me and it was like a hurricane sweeping through, 'Thwack, bash!' They're lying on the floor and there's blood everywhere, broken glass. He dropped a fellow at the bat of an eyelid.

Hickson alleged that while in the police station where he had been taken by P.C. Torney on a charge of having stolen 10s. from the pocket of his clothes in a cubicle at the Corporation Swimming Baths, the constable gave him a violent blow to the eye, and followed this up by two blows to the body . . . he was subsequently acquitted on this charge. P.C. Torney claimed that Hickson's story was fabrication, and said the youth was prancing around the room at the police station, boxing and boasting of his prowess as a boxer . . . as a result of the boisterous behaviour, he caught his eye on a window-ledge. (*Liverpool Daily Post*, 1936)

K. M. On one occasion, there was a chap—not been long on the job—ex-Artilleryman. He was getting on a bit, transferred in to the Mounted. Used to call him 'Major'. One time we were on some stunt on the airfield and the people were encroaching on the ground and we were told to push them back. Walked towards them and they started to go back, flock away. This chap, Major, when he heard the order, he got his big staff out—our staffs were about three foot long—and he was going along waving his staff about, and laying into people. A couple of us went over to him and said, 'Put that flaming thing away.' He thought he was doing right. We'd have cracked somebody's head if we'd used them.

Violence against bucks, male and female, could always be rationalized.

S. H. I was in Lime Street one night, and a prostitute came along there. I said to her: 'I saw you talking to that fellow, and I'd warned you.' Do you know what she did? She stepped right in my face. I looked around and I hit her such a bloody fourpenny one that I knocked her flying. She went on the ground and I picked her up and a couple of fellows came along, saying, 'Do you want any help, officer?' I says, 'Just give us a hand to this Box.' I locked her up for soliciting, disorderly behaviour, and assault. She says to the sergeant, 'Look at my face.' I says, 'Tell the sergeant what you've done to me. You dirty so-and-so, you stepped right in my face.' Sergeant says to her, 'If I'd been there, I'd have done the same.'

Successful tests of bullet-proof shields have been carried out by members of the Liverpool City Police Force . . . policemen armed with these, faced with equanimity revolver bullets fired by colleagues. Two men, each carrying a heavy shield on his left arm, rushed as storm troops at the supposed criminal gunmen, firing themselves through a slit in the shield. Eye protections are provided in the shield, and tearbombs are added ammunition.

(*Police Chronicle*, 1928)

Documenting such violence in police–public relations through the medium of oral history is especially difficult. On one hand, experiences of the beat could differ greatly. An officer who spent his career patrolling a middle-class suburb would only in extreme circumstances be involved in a physical encounter. Conversely, in the inner city, the use of the stick could be a regular practice. However, the picture is confused further. On no other topic were these former officers of the Liverpool City so reticent. A few took pride in their resort to stick and fist. Most, however, felt that such practices were not topics to be made available for public scrutiny.[33] *Similarly, the information they provided on the question of bribery was open to some reservations.*

'BEWARE OF THE MAN WITH THE BOTTLE'

You were not likely to get rich from policing the street. Inducements from the public were rare.[34] *Surviving on the social margins did not allow much surplus to use as a bribe. There might be the very occasional gift for a personal service, but the bottle of beer from a few householders and especially from the publicans was the only obvious economic transaction, and was rarely ennobled as a 'payment' for services rendered.*

D. A. Never had any gifts. I did all my service round Garston. There was never any call for inducements because there was really nothing for people to break the law with. They had nothing. People on the parish only got ten shillings a week to live on and I often used to wonder how those who got drunk could afford it.

K. M. Bribes weren't what you might call rife. Bottle of beer's not a bribe. It was the custom—a given thing. Nobody's ever offered me a bribe. The pint of beer on the doorstep was the only perk that there was—you didn't find anything else. No question of hand-outs. It didn't happen because there was too much at stake.

H. P. Some people would get a bottle of beer—we'd had a lot of fellows come out of the army and they were fond of their drink and there's no doubt that they could get it. They knew the licensees. They weren't angels, none of them. You had certain of them that knew where you could slip in—you could slip in for a smoke and a cup of tea, so long as you weren't caught. The sergeant was chasing you round and if they came round and saw you coming out of a shop, you had to have a good explanation.

M. B. No official bribes. People you'd been helping might offer you something. For instance, if you're on a traffic junction outside a railway station like Lime Street, you won't be there five minutes before you're approached by some hotelier saying, it would be worth your while to send them up to his hotel. Or, for instance, the floating roadway where traffic was going down on the barges to go across the river, it would be well worth any particular company to have a word with the officer on the floating roadway to let their vehicles through first. But no gifts to any great extent. You might get ten bob or so—not very much. I don't think I had a Christmas present all my blessed life. All sorts of people held their hands out to me but I don't think I ever got anything.

One fellow gave me ten bob once—he was a tram-driver. I was called to a house and there was a man in agony. I was on my way home again as usual. He had tripped on a gas-lid in the road and fractured his patella so his wife was busy bandaging him up. She made an awful job of it—ten times worse. I took this bandage off and put a cold compress on, making a proper patella dressing, got the ambulance and got him off to hospital, and put in a Report about this broken gas-lid. Two months later this tram-driver stopped me: 'I want to see you for a minute. Come to my house.' So I went round after I had finished.

He and his wife were there. He said: 'I owe you a lot for that. I'm employed by the Corporation so I couldn't sue the Corporation. But your Report that it was a gas-lid—I was able to go ahead with it and I got compensation.' His wife says, 'Go on—tell him what you got.' 'I got a £100'—which was quite a lot then. He gave me a ten bob note and a bag of tomatoes. But that's the only thing that I ever remember getting.

A publican had to make sure that the gift was not too obvious.

S. H. Offered cash many a time. I'd say: 'Push your bloody money in your pocket. I don't want it.' I had a fellow come rushing out to me, point duty outside Legs o' Man pub one night, when I was directing traffic, puts a bottle of beer down by the side of me. I says, 'I'll give you two bloody minutes to take that bottle away.' He bloody soon took it away. It would have been a problem for me if the bloody sergeant had come along and seen me drinking beer or seen that bottle beside me. He might have thought I'd had one previous. If they said, 'Officer, there's a quid to square it'. I'd say: 'You'll square nothing with me. I do my bloody duty.'

But the perk—the bottle of beer—was a payment in kind. It might not induce a particular favour from a police constable but then, as now, it ensured a level of co-operation. It was in the publican's interest to keep the constable sweet, to help with rowdy customers.

W. S. Irish was tough. On a Saturday night, there used to be at the bottom of Scotland Road—Byrom Street—all the Irishmen. They used to come over for the spud-picking and go to Ormskirk and live in a bothy and would come to Scotland Place because there were so many wakes. There may be ten of us on Scotland Place on a Saturday night when the Morning Star got chucked out and the licensee was a feller called Pat McEwen (he had a marine store dealer's in Chaucer Street and took that pub). We had ten bobbies in five pairs waiting for them coming out. I've seen thirty men with their coats off fighting—getting on the trams and dragged off. Then you'd see old Pat McEwen's wife looking out for you. You'd go to the back of the pub and sit down. 'What will you have, Jock?' 'I'll have a jar,' and it was real good.

In accepting the unofficial payment, the hierarchy had to be respected.

H. P. We used to keep an eye on pubs where the sergeant and the constable used to do a month at a time, visiting the cinemas, theatres, and public houses, licensed places, and do some pubs, night after night—just checking things, and at five past ten, you'd be right in checking they were keeping to closing time. We'd clear them out for the licensee if he was having trouble. Licensees would offer you drink after drink if you wanted—lot of them did. If I said 'No' as a sergeant, the constable wouldn't get a drink; but if I said 'No' as a constable, the sergeant would have it.

T. B. There were some bright lads on the job—boozing a great deal. All your licensed premises on your area had to be checked at least once a week (in uniform) and the sergeant would pick you up and take you visiting these various posts, and I used to take a glass of beer. You'd go through to the back place and as soon as the licensee saw you, there's two pints. I'd only drink half a pint, so I was in great demand—the sergeant would have the rest. Same when you visited the cinemas and dance-halls, watching the dancing. They were licensed premises.

T. D. We cleared a little thing up—back end of a wedding. You'd look at the sergeant and if he O.K.d it, you'd have one but if he didn't, you bloody wouldn't.'

The ex-CID officer was more reticent about the perks of the job, more willing to see those offers as the practice in other forces.[35]

G. E. I was offered money many a time. I only pinched one feller for bribery because he was a nasty feller. One thing about it, I don't recall any CID man in my recollection, while I was serving, ever falling for taking money off. In London, there was a lot of it going on. You used to have to go to London to the Old Bailey, giving evidence and anything like that. I used to go out with the London detectives, and these Cockney fellers down in London, they'd take money off anyone. It opened my eyes when I first went there. I was at the Old Bailey, spent about two weeks there—I had the London detective with me. I was staying in the police house—they had several police station-houses for CID men staying, instead of going to a hotel.

These young London detectives would come out with us for a meal, after we'd finished the court-work, go down to several famous pubs, and order several drinks. You'd always put a ten bob note in. They'd come back with change for a pound, knowing he was a London detective. That was regular, speaking from experience. Didn't happen any town that I knew of except London and I can understand why they did it in London—very expensive place for a young detective to make a shape—cost too much money keeping in front of your job there.

In Victorian days, the Watch Committee regularly placed adverts in the local newspapers in early December: 'Shopkeepers are advised not to give Christmas Boxes to police officers.'[36]

T. D. Christmas Boxes? there used to be a read-out at the parade before Christmas period—the Chief Constable himself would come down and say: 'Be warned —beware of the man with the bottle'.

For the poor, there was rarely anything tangible to offer in a transaction. For some of the street entrepreneurs such as the bookie or brothel-keeper, the shopkeeper or publican, there were some minor ways of keeping the police sweet—rarely anything that could be dignified with the name bribe. The police authorities might look askance at the bottle of beer but to the constables it was seen as a legitimate reward for a little extra service.

FROM SERVICE TO DEFERENCE

This gift relationship related directly to the form of class relations in the city. In general, the gifts came from the shopkeeper or publican class. But further up the social scale, unrewarded deference was often required, often with the constable being treated as simply another flunkey in uniform, an attitude that might provoke a retaliatory reaction.

S. H. We were treated with a considerable amount of respect by the middle class. Very rarely you would come across a person that seemed to think that you were beneath them and ought to do as they said. It did happen at times but they were usually people who fancied their power, such as city councillors. The factory owners and shopkeepers would come and have a chat with you.

There was a fellow came up to me in Lime Street and said: 'Hey, get me a taxi. I'm a ratepayer. I pay for the likes of you.' I said: 'Getaway, you pay rates do you? I pay rates. Let me tell you something, mister. I'm paid to keep you in your place. That's what I'm walking the streets for.' I got hold of him by the scruff of the neck and took him along to the police box and rang up for the wagon. He says, 'What's this?' I says, 'Here's your taxi.' I took him round to Cheapside and booked him for being drunk and disorderly.

Some reticence was necessary in dealing with the middle classes—you were never quite sure what influence might be brought to bear behind the scenes.

D. A. I was on a school-crossing duty for disabled children and I held up my hand for a motor cyclist to stop and he rode right past me. I called him to stop and said, 'I've got to test your brakes.' I found that the front brake was inefficient owing to lack of adjustment. I said, 'I've got to summons you for driving amongst children.' So he went before the court and pleaded 'Not Guilty'. I gave my evidence—he adjusted the brakes in my presence after I found them inefficient. So the magistrate said to him: 'You heard what the officer said. Do you agree with that?' 'Oh yes.' And I couldn't believe my ears—'Case dismissed.' The only thing I could put it down to was his father was a big Mason and he was Freemason on the Bench. Strangely enough, that young man was killed on the same motor bike within three months of that—killed within two or three hundred yards of the same spot.

Such accounts often contained a moralizing vengeance—as if, occasionally, there was some supreme being able to impose a natural justice.

There were some rare contacts with an élite that transcended the urban class relationships.

J. V. Lord Derby—he was Lord-Lieutenant—made ceremonial trips into town from Croxteth Hall, every Christmas. Each constable at every junction of the street corners down, used to be given a game bird. No traffic lights then—these men used to give him right of way.

But there were intimacies at the opposite end of the social scale—in which a barrow girl might fancy a young police constable, or a socially mobile 'buck' might seek advice from the local fount of authority and knowledge.

T. D. People were scared of you—didn't matter whether you were a big man or a small man. It was the uniform. They were brought up to respect us and to go to a policeman when they were in trouble. I remember one feller that came in—a respectable buck, a docker. Comes to corner of the street for a breath of fresh air. His hair was all tousled, a scarf round his neck, touching his braces. This fellow Dickerly says to me, 'Can you give me a bit of advice, officer?' 'Depends what it is.' 'My son has just passed his exams to go to St Francis Xavier. What would you do if you were me? Let him go or pass it by?' 'Entirely up to you—if he goes there, it will cost you a heck of a lot of money. He'll want certain clothes, certain books. He'll want a push-bike like everybody else. He'll want togs for football or cricket. It's up to you to weigh the situation up as to whether you can stand it.' About twelve months later, I was walking around the Dingle and saw this chap coming down the road, brand new suit and all the rest of it, with his wife and kid. Stopped me and told me he'd let him go to St Francis Xavier's. He says: 'I can manage—course I can't live down there where I was. I'm a respectable man now.'

A. T. You always got respect from the people on the ground. They'd come and ask you for advice and you'd tell them and help them all you could. I hadn't been in the force very long and my sergeant met me and said, 'That chimney's smoking.' I said, 'I'm going off duty soon.' He said, 'Go and do them.' So this was an order and so I had to and a young woman opened the door—about eighteen years. I said, 'Do you occupy this house?' 'No, it's my grandmother's.' 'Do you know that your chimney's on fire?' 'Yes.' 'Well, I'm sorry but the sergeant's out there and I'll have to report you.' So I took the name and address and so eventually a summons came through for this old lady. So I served it. Lo and behold, when I got to court, this old lady was there and I felt so ashamed and so sorry for her. I said, 'How are you going to get home, love?' 'Oh, I'll go on the tram.' I says, 'Come on, I'll pay your fine.' And I paid the first fine that I ever did. I never paid another one. But for that old lady, I had been ordered to do her for the fire.

M. B. Even in the 'bobby-bashing' neighbourhoods, they were friendly towards you. This street—I patrolled it at night. I remember walking down there at night and I had a cough. This old lady came out and said about the cough—she gave me a dose of cough medicine. They called me 'baby-face' when they were annoyed, but generally they treated me with respect. You had authority in those days. You made people move on and they went.

W. S. Great Homer Street—it was the busiest place in the country. You could have walked on their heads on Saturday. The butchers would open at one in the morning. The girls used to come out with the barrows and the people with the shops used to complain. Liz Edmunds—they were fruit people—she was a nice kid. She had her eye on me. I used to put my cape on the railings. When you went for your cape, it would be full of apples and pears. They were real good.

Attitudes to the police historically have been documented thoroughly in the revisionist accounts of policing.[37] *This Liverpool evidence—the patronizing condescension and occasional bullying by the middle classes and the supplicant individual contact from the occasional member of the lower stratum—is congruent with the overall profile of class relationships to the police in Britain.*

FROM DEFERENCE TO CONFRONTATION
(AND BACK)

Street encounters—both between the lower classes and the police and amongst the former—embodied all the elements of contrariness produced by a culture of desperation and survival. A combination of poverty, street recreation and entrepreneurship, the delights of beverages such as 'red biddy', collective solidarity, and individual dispute entailed a spasmodic relationship which veered from passivity and deference, on the one hand, to violent assault, on the other. But the ultimate common denominator was a realistic trepidation in the face (at least) of the all-powerful police.

M. B. The Scotland Road area had a name for violence to a certain extent —drunkenness you know—not a lot. Trouble was mainly due to poverty. Only one in a thousand had bathrooms in their houses. The people round there drank red biddy and that sort of thing. It was like methylated spirits. It was a wine that they paid about a penny or twopence a glass for. They would drink that in some of these pubs and, of course, as soon as they got out in the fresh air, it hit them and they were away. The men used to go paralytic and put windows in. We would have to deal with it then. You got the women, the 'shawlies' we called them, drinking this and then they would come out fighting drunk. If you locked up one of these shawlies, as you were coming away from the Main Bridewell, you would usually find a deputation of shawlies coming running down the road. 'Where is she, sir? Can we come and bail her our?' They'd do that. They helped themselves. The poor helped the poor.

K. R. I saw a fellow having an epileptic fit and I got down to hold him while he kicked out. Let him kick it out as long as he didn't injure himself. I was just holding him down and I got a hammering from the locals. They thought I was having a fight with him. It wasn't me molesting them. It was them molesting me. It was a natural thing for them to do so I didn't take any action—told them in no uncertain terms that this man was ill and he eventually came to and everyone was happy then.

At the end of the day, there was no love lost between the street people and the representatives of an all-powerful State.

T. D. The ordinary working-man and his kith and kin, unless he was in trouble, he didn't want to know you. But if you did something underhand, they'd shout about it. I had a smoke and somebody would shout: 'Hey—copper's smoking.' General feeling was 'once a policeman, never a man'.

Policing the street was the bedrock of urban policing. On that terrain, the patrol constable gradually learnt the tricks of the trade—the verbal tricks to diffuse confrontations, and when to use the ultimate omnibus body of legal weapons, backed up by the stick and the fist. In using those techniques, the essential purpose was one of social control. Moving-on, on the surface, was a pointless ritual. Its latent function was to ensure that the lower classes fitted in with the designs of their betters. They were to be confined to a moral order that suited the exhortations of the urban middle class. Police regulation—of which law enforcement was only a tool—was about confining the 'troublesome' poor to their quarters and ensuring that their nefarious characteristics were not contagious. Policing was an urban prophylactic. In that process, individual police experiences might differ—the Instruction Book and the stick in one hand, the bottle of beer and the barrow girl's apple in the other. Only with the more entrepreneurial activities of the lower class—from bookmaking to thieving—did the gospel of urban moralizing combine with an economic imperative.

5

Regulating the Lower Classes

THE street life of the urban poor in England between the wars consisted of two interrelated elements—the social and the economic.[1] On one hand, the street was the arena of recreation, where kids played football, gambled at pitch-and-toss, where men gossiped on the corner outside the pub, and where working-class women chatted with their neighbours and kin.

But an overriding feature of Liverpool in 1919, about to be overtaken by London as the busiest port in the UK,[2] was the street economy. This was the system of economic and social relationships from which the urban poor, and some of their betters, scraped a living. It involved a variety of pursuits—casual employment in the docks, in transport, in coal-carrying, and in the building industry—and a variety of life-styles—from living 'on tick' at the grocer's to pawnshop credit, from public houses to the rag-and-bones trade, from the street market to the public wash-houses, and from buying clothes on the never-never from the doorstep salesman to saving for a Co-operative Society funeral.

Street trading and similar activities flourished in the space left behind the primary economy. The traders survived in the economic void created by a system in which small shopkeepers, facing a combination of bad debts, relatively high overheads, and small profit margins, charged prices above the heads of the casual poor. A living could be made, repairing and (with the assistance of the rag-and-bone trade) recycling household goods.[3] The street economy also included, for some, prostitution and brothel-keeping spawned mainly by the shipping industry. For others, it involved occasional employment as runners and lookouts for the bookmakers. For a small minority, it meant casual and intermittent thieving.

This street or secondary economy was integrated with the official, primary economy of the city, the system of taxable, regular employment, production, and transaction.[4] Liverpool's trade required the provision of a pool of surplus labour in all the industries related to the port. This reservoir of employables was characterized by casual availability, and by consequent low pay.[5] The secondary economy provided the necessities of life and some of the recreations for a major part of the population that had insufficient resources to purchase life-styles through the approved channels. In the eyes of that class, street markets and associated forms of economic exchange supplying services and materials at low cost were the only affordable source for purchases.

What all these activities, social and economic, had in common was state intervention. Where they were not illegal, they were severely regulated. In particular, the bookies and brothel-keepers were open to apparently arbitrary but systematic police assault. For others—in the dance-halls, in carting (where the owner's name had to be stencilled on to the contrivance), in the public houses, in peddling, and in market trading—there was regulation by licence. Even singing in a public house was liable to legal reprimand. The moral hangover from Victorian England,[6] as well as the demands of the respectable shopkeeping class, required that street life be policed—whether it be passing the time 'doing nothing' on the street corner or threatening the profits of the shopkeepers by itinerant trading. Hence a Home Office spokesman, referring to the Street Betting Act 1906, said it had been passed 'for the protection of the working man against himself'.[7]

The superficially ramschackle, but organized, street economy, unlike street recreation, could only be regulated through police departments with particular mandates. A Plain Clothes section confronted the brothels and bookmakers, checked the public houses, and regulated trading. Criminal Investigation Departments policed petty theft and more serious offences.

PLAIN CLOTHES

Compared to the beat, anything was attractive. Plain Clothes work, policing bookies, brothels, and bars, offered some variety, a degree of freedom from the clock discipline of the beat, and status—a sign of some imagination and proved ability. Major aspects of Plain Clothes work were regarded as requiring special skills and motivation. With regard to apprehending street bookies, for example 'men must be specially detailed and must devote a considerable time to observation . . . it is not by any means every policeman who has the ability, or indeed, desire, to carry out the duty'.[8]

Plain Clothes work entailed singling out particular street activities for legal proscription. It often involved working against an actively hostile community. A 'considerable section of the public opinion regards the present law as class legislation, and supports the street bookmakers and the small backer'.[9] The Plain Clothes officer had to manage without any form of communal approval, and with more hostility than even that encountered by the street constable in the lower-class district. Some benefits might occasionally accrue from the work of the constable, but it was difficult to recognize any local value in the work of the PC officer.

B. A. Everyone wants to be in Plain Clothes. You do twelve months' work in PC after you've proved yourself an efficient policeman. So I was selected—eight of us. We used to go in twos. You're looking at brothels and things like that on late duty. It was all advanced work, enquiries from other forces, reports that had to be dealt with that couldn't be dealt with by uniformed men. Also we were responsible for all kinds of vice—prostitution, gambling, club offences, anything of that nature—fairly tightly scheduled. Mainly vice but any mortal thing and to a certain extent the Plain Clothes sergeant was the right-hand man of the superintendent. He would be called in by the superintendent to deal with any matter that needed attention. For example, in Plain Clothes, the sergeant might be called in with his men to deal with an incident in another division—maybe a brothel or a shebeen—where they suspected that a little bit of information was leaking.

P. P. Did about nine months on the beat and then I was posted straight to the Plain Clothes Branch as a temporary detective. All you did then in the Plain Clothes department was you attended the bookmakers and the brothels. In PC, you worked split duty on alternative days, then on the next day you would work nine to six. You had much more freedom. You were allowed to go anywhere—it was a very good job. I had sufficient of a baby face to go and do the clubs. They trusted you. You got extra money—Plain Clothes allowance. Discipline wasn't quite so severe. I had quite an interesting time in PC. We were interested mainly in prostitutes, brothels, betting-houses, street betting.

H. P. In a police force, like any other job, you have all sorts of men, some as thick as two short planks. Some are keen, some are not. Some are quite content to stand on the Dock gate all day, watch the world go by—that's monotonous. You get a chap who isn't afraid to do this job, so they're selected in each division—six men in Plain Clothes and a sergeant in charge. They've got complaints coming in. If you've got complaints from the public or disorderly houses, noise outside pubs or information from your colleagues, these came to the PC section. You'd have this report and within a fortnight, you had to report what action you had taken on it.

In practice, the bulk of the work, regulating—prosecuting and persecuting—bookmaking and prostitution, did not afford much variety.

Regulating Street and Club Gaming

Chief Constable Caldwell of the City Police had combined moral and economic imperatives in his condemnation of the bookies. It 'destroys home life, it brings poverty into the home many a time. It also leads . . . to many cases of embezzlement and the misappropriation of money'.[10] *Outright suppression was impossible. All his Plain Clothes officers could hope to do was to keep the lid on, by intermittent assaults. Those practices brought some relief to bobbies who had graduated from the monotony of the beat to the stimulus of a specified target.*

G. E. Great game of hide-and-seek with the bookies. Street bookmaking was regarded as a serious offence in those days. You'd be sent out in plain clothes. Somebody had got the information that a bookie was making a stand at the bottom of West Derby Street and you'd be sent out in twos—one to corroborate and one to keep watch on the bookie. Well, you wouldn't see the bookie because he would station himself at the bottom of the street, taking the bets, and we'd pounce on him when we saw him take a few bets and take him in and charge him. They got heavy fines in those days.

P. P. Street betting was a relatively simple matter. You got to know who was standing—there were plenty of touts who would tell you who they were. Then a matter of watching from a distance and seeing how many slips they took, and careful they didn't get rid of them before you got out to him. You let him take about three or four slips, then pick him up and take him in. They used to work all sorts of things. Street bookies used to be on street corner, and as soon as they put their nose around it, there was a whistle and away. Never got near them. Bookmakers used to have cloth bags.[11] If you've got a runner, you had to make sure that the money was in the bag before anyone was winning and sometimes the bags didn't come in till late—used to have a key and use a check to seal it.

Police action against bookmaking was not aimed at eradication. It was a strategy of containment. Officers on the ground, faced with the impossibility of total enforcement, worked out their own solutions to meeting force goals. In that process, informal strategies were agreed, relations in which bookmakers and police would come to an understanding, sometimes for a backhander, sometimes not. It was common, for example, for bookmakers to arrange for stooges to be arrested in order to satisfy police demands for a quota of convictions.[12]

T. D. There was a lot of bookmakers would set them up and leave a man out to be picked up. They thought that if a man was picked up in that area that would keep the rest of them clean for a while—police wouldn't come back again.

T. B. We knew all the bookies. They used to set themselves up to get locked up every so often so the police would have a victim—it was so-and-so one week and somebody else the next. We knew that unofficially. It got to a routine—they'd set fellows up to get locked up. The fellow got fined a couple of quid for acting as a street bookie and it lessened their convictions. Yet it still showed that the police were carrying the job out.

The formalization of these relationships between bookies and police could occasionally result in trouble for the latter.

A. T. There was a chap called Billy. He was a favourite bookie around there. Everybody trusted him. He was as honest as the day is long with their bets—we more or less proved it. The day I got him, there were three of us went round. The sergeant was on a bike and I walked down. I had an old mac on—scruffy as could be—Derby day. I got hold of Billy. 'For God's sake, let me go.' I said, 'I can't let you go Billy, you know.' He said, 'I've got all the CID bets in here.' 'Oh,' I said, 'don't be daft.' 'I have, honestly, can I put them in your raincoat pocket?' I said, 'I'm not going to carry them for you.' Then I thought: 'If so-and-so [from the CID] comes up, what is he going to say to me?' So I put them in my inside pocket and walked him into the station. They emptied all his pockets, and his coat had been ripped, specially made, and he had all this money all the way round the inside of it. Terrific amount of money, he had. So I said to him, 'Hey, what about this?' pulling out his packet from my pocket. He said, 'You'd better keep it.' 'I can't keep it—I'll go and tell the bridewell sergeant.' (This is all happening in the middle of the station). He said: 'Me brother will be coming shortly. Give it to him.' And I thought: 'What am I getting into? I'm going to get the sack here.' But his brother-in-law came in and Billy must have told him and he came over to me saying, 'I believe you've got some bets of Billy's?' I says, 'Yeah—if you put your hand in there without anyone seeing, bring them all out and get to hell out of here.' He did that and I found out that when he brought them out there was a pile of money in as well—I only expected betting slips. There was the CID money in it. Anyhow, I believe he paid everyone out for all the bets that were confiscated.

More serious trouble was not uncommon. A major Metropolitan case of corruption was followed by one in Liverpool.

P. P. There was a big scandal while I was at Essex Road when the Plain Clothes Section came up before the Assize—six or seven of them, for corruption with the bookmakers. The bookies would arrange that they arrested so many but the individuals they arrested had no record, so the amount of their fines would be for a first offence.

The trial of the Liverpool bookmaker and nine ex-Constables of Liverpool, concluded at Liverpool Assizes on Monday, all ten being found guilty of corruption and conspiracy. The allegation was that all the Policemen . . . accepted bribes from [a bookmaker] so that he might not be interfered with in carrying on street betting. One of the constables, when dealing with the arrest of a 'dummy' said four officers were working together, and one officer made up his notebook for the purpose of his evidence. 'We would all make it up the same. That was a matter of form.'
   Mr Justice Swift: 'I have often heard it suggested that Policemen do these things but I have never heard a Policeman on oath say that he did them.'
   Constable: 'Well they do. It does not say we would say exactly the words in our notebook.'
   'Are you saying, as an officer of seven years' experience, the usual thing is to make items agree, whether it is true or not?' 'If I had to go into the witness-box, I would make my notebooks up true.'   (*Sunday News*, 1927)

The forms of corruption were of two kinds, receipt of monies a week on consideration of a partial stay of police action . . . The other, an arrangement whereby certain arrests were made, followed by pleas of Guilty and convictions of men provided with betting slips for the purpose so that complaints of street betting in particular localities might be satisfied, meanwhile there would be immunity from arrest at other places. . . . The bookmakers carefully selected men to be convicted who had no previous convictions, so that light fines should be inflicted.   (*Chief Constable's Report to the Watch Committee*, 1927)

In a Metropolitan case, the payments are standardized.

the two constables who were watching Bottom (described as a race frequenter) as a suspect
. . . saw him hand a silver coin each to the accused Constables who then walked away.
When Bottom was arrested, he shouted 'Fetch the Sergeant. He'll tell you I am alright.'
The two constables came up and said 'yes, he's alright. We know him.' Not satisfied, the
watching officers took Bottom to gaol, where they found on him a piece of paper with the
following notes 'Sergeant 5s. Busy 5s. Three Flatties 7s. 6d, Private Flatty 2s. 6d.' 'Busy',
explained the prosecution, was slang for detective, 'flatty' was for constable.

(*Police Chronicle*, 1926)

Toleration of bookmaking could lead to some odd situations.

A professional bookmaker named Morris Michaels was charged at the Liverpool Police
Court on the 1st inst. with betting at the Liverpool Police Athletics Sports. The sports were
held at the Police Athletic Grounds and . . . Michaels was shouting the odds and was seen
to receive and to pay out money.

(*Police Chronicle*, 1936)

*While bookies were tolerated by the beat constable, if more arbitrarily by the specialist Plain
Clothes squad, that tolerance could be disturbed where a bookie appeared to step out of
line—an opportunity for the beat officer to garner some public credit.*

K. M. I was on the East Queen's Dock and there was a crowd outside on the street,
and I went there and there had been a row and a woman playing hell over it. She
said this bookie making the bets had fiddled her out of the money. The bookie in
this street used to be in an entry right of the street going in, and he had a look-out.
Day after this, I walked down with a mate of mine and I said to him: 'When we go
down towards the bookie, turn into the street and you go into the entry opposite'
(which went round and came out at the far end). There was a small patch of ground
next to the entry where the bookie was. My mate circled round. I just went
straight in, towards the bookie. By that time, the look-out had spotted me and I
was still walking—so I nipped straight in there. Instead of the bookie running the
other way, he ran towards me and passed me, he ran that quick, and I caught him
up by swinging my cape and sending him flying. He lost his footing and went
down. I took him round to the Dock hut and asked what he had there, and he had a
'paying-out' sheet and some slips. So I got them for evidence and then got in touch
with the Plain Clothes. He went down to court and was fined. Everybody around
was delighted, and this woman especially.

*In any case, even when there was little police co-operation, bookmaking could be a highly
organized business in which the bookies could not afford to leave police operations to chance.*

P. E. There used to be chaps with the betting who were watching, waiting for the
Plain Clothes—they knew our duties and they'd see us go out, see which direction
we were going in and they'd tip the runners off at the different places, all being
paid by the bookies. It was a good game matching their wits against ours.

The look-outs ('dowzies'[13]) could normally count on community support in their defence of

street pastimes, whether in betting or in pitch-and-toss. Ayers quotes of a bookie's look-out:
'One day the Black Maria came whizzing down and a dozen policemen whizzed out of it
along the entry and Gerry hadn't been given the tip-off but he run through the street and he
got as far as the outhouse and my dad was standing at the door and Gerry shot up our steps
through our house and out the back. When the police got to our door they went to go up the steps
and my dad said "Not through here, not without a warrant." '[14] Of pitch-and-toss, Woods
relates: 'The police never had a great success rate, as neighbours would always help the
players. As far as the latter were concerned, the men were doing no real harm. Thus it became
standard practice to leave backyard doors open so that players could run in during a raid. It
all seemed quite normal for us as children to be sitting down for a meal when a man would
dash in, throw off his cap and coat, quickly grab a chair and make himself at home. If the
police followed . . . all were prepared to swear the bloke had been in the house for, oh, half an
hour.'[15]

In turn, the police developed, their own techniques:

P. E. Method of catching bookies? We used to have the 'silly' chap who worked
for us, and he'd go into a pub and he'd watch somebody taking bets. Then he'd
come out and raised his hat over the feller, and we'd lock him up with six betting
slips on him. When we were locking him up, he'd say, 'You didn't see me taking
bets in the street.' I said, 'Well, where did you take them?' 'In the pub.' 'You go
and tell the feller, what you told us—you won't last much longer.' (The pub
landlord would be summonsed.) We always planted men in the pubs.

Clubs could reputedly combine the bookmaker's functions (and finance) with prostitution.

H. P. . . . a lot of illegal clubs—shebeens. We had all sorts of funny clubs going.
If you were going to raid these, you kept it hush-hush. You didn't trust your
colleagues and you didn't tell the uniform men in case they were pally with
somebody who went there. You'd get the warrant. You'd all be brought in but you
didn't necessarily know where. You'd be kept in because people used to follow us
around even though you were in plain clothes.

In some of the Liverpool clubs, ordinary amenities are almost entirely lacking . . . Clubs of
this kind exist solely for drinking and betting and are run by bookmakers. The Police
experience great difficulty in obtaining evidence. The closest scrutiny of entrants is
maintained by officials of the clubs, spyholes are cut in the woodwork to enable doormen to
examine persons seeking admission, and systems of electric bells are installed to give alarm
when necessary. If the police resort to clandestine methods to defeat these means of
covering grave breaches of the law, it is because, as the law stands, there is no alternative.

(*Chief Constable's Report*, 1936)

P. P. We used to raid houses where the bookie business was being carried on.
There was a lot of houses collecting for the bookies. You may execute warrants on
one of those places in the afternoon when the racing is good. Then you might be
brought out at night to raid another club. You never counted the time then—you

expected it. It was exciting to think that you'd matched your wits against them and beaten them.

The Royal Commission had noted that there was no section of the local police as likely to be subject to so many 'temptations and to which the police sometimes succumb . . . no department in which accusations of dishonesty are so common'.[16] Careful selection from the rank and file, appointing to Plain Clothes only those officers with unusual qualities, was little proof against the temptations. The combination of unpopular penal legislation and ready cash were material inducements to overcome any organizationally approved personal qualities.

Prostitution

The second major imposition of moral legislation related to the policing of women. Historically, beat police work reflected the male chauvinism of a legal code that was often construed in ways that favoured men.[17] Whether as victims—the case of forcible rape—as potential offenders—as in prostitution—or simply as single women abroad at night, women were viewed in both Instruction Book and within the police culture as inferior beings, childlike, often unaware of the consequences of their own actions.

There was a vast legal armoury, apart from the unwritten powers of the Ways and Means Act, to deal with prostitutes. Unlike the Metropolitan Police, the Liverpool City Police had never possessed the formal powers contained in the Contagious Diseases Acts of the Victorian period. There were, however, powers enough.[18] Prostitution in itself was not illegal. But it was easy to find a relevant charge. Under the Vagrancy Act 1824 (Sect. 3), if the male constable regarded her as behaving in a 'riotous or indecent manner', she could be locked up. Under the Town Police Clauses Act 1847 (Sect. 3), if he considered her to be obstructing passers-by while she plied her trade, he could arrest her. Further powers were provided by the Criminal Law Amendment Acts of 1885, 1912, and 1922 (especially concerned with brothels). The constable required no specialized legislation in order to wield grace-and-favour power over the prostitute.

Street prostitution was largely the province of the beat constable. Plain Clothes dealt mainly with the brothels. For beat officers, prostitution was usually something to be tolerated. As long as the woman did not go out of her way to solicit customers, it was recognized that she, too, had a living to make.

M. B. Knew quite a number of regular prostitutes. They had prostitute lodging houses down in Kempston Street and other areas. They were all right. They never caused trouble. I've never arrested a prostitute in my life. It wasn't exactly tolerated. If they made a nuisance of themselves, they would be arrested. But as long as they were discreet, they were just left alone. If a girl was being blatant about it, pulling up men right, left, and centre, then she'd find herself arrested. But as a general rule, they had to be warned once before you could contemplate taking them in. And of course, you had to prove that they were a prostitute. That wasn't easy. You had to know that they had been arrested for this offence previously and had convictions for it. Otherwise, it was very difficult to say, 'This woman is a prostitute.'

There were other reactions to prostitution. In Plain Clothes, where the work was obligatory, practices were routinized and often tedious.

B. T. We done quite a few brothels up Mount Pleasant in a couple of hotels there. Lord Nelson Street. They were a bit monotonous doing them because you had to get a place of observation, generally right opposite, and you had to know the prostitutes, mostly by name, and you would sit there from about eight or nine o'clock until about twelve taking observations on the men entering the building and when they left.

The police kept observation on the premises—a licensed refreshment room, on 12 nights . . . between the hours of 7.30 and 10.40 . . . 35 women of a certain class, 30 of them known to have been convicted, were seen to enter, generally alone, and to leave in the company of men   (*Liverpool Echo*, 1920)

W. R. Plain Clothes always had a list of brothels to watch. You'd be sent by the Inspector who'd give you an address—we were told there was a brothel at Ashton Street. I did one up in Pembroke Place. You had to keep three days' observation on it and we'd count the number of men coming in and the number of men as they come out. You'd go in the brothels about two or three in the morning. Then you'd make your evidence out and go down to the Magistrate's, who'd give you a warrant to raid the brothel. We'd get a warrant and go on a suitable day—usually towards the end of the week when men had their wages. I was doing a turn in Elizabeth Street, just doorways for observation and watch round the corners all the time. Nobody seemed to bother. You were in civvies so nobody took any notice —probably think you were a fellow waiting to pick up a girl. We'd watch it till we saw a couple of men go in. We'd immediately follow them in and arrest the woman as a brothel-keeper and of course the man was always allowed to go away.

P. E. Used to know quite a lot of prostitutes—about a dozen of them. Never caught them in the act. But where I did catch was in a brothel we raided once in Albany Road. The back door was painted white so they could find the place easy, down the back. Locked the feller up and his wife and daughter. The feller got fined £500.

A few beat officers saw themselves on a crusade against prostitution. Moral indignation was compounded by physical repulsion, and reinforced by the reservoir of legislation.

Morality
repulsion
legislation.

S. H. I used to lock them up ten a penny on Lime Street. Used to come across them all the time. When I saw one, I'd go up to the fellow she had accosted and say, 'Excuse me, can you tell me what that lady said to you?' 'You must be—I don't want to be brought into it.' Or, 'She asked me if I wanted a short time.'

'Would you care to give me your name and address?' 'No, I'm not interested—I don't want to go to court.' So that was that, and some said, 'Yes, I'll go to court.' But a lot of them didn't want to be mixed up with prostitutes. I've locked them up ten a penny. I've locked them up out of the bloody gutter, drunk on methylated spirits (we used to call it 'mojo').

H. P. I've locked up a hundred prostitutes but the fines weren't excessive (there wasn't the money for bribes from them). <u>They were dirty, filthy women—the lowest of the low in their dress and cleanliness.</u> They'd go with some chap in a doorway. You used to get a lot of it out on the street and these were filthy old women there, and the chap's had a few drinks and he goes there with one of them. Being caught with her and having to give evidence, when he hears their record in court read out and the Clerk says: 'Best thing you can do Mister is to go to a Clinic.' In Plain Clothes, you know the dives and doorways they used. We could pick them up easily and some of them—Selena Sefton was one—you had to be drunk before you went with her, a right old hag. They got an awful shock the next morning when they saw what they had been with. She had well over a hundred convictions for prostitution over years. And some fellow thinks suddenly, 'I've got a wife at home and that's what I've been with.'

Plain Clothes practices and individual obsessions were not always viewed sympathetically by colleagues.

A. M. Plain Clothes officers were a bit cruel with prostitutes, picking them up without cause. Unless you saw them importuning, it was better to leave them alone. They had their own places to work and if you didn't trouble them, they wouldn't trouble you.

Occasionally, catching a man in the act could be an occasion for banter, breaking up the tedium of the night beat.

H. P. I was working one time in uniform at night. When you found a car parked, you had to enquire into it—whether it was stolen. There was a car parked—and I'd been there a short while making enquiries, and a chap came out of a house there which was already on our records. When he came out, he recognized me. I pulled his leg about telling his wife—had sent up a message to the house about the car being there.[19]

With the power of men generally and of police over prostitutes—able to arrest or ignore almost at will—the temptations were available, the prostitutes forced to pay an unofficial price. The lesson of the Metropolitan Contagious Diseases Acts (by which any patrolling officer could demand that a single woman, on her own at night, be forced to prove her innocence of prostitution and subject her to a degrading physical examination) had been that discretionary law enforcement in relation to sexual offences could be grossly abused.

H. P. I know one or two cases where a policeman would jump into bed with a different woman every night. One instance, when I was a young PC in town—we had one young policeman (he'd been in the navy) and he gave us so much information in the Plain Clothes section, about prostitutes and where the brothels were, we suspected something. This was so good that we recommended him to the boss that he should have a spell in Plain Clothes and he was actually down in the Superintendent's Orders to be posted to the PC section. Round Christmas time, his wife had been to see one sergeant complaining that he hadn't been home over Christmas and this sergeant said, 'Well, you know what sailors are—he's been to a party,' and was a bit flippant about it. Really, he should have made more enquiries, because if we were going to be away over night, we had to put a report in before we went. I got a call to a house—the tenant was a foreigner—low dive. The bobby was dead in bed with a prostitute—the gas had been on. This was the party he had got in with and that was how he was able to feed information back to us.

Prostitution, like street bookmaking, presented an obvious dilemma for Plain Clothes officers. The injunctions to act against it were severe. But live-and-let-live was a saner policy for the pragmatist wishing to survive an unpleasant range of work tasks. The sheer volume of prostitution and the array of permissive legislation, when backed by the male chauvinism of police culture, gave the police officer enormous discretion over women on the street. Convictions were easy, as a means of keeping your street clean and of filling the unwritten quota of arrests. Different officers resolved the dilemma in different ways.

Inconsistencies in the moral crusades of their betters were obvious. The middle classes might moralize about the evils of lower-class vice—but magistrates were quick to censure officers who carried out impossible judicial demands by improvised devices.

a Liverpool Magistrate . . . explained that he would not inflict any penalty because of the way the prosecution had been brought about. He referred to the evidence of a Constable who had asked for a drink when the bar was not open. 'I cannot express my disapproval too strongly of this . . . It may be necessary for Police Officers to resort to subterfuge to obtain admission to such places, but I strongly deprecate the conduct of the officer this time . . . The Police should be particularly careful not themselves to provoke a breach of the law.'

(*Police Review*, 1929)

'I suppose the police have to use these methods but I contend they are diabolical,' declared Mr. J. A. Behn defending at Liverpool when a public-house barman was fined £2 for selling an Irish sweepstake ticket to a woman sent in by the police . . . 'woman spy' induced him to sell her a ticket by showing him a Roman Catholic holy picture.

(*News of the World*, 1937)

Late Victorian morality dictated the prime tasks for the new Plain Clothes departments. The moral issue was also a class issue. It was not a moral perspective with which working men in police uniform had much sympathy. The outcome was idiosyncratic, individualistic, survival policing, which satisfied none—religious pundits, lower social classes, or specialized police officers. Some tasks, however, were less convoluted.

Odd-Job Men in Plain Clothes

CID officers may have been 'jacks' but Plain Clothes had to be 'jacks-of-all-trades'. There were possibilities of travel—but it was not so much a perk as a tiresome duty with little compensation in terms of pay and time off.

T. B. Two prostitutes lived on Smithdown Lane, working the district. The coloured fellows were coming in those days, and the two of them, one white, one Chinese, wanted to take in a coloured fellow. One didn't want it and when she was coming home one night the other one had skipped, taking everything she could lay her hands on—the other's clothes, everything. So I circulated a list of the stolen goods. A few weeks later, she was arrested in a raid in Manchester. They notified us and I had to go on Sunday afternoon, taking the wardress with me to bring her back. Went to Manchester, went in the police station, and had a few bottles of beer, and then the wardress said, 'I want to go home.' So they ran us to the station in a van. Got on the train and I was bursting for a 'Jimmy Riddell'. 'Blimey, I'll burst if I don't go soon.' (The trains those days had no corridors.) 'Oh,' she said, 'do it out of the window'—said it wouldn't be the first one she had seen. Anyhow, when we got to Lime Street, I slapped down two tickets for the wardress and the prisoner and dashed into the gents. It was about five minutes before I could do it—I often wondered what would have happened if the prisoner said in Court: 'The detective peed out of the window.'

Tragicomedy percolated through the accounts. As a recounting technique, it retrospectively neutered unpleasant experiences.

W. S. We did things like indecent exposure. In Green Lane, there's a Labour Exchange, and there's a young woman there one morning, alone. A feller just exposed himself to her. We got to know who he is—picked him up and he's bailed to appear. But we find out that he lives just over the City boundary. My mate, Stoker Smith—he was a judo expert—and me went to court. He didn't appear. 'You'd better go round and see this man.' So we get to Old Swan on the tram-car. Stoker Smith says: 'I'll go and fix up the book with him and you go and deal with the family.' I got out to this feller's family and I'm walking up the street. There's two cars outside the house, so I went up to the door. I could see bobbies' helmets inside—went up and knocked on the door. Woman answered: 'I don't want any more of you here this morning—we got trouble enough as it.' I said: 'I haven't brought any more trouble. I'm Plain Clothes from Old Swan. I've got to come in.' He'd committed suicide. He was dead when I got there.

J. V. There was one time I had trouble in Woolton. It was a big man. He had a big sausage company. I was coming down Woolton Road. He was playing merry hell, shouting and so on. So I went over to him—wife trouble. He was a rather bellicose fellow, so I told him to pipe down and warned him. Divorce proceedings had just started and it was just as well I had made a note of it, because I was eventually called to give evidence in a big divorce case in London on the Wednesday morning. I didn't even know where London was. I could only give me evidence at the court that I was called to a disturbance—never gave it a thought after that. I'd left Liverpool and out in digs in London for two days, and returned to Liverpool the next day. I was only allowed four hours off duty for being engaged.

B. T. We also done a lot of escorting aliens. I've been all over—down to Newhaven, and Dover, Hull, Southampton, Swansea, Newcastle, and take aliens. If they were undesirable aliens being seen out of the country, you had to put them on board ship and stay by the ship until it sailed. You had to put in your report that you saw it sailed with the man on board. What we used to do was to go on board and tell the captain that and he would lock the alien up in the cabin until the ship went. Some of them wouldn't do it. We would get your expenses and probably stay overnight and travel back the next day but turn out for duty just the same. In Plain Clothes, you never got any time off. Even when we were doing observation on those brothels, we would have to parade on mornings and do a split shift nine to twelve, go home and come back at six, and right through. It might be 1 a.m. before you had finished.

T. B. A Spanish ship docked in Garston and one of the crew (an Austrian) had been found by the Captain broaching his brandy. Captain threw him ashore and Immigration refused him permission to land and my mate and me had to take him down to Newhaven and put him on the cross-Channel steamer.

P. P. I remember going across to the Isle of Man. They wanted some policemen there to do the shebeens and hotels. How they would work it then was to make some arrangement for a couple of PC men from here to book in the same hotel. You'd do your own booking from here to the hotel you were supposed to do. One one day, and one the next, so they wouldn't know. Any difficult betting job they had there, we had to do, too, when we were across there.

Colin Arthur Brown, proprietor of the '45' Cafe in Hanover Street, Liverpool, was fined £30 for permitting disorderly behaviour on the premises . . . the behaviour of young men with painted and powdered faces who . . . openly addressed one another as 'dear' and 'darling'. P.C. Plank gave evidence of what he had seen when he visited the cafe with his face powdered and painted, and wearing horn-rimmed spectacles . . . 10 young men and 7 girls entered the cafe at 2.10 a.m. . . . in fancy dress. Two of the men in fancy dress called themselves 'Julius Caesar' and 'Nero'. P.C. Plank alleged that Julius Caesar later threw his arms around his neck. Robert Little for the defence explained that he was a dress designer . . . On the night of the School of Arts Ball, he took a party from the Ball to the cafe. They were all his friends and they were dressed in the costumes of the Roman period that he had designed himself. Mr. Karmel: 'What sort of men were in the party? Were they moral perverts?' . . . Brown then gave evidence—said he was a graduate of Liverpool University, an architect practising in Liverpool . . . he had been proprietor of the 45 Cafe for 12 months and he had never seen any of the behaviour inside the cafe with the exception of the night of the Arts Ball when there was a complaint about a man who had a powdered face and painted lips. This proved to be P.C. Plank . . .   (*News of the World*, 1935)

Alexander McLeod was charged with using indecent language at the Shakespeare Theatre, Liverpool . . . McLeod, a comedian, was telling his stories while spinning a rope. It was the language he used and the things he said that were the subject of complaint. Evidence was given by P. S. McKenzie . . . he made a note of some of the anecdotes told by McLeod. The Sergeant then proceeded to repeat ten of the anecdotes. The jokes referred to Mr. Lloyd George, Gandhi, Hitler, Belvedere beans, nudist colonies, Mae West, and the invisible man. McLeod then gave evidence, 'He has got them down wrong. It sounds terrible the way he explains them . . . the Mae West joke he has got completely wrong.'

(*News of the World*, 1935)

G. E.   You'd be amazed at the sort of things we were in to. When I was put on PC, we were mustered one night. We all had to muster at Prescot Street, 6 p.m., and we were each issued with a warrant to arrest, say, Seamus McKell—any Irish name as a rule—to go and arrest him with a signed warrant from a magistrate, take him into custody. I was given a chap who was a teacher in a Roman Catholic school down at the bottom of Fontenoy Street. Pretty nice fellow—a member of Sinn Fein, and the Government had got the addresses of all the Sinn Fein. We arrested them all. Took them down to the Main Bridewell, shipped them to Ireland —transported. The trouble was that the Government had made a mistake. The Home Office authorized the arrests but it had no power to do it—before the Free State. And they found out (probably one of their MPs) that it was an illegal act, and they had to release them all and they all got £80 compensation—a lot of money then—and they were back in the schools and doing their jobs. So they thought it was great.

Humour, the occasional crack at those on high who specified the duties, the dodge for obtaining some light relief, allowed Plain Clothes officers to survive the contradictions with some retention of respect for self.

THE 'JACKS' OF CID

CID was the self-confident élite, priding itself on its freedom to work the hours it pleased, luxuriating in the information brought in by the beat bobbies, and enjoying a reputation as the section with the most quick-witted personnel. However, its crime-fighting image contained more hype than substance. Liverpool crime, according to contemporary accounts, was petty. There is no evidence of the relatively organized and serious crime that appeared in the Metropolis at the period.[20] Theft of a side of bacon from the Docks, faking cancer symptoms to feed a heroin habit, and the occasional breaking and entering at a pawnshop were not the stuff of media representation of CID work.

The recorded juvenile crime rate for the city for the 1930s suggested a crime wave of epidemic proportions—three times the national average, half of the cases involving housebreaking and shopbreaking. The reality below that surface was a little more prosaic. Two-thirds of the cases involved goods valued at £1 or less. A quarter of the children (eight to thirteen-year-olds) convicted of crime had stolen goods worth one shilling or less.[21] Like beat work, there was not a lot of glamour about the Criminal Investigation Department.

Initiation into it had its own ritual, and reflected its policing status. The CID craft was imbibed—often literally—from the old-stagers.

An entirely new type of Detective is being created in Liverpool. The authorities have selected from among demobilised officers men of education, intelligence, and discretion, who are not of the 'military' type—those who have been in the clerical or intelligence department of the army. For training, they are sent out in company with experienced Detectives who make them acquainted with the various districts of the city, and initiate them into the tricks and subterfuges of the criminal classes.

(*Liverpool Daily Courier*, 1920)

G. E. When I was promoted to CID, I was posted to Prescot Street and I walked there. The senior sergeant was a fellow named Hayes. In those days, the CID constables were in one room and the CID sergeants in another. Walked in the Constables' Room. There was a big fellow sitting there. He was a detective sergeant and he said, 'What's your name, lad?' So I told him—he knew I was posted to the place. He said, 'How old are you?'—said, 'I'm nineteen.' He said, 'Christ, they're signing on Boy Scouts.' I was about the youngest ever appointed to CID. I was given a piece of territory. If anything happened there, it was mine. If it happened there, it was Sergeant so-and-so's. Used to get 7s. 6d. a week for clothes.

The status and work privileges of CID provoked enmities.

K. R. The inspector came through one night. He said, 'Are you smoking, 125?' 'Not smoking, sir.' 'Well, you should be, and I'd know you were awake.' Month later and I met him on Pitt Street. 'How would you like to go on the Plain Clothes?' 'Very much like it, sir.' 'You can go. You're no bloody good to us.' That's all the conversation I had, except that when I went off, the bridewell sergeant told me to report to the station sergeant at Essex Street, and he got a message from the chief superintendent to say I was to parade at the CID school at 9 a.m. the next day. This was the probationary department down at Dale Street. We reported to the superintendent of CID and he attached us to one of the sergeants. We just went round with him. All shopbreaking, officebreaking. The ordinary policeman did not do enquiries into shopbreaking. He just took the facts from the complainant and the detective went along and took it from there. The older detectives could tell by the way the job was done that it was one of five persons. Just experience. The *modus operandi*, as we used to call it. You learnt the trade from them—as you are walking to a job or coming away from a job, they'd be telling you anecdotes about what happened in the past. You learnt the trade like that.

One Saturday afternoon, the telephone rang and I answered it. It was from a pawnshop to say: 'We are detaining a man with a microscope to sell—he shouldn't really have it.' I looked round the station but there wasn't a soul in sight. I had to go myself. Frightened to death. No idea what to do when I got there. Went into the pawnshop, just like a customer, and after a few minutes, says to the fellow: 'Nice lens, have you got any more?' 'Yes.' 'Where's the objective lens?' 'What are they?' 'Don't seem to know much about microscopes.' (Didn't know whether I was right or wrong). Got talking to him and said: 'That's not your mike—you don't seem to know how to use it. Where did you pinch it from?' Right on the ball. He was a removal man. He'd taken it in the course of his duties and was trying to sell it. I'd got him—got a confession. Took him in with the microscope to the bridewell. 'Charge this man with stealing a microscope.' 'Where from?' 'I don't know.' He's stolen it from his employer. That's the way I learnt the job.

But, like the beat, CID had its own routine. Occasionally more exotic, the precise designation of the night and day rota of the beat constable's was exchanged for the unpredictable chaos of irregular duties. CID work included a medley of jobs, some routine, some titillating, some depressing.

G. E. In the morning, we got all the reports from the uniform branch. You'd get a list of the shops broken into in your district, sent up to the CID office where the senior sergeant would allocate which shopbreaking you went to and—I'm not joking—I would normally have six or seven shopbreakings to attend. I've come on one morning in particular and I had twenty-eight shopbreakings allocated me. I had to go to twenty-eight different shops—take all the lists of stolen property, descriptions—and we had no typists in the police force in those days—no women—you did your own typing. I was pretty efficient on typing (when I was going away to sea, I was the Chief Steward's batman and I learnt to type in his room). The police had their own printing press in Everton Terrace. It would print [the lists to] circulate around every police station, so the local detective could go to the pawnshop and say 'such-and-such gold stolen from so-and-so'. I had to go and visit every chemist once a week in my district. Lots of duties like that they don't do now. You had to go to every chemist to work out who was using heroin. Every chemist had to keep a DDA [Dangerous Drug Act] Book—had to be in a locked cupboard. They'd open that for us and we'd always look down the prescriptions. You'd see some woman using terrific doses of heroin. You had to make sure that she wasn't a terrific drug-taker. So we'd enquire of the doctor who had signed the heroin. It was sometimes a drug-taker faking cancer, and the doctor being stupid enough to write her out a prescription.

K. R. Did all crime duties—anything that was reported to us personally—for the most part brought in by a uniformed man who'd been given the brief details by the complainant. The boss sorted out who was to deal with what. You'd get over and go out. Start whizzing round trying to work out 'who' and its surprising how you get to know. A good detective can go to, say, so-and-so Street, enquiring into a crime and get somebody in eventually. Take him down to court and he'd be put on probation. Then you go up to him as soon as the court's finished. You'd make a pal of him—which you could do by intrigue or otherwise. He'd think you a good fellow. You remembered him the next time you were in that street and sometimes he would come out with information. You could go into one street and you'd know a dozen fellows after a few years. You could go to any one of them—there might be a few awkward encounters, but not many.

G. E. Licensed brokers and secondhand people used to have licences and you had to keep a check on them, sign a book for them. Pedlars licences and all that—we used to check on door-to-door pedlars—see that there weren't any convicts amongst them.

CID work was partly envied because of its machismo, its free-drinking style, its marginally higher pay—and mainly because of the freedom from the discipline of the beat and section sergeant. It cultivated discretion and work autonomy. It was at the opposite pole from the dead-hand of the quarter-hour points. However, it was still regulated and resented —structured by the uncomfortable split-shift system, by the time-consuming rigour of report-writing, and the infinite number of offences that could be listed and monitored as the detective's case-load.

G. E. You had absolute freedom in CID. The CID man usually worked split duties. Be out in the morning to visit pawnshops and chemists (had to work his eight hours) and in the evening—that was when most crime came in. The afternoon was your own. Some fellers used to go home and have a sleep in the afternoon because you were out late at night, but I never bothered. I used to go to the pictures in the afternoon to fill my time up . . .

You had a lot more freedom in CID, but everything had to be put down in writing. The first thing you did when you got a job, you wrote it in the book, and that book is termed the 'mirror'. 'Bring your mirror in to me.' The boss would have a look. 'You've had that, that, and that—and you've cleared up that and that—not so bad.' That's all there was to that. He'd try to ease the load as best he could.

There were, nevertheless, still penalties for domestic life.

G. E. No permanent nights on CID. It was very awkward—day duty one day (9–5—a nine-hour day) and it was split duty the next (9–1, 6–11). That was really awkward. You couldn't make appointments, arrangements, so that you'd have to work out what I was on next Wednesday week—varied every day.

The use of informers—'snouts'—was the major peg on which detective work hung. The payments for information created an uneasy alliance but also, paradoxically, helped lubricate the street economy. Dealing with snouts also allowed detectives to indulge their professional contempt for the lower life of the streets.

G. E. Each detective used to have a couple of good snouts. I always used to have a couple—couldn't afford any more. Got regular information from them. They lived on it. Their beer money for shopping their mates. I've paid up to £25. In those days, you could almost buy a house for that and if you were sure that you were on a good job, you'd go down to headquarters and ask for it. If you asked for anything over a fiver, you had to go to HQ (Winstanley was the head of CID then—became chief constable afterwards). I'd go and see him and had to convince him that it was a genuine good snout. If you got on in CID quickly, or got into the top rank, you had to be a drinker because if you met any snout, he would only meet you in the pub. So you, quite necessarily, even if you were a teetotaller, if you ever met a snout, and he was having a glass of beer, you've got to have one or he won't trust you. A matter of human failing, that.

K. R. If you paid a man a pound for some information, you had an awful job to get it back. You had to put it in writing, make a full report which was criticized by the inspector and transmitted to the chief superintendent and back it would come 'refused'. Sometimes, you would have to go and explain it—it was normal to pay informants. But it is surprising what you can do with half a crown. You had a string of informants but a lot would do something for nothing. But you did get a lot of snouts. One would come along and say: 'Have you got a jemmy? Got some fellows want to do a job in Scotland Place tonight.' He'd want my jemmy and, armed with it, would go along with the others—make himself scarce when the raid took place. He'd set them up. Mind you, the guilty intent was there. They'd come along just for a few coppers.

In the witness box. Laverty swore that he bought some of the whisky alleged to have been stolen . . . on the express instructions of the Liverpool City Police, who wanted to catch the thieves . . . He said he knew the whisky had been stolen when he bought it, but he was merely trying to help the police officers with whom he used to drink.
Recorder: 'What I can't understand is why, when you were arrested, you did not protest against being so shabbily treated?' Laverty replied: 'The officers told me how to act and just to plead "Not Guilty". I thought they were being my friends.' Detective Constable Corkhill told him: 'Don't worry. You are alright. We will have the charge withdrawn against you . . .' He also told him 'to cook' a story in the Police Court, and he did that.

(*Liverpool Daily Post*, 1922)

Suspicion of dubious CID practices is supported by adequate historical and present-day evidence.[22] *They were practices justified by the character of the 'client' population.*

G. E. They're not faithful to their mates. They'd shop them if they think they can get any benefit from it. Always remember a feller who lived in Park Road. They pinched about 500 rings from John Brown's pawnshop. A lot of money. I got hold of my snout and said: 'I want these rings. Joe Brown has promised me £25 if I get them back.' Save him claiming on the insurance because they were nice rings and they couldn't be replaced. 'If you get these rings back, there's £25 for you.' He said, 'Have you got that £25?' 'No, but I'll have it at the weekend.' So I met this snout in a pub in the city and said, 'Here you are.' He give me the address. Said they'd be in the second drawer of the dressing table. Off I went with a young assistant. They were there all right. You didn't need a search warrant if you've got proof they have stolen goods. The rings were there but the address turned out to be the snout's brother—he got four or five years and his own brother shopped him for £25—that's the sort of people they are.

If beat work was analoguous to semi-skilled manual work, being a detective was a craftsman's job.[23] *Not only did you learn and utilize particular skills, you also had the occasional reward of turning the raw material of reported crime into the finished product of a conviction. Licensed deviance—bending a few rules—was accepted because you learnt to despise the class you were dealing with. In the jack's eyes, they did not deserve any rule-bound respect. On the other hand, there were some types of presumed offender to whom you gave a measure of respect.*

Licensed deviance to bend rules no respect

Search Warrants—Sinn Fein Episodes

Irish 'troubles' affected the city in bouts. CID was instructed in searches and in deportations both during the early 1920s and in the countdown to World War II.[24]

G. E. We raided a lot of the IRA fellers once. I was issued with a warrant by the Super. He was allowed under the Act of Parliament to issue warrants to go to the house of the local Sinn Fein man, who lived in Rishton Street (he was an Irishman) to search his house and if we found any Sinn Fein literature or the makings of bombs or anything like that, we were empowered to arrest him. Searched it—couldn't find any papers around. So I pulled every drawer out and tipped it up. (You see them doing it on television now. People think that's terrible—'the brutal work of CID', and doing it deliberately to upset people. You're not. The only way to search a drawer is to pull it right out.) Because I was in his sister's house, in his bedroom. I pulled it out (I had a young jack with me, showing him how to go round). Pulled every drawer out. Now the back of the middle drawer was pinned up with drawing pins, in a nice envelope, all his orders. You never saw it until you pulled out the drawer. I arrested him, took him in custody, had the papers to prove it. He went to Manchester Assizes. He refused to plead, so he got twenty years. He was lucky because the war broke out within twelve months and they were all released from Dartmoor on signing a sworn statement that they would not come to this country again, stayed in Ireland. But they were all very fortunate those fellers.

By the courage and resource of a Liverpool police constable, who gallantly fought with four suspected men in the early hours of the morning, it is believed that a Sinn Fein raid, similar to those perpetrated a fortnight ago, was frustrated.

It was shortly after two o'clock that Police Constable Read, who was on duty in the Kensington area, saw a motor-car containing three men and a woman turn out of Kensington into Gilead Street, where the party got out of the car. The constable had his suspicions aroused, and went to Edge Lane for assistance. He then returned but the strangers had disappeared. After a search, he came into Ling Street, off Holt Road, and there he saw two persons whom he took to be a man and a woman dressed as a nurse, standing in a door-way on the opposite side of the street. He went up to the man and his companion and asked them what they were doing. The man moved his hand to his hip-pocket whereupon the policeman struck him and closed with him. A fierce struggle ensued, the 'woman' joining in. The two other men ran across the road, and one of them drew a revolver and fired three shots at the constable, but fortunately missed him. Read put up a plucky fight but was overwhelmed and eventually collapsed. His escape from injury from the revolver bullets was most probably due to the man who fired being afraid of hitting his confederates in the rough-and-tumble, and so became confused . . . in his struggle with the party of four, the policeman made the startling discovery that the person dressed in nurse's clothing was, in fact, a powerful man.

The mysterious strangers are believed to have been under the impression that a resident in the street had a relative in the R.I.C. and intended to wreak vengeance in accordance with the extensive campaign recently carried out in Liverpool.   (*Police Chronicle*, 1921)

Irish 'troubles' were part of the memorabilia of the City Police—from the Hatton Garden bomb-planting of the 1880s[25] to the incarceration of one Brendan Behan in the Main Bridewell in 1940,[26] the stuff from which police careers could be carved, reputations of both individuals and of department enhanced.

Élitism and CID

CID represented the occupational summit for ambitious constables. CID prided itself on being an élite, an apparent world away from the humble beat constables and Plain Clothes officers. Different criteria might be deemed relevant—here, local 'streetwise' knowledge could be an asset.

G. E. The real CID men wouldn't look at a brothel case or a bookmaker's. They kept themselves for serious crime. They were the élite and usually they were the most intelligent people. That was why they were picked. I'd be boasting if I said I had brains—the senior men would soon pick up a good fellow. If you had any intelligence, you were picked out very quickly. Many of the policemen in those days were from country districts, from Scotland or Wales and didn't know much about city life to start with. So we were chosen because we were quicker-witted.

It was an arrogance built on dealing with the cream of the street economy, regarding petty offenders as the flotsam to be discarded in any real police work. In part, CID unpopularity with their colleagues was a consequence of their final role in police work—whoever did the donkey work, the 'capture' belonged to CID.

S. H. Once you had a job over to CID, you don't get to know any more unless they want you for a witness. I did get frustrated once. Behind Tithebarn Street Station, one night, there was an electrical goods shop. I saw this fellow cross the road, and I thought, 'Watch this bloody fellow, it's late at night.' He was just going to break into the shop. I thought I'd got a bloody fine capture here. He went in and just as I was going to grab him, somebody grabbed me, and two bloody CID men, they said 'All right, leave it with us.' They wanted this bloody fellow and they robbed me of the bloody job, and of a recommendation.

Detectives saw the division of responsibilities in a rather different light.

G. E. We sometimes asked the beat constables when we wanted information. Some of the old coppers had been on the same beat for twenty years. They knew it backwards. They'd tell us what we wanted and that's how we kept in touch.

To the uniformed constable, CID work represented a relief from the tedium of the beat. But there were moments of anguish. crimes 'solved' have a different meaning when subjected to the imagination of the CID tradition, with its fictitious 'clear-up' rate.

D. A. I didn't like working in CID at all. There were so many reports of crime and you had to get 'write-offs' for so many unsolved and to make excuses for not getting a prisoner.[27] I said to myself: 'I just hate this. Writing excuses for not enough of solving a crime.' And that system applied all over the country.

T. D. CID was terrible buggers, coming home three or four in the morning —drunk up to the eyebrows. It grew less but half the time they were drunk.

There was, however, pride in certain specialist skills and casual cynicism about their object.

G. E. When I left I was one of the senior sergeants. I was noted throughout CID for my capacity to interrogate people properly, which is an art. I've been knocked out of my bed at two o'clock in the morning to go to Rose Hill to interview a feller who was making counterfeit half-crowns (put them in cigarette machines). Counterfeiting of coins was very common—it was worth while making a half-crown in those days. He'd refused to speak to the detectives holding him, for four or five hours. So they came and knocked me up in the middle of the night. I had to go in the CID car, so I just put an overcoat over my pyjamas. As soon as I walked in the cell at Rose Hill, this feller was sitting in the corner. He said, 'I'll tell you, boss, I'll tell you.' And he gave me the name and address of where he had made the coin-making machines. Coughed to me because I frightened him—the look on my face—I had a black growth of beard. I must have looked a frightening object. I wasn't pleased about getting out of bed in the middle of the night. Most of these criminals are not very intelligent. They are easy questioned. You can easily trip them up. You interrogate them and about an hour later, go back and go through it again and he's forgotten what exactly he said but you haven't. Trip him up, like that. And of course, realizes that the game's up.

Cynicism could be covertly expressed in official circles about those interrogation techniques. The Royal Commission of 1929 had noted a number of possible reasons for a post-war increase in the number of 'voluntary' confessions. Enhanced war-time powers with regard to suspects might have 'bred in the Police a war mentality which has not yet been erased . . . the growth of education amongst the criminal classes has made them more anxious and better able to give long statements and the higher education of the Police has made them better able to make more use of their powers than before . . . the Judges' Rules has encouraged the Police to question suspects more freely than in the old days when they were deterred by the uncertainty of their legal position.'[28] The Commission also noted certain dubious strategems—keeping the suspect in the dark, constant repetition of the same question, bargains offering less charges or sentences, and the role of 'bluff'. 'Some of the CID evidence on this subject . . . is disquieting.'[29]

There was some work you could take pride in. Professional coppers prided themselves on their handling of professional villains. Other work was the reverse—bureaucratic and personally repugnant.

G. E. The fraud men were different people. You had to use different tactics. A fellow running a bucket shop was a clever man—that's hiring an empty shop and setting up in business and giving orders for the stuff to be delivered to the shop. The vendors think that there is a good business starting. It's not. As soon as the stuff's all arrived, they put it in the car and away—left an empty shop. There was a lot of them in those days.

Revolvers, a bottle of chloroform, a false moustache, a blow-pipe, bottles of oxygen and acetylene gas, and 100 feet of rubber tubing were numbered among a collection of exhibits in Court when the case was brought against two men on a charge of breaking into the Midland Bank, Great George Street, Liverpool.   (*News of the World*, 1933)

G. E. You had all kinds of work. A lot of it was absolutely boring. A lot of it was sickening things—you had to deal with a lot of incest, which is a boring job for a detective. It was rife in those days. There was a new Act of Parliament—passed in 1907. You had a lot of writing. You had to apply for a fiat from the Attorney-General to prosecute. One or two of those during the week, and your time was occupied with these women, taking statements, writing to the Attorney-General. (You had a lot of mundane shopbreaking things to attend to at the same time.) These things were a damned nuisance. I used to curse them and nobody except a detective to attend to them. Can't delegate the incest work to a uniformed man.

But there were moments of exhilaration—when a job could be seen through to the end, when an action had a desired result.

G. E. Clearing up a good job was the best things you did. We used to have gangs of safebreakers going round doing safes. If you could get one gang of safebreakers, you could clear up about twenty-eight different jobs. They used to steal the safes bodily. They'd break into a place, take the safe, and open it down in a cellar. No safebreaker would open a safe by the door. He'd turn it on its face and make a hole through the back, cuts diagonally and makes a hole so that they can get their hand through. I've done it myself.

The crime-detection role achieved its pre-eminent position in the status hierarchy of policing through several practices. One reason is that it gave practical freedom to detectives—a degree of control over their working hours, some power to decide how to fill them, to wear their own clothes, to enter pubs, to mix with the criminal underworld, to cultivate informants, and a more freebooting life-style.[30] *However, under that surface lay considerably more routine tedium than the image of a Criminal Investigation Department normally conjures.*

Reservations

Not all uniformed officers shared CID's view of its princely skills and status. The Royal Commission phrased it succinctly: 'There is a tendency amongst this branch of the service to regard itself as a thing above and apart, to which the restraints and limitations placed upon the ordinary Police do not apply.'[31] *Plain Clothes work might seem one-up from the beat, but few could take pride in dealing with the detritus of city life. CID practices rarely matched the public image. Some civilians too were unimpressed. The most articulate criticism appeared from the socialist press of the period. The Independent Labour Party, especially, in a series of cartoons and satirical comments on the national policing scene, had some pungent observations in its weekly journal,* The New Leader.

INTENSIVE CULTURE OF COPS
by Yaffle

It is my privilege to have seen justice done. I may say that she was more than done. She was done in: some say she was done for. All agree that she was done. This trial of George (Fifth) v. David (Kirkwood) will live in history. It is the greatest thing since Magna Carta. I'm not sure it isn't the greatest thing since Dan Leno.

Never has the principle of Free Speech been established so firmly. Hitherto speech has never been entirely free. One was always liable to be interrupted. But after this, speech will be absolutely free for Tories. Henceforth anybody can be arrested for Sedition so long as a policeman writes down on a piece of paper what he didn't say. Such is the speech-making principle upheld last week by the eleven magistrates of Renishaw, as fine a body of men as ever carried language a step further than 'Tu-whit, tu-whoo' and took to judging the sins of men on the strength of it.

But the trial was, after all, something more than the establishment of Free Speech. It was the final triumph and vindication of Jix [Home Secretary Joynson-Hicks]. Prior to his regime, the police had been trained to regard murder, theft, copper-bashing, and being without money as the chief crimes they had to deal with. Jix altered all that. The only crime that really matters, he said, is Disaffection.

Now it is very difficult to decide what Disaffection is. It requires men of subtle perception and great intellect. And the old type of cop was chosen rather for physical fitness. He was selected for his ability to adhere to a collar or clip on the ear, and no man was accepted who could not absorb at least four standard steak puddings at a sitting. Such men, Jix found, were unfitted for detecting Disaffection. They confused it with Disinfection, and were continually arresting innocent drain-inspectors.

So Jix decided to train a new type of man, known as the Super-Cop. They had to be capable of listening to a speech and deciding what part of it was Disaffecting. To encourage this, I learnt that any Cop who comes away from a speech without having found any Disaffection in it is sent to bed without supper.

Three of these men were sent to listen to a speech of Kirkwood's. The result was startling. Let us recall the facts. Three Super-Cops stated that Kirkwood said, amongst other things, that 'he would not only flood the pits, he would destroy them'. Kirkwood said, on the other hand, that what he really said was that if he had to choose between driving the miners to slavery and flooding the pits, he would not only flood the pits but would destroy them.

Which was correct? Here were three men not only agreeing that Kirkwood did not say what he did, but also agreeing as to what he actually said. Could this have been coincidence? Could the six ears of three cops (two apiece) have been deceived in exactly the same way? Surely not. I know the great possibilities of coincidence. Three weeks running, for example, I have had rice-pudding on a Monday. But surely coincidence would jib at causing three policemen to misinterpret the same speech in exactly the same way.

However, the Bench knew what the public will soon know if only they will stop flapping their ears and listen properly, namely that these men are the fruits of Jix's Intensive Cop Culture. They are selected from many thousands by reason of their abnormal intellect and intuition, and then highly trained by a special forcing process till they are able to say what a man ought to have said inspite of what he did say.

Is this supernatural? you will ask. I do not think so. I think it is very largely due to careful diet. The secret of this diet is strictly guarded by the Home Office but I have heard, for instance, that every policeman is obliged to eat his carrots raw, because boiling neutralises the action of the sillyassic assid which stimulates the brayin' and feeds the cells . . .

We now come to the most convincing proof of the efficiency of the police . . . I refer to their capacity for taking notes under their clothes. This form of athletic exercise is new to the public, whose attention is too much engrossed with footballers and trapeze artists.

At the trial, the court was much impressed with the incredible accuracy of the notes taken by the two men who were in the hall at Kirkwood's meeting. When, however, it became known that these notes were taken under their overcoats, the court was struck all of a heap. The Bench was already in a heap, but it was struck all the same.

The public will readily understand that a policeman in plain clothes prefers not to be seen taking notes at a meeting, as it might get him disliked, and what a policeman desires above all things is Love. So he has to take them without being seen. Policemen are therefore trained for what is known as Underwriting, i.e., writing speedily and legibly under any outer or middle-to-outer garment. Although, of course, undies would seldom be called into use in ordinary circumstances, I believe that no policeman can get his full certificate as an Underwriter until he can conceal his literary creations from view clad only in tight-fitting Jaeger.

I trust now that I have shown that with a police force of this kind, England is as safe as a parrot-cage, I would only ask that you all stand for a moment with bared heads and remember the man who has made a policeman what he is, and thank God for Jix—Jix the greatest man England has seen since Scatty Wilkins, who used to go about with his hat on sideways, and spent the last five years of his life trying to convince the doctors that he was Napoleon. *(The New Leader, 1926)*

Specialization in police work grew to meet identifiable targets. Detective work had originally risen in the Metropolitan Police in the 1860s to combat the Fenian campaign.[32] *Echoes of that thrust appeared in the episodic clashes of Liverpool City Police with Irish republican sympathizers. But that political motivation for police specialization distracts attention from the economic imperatives and the moralizing injunctions that determined the nature of both CID and Plain Clothes police work in Liverpool.*

The city's street economy subsidized the primary economy of the port and related industries. Individual entrepreneurship on the street was a necessary feature of a low-waged, casual economy. The motivation for those street practices was twofold—individual survival required solutions in the collective milieu of the lower-class city. Provision of goods and leisure pursuits was essential for those who had no access to more legitimate resources.

Contradictorily, such provision, though functionally necessary to the city, was perceived as a threat by the city's middle class. Economic activity outside the formal realm threatened the participants in the primary economy. Shopkeepers' trade was undermined by itinerant traders. Street gambling recycled cash resources outside the approved channels of distribution: if you spent your earnings on games of chance, you had little to spare for the consumer goods in industrial society between the wars. Economic threat was accompanied by moral fear. Vice, the assumed proclivity of the lower class, was viewed as a contagion—not just supposedly undermining fitness for industrial labour, but costly to the rates of urban property dwellers through parish relief. Vice among the lower class was seen as a potential epidemic that, unless contained, would spread to infect the fabric of the city, and by implication, of the moral order that underpinned the state, and the Empire.

Specialist police departments expanded in response to this contradiction: Plain Clothes officers to regulate and contain the cultural and economic life of the street, CID to maintain the legitimacy and security of the property relations of the householder and shopkeeper which—if only symbolically—were the linchpin of a city committed to the sanctity of trade and economic contractual relations.

6

Troubles: Domestics, Injuries, Race, and Politics

FOR most officers, the main features of work-life had been the stultifying, unending boredom of beat patrol as they followed the updo, downdo principle. Plain Clothes and CID officers enjoyed rather more variation but even there, work was largely humdrum in practice. Consequently, especially in the retelling, work-life as a police officer could be mitigated through the occasional out-of-the-ordinary interruption. These occasions were memorable partly because they broke up that tedium and sometimes because of vivid personal consequences. That interruption was, to the individual officer, their only common element. He was not concerned with locating the incident within the larger seamless web of the problems of the urban milieu.

All regarded 'domestics' as an arena not just of trouble but also sometimes of dramatic tragedy. There was little joy in dealing with a battered wife or a family in communal suicide.[1] There were individual 'troubles'—the accident that might destroy both a man's career and his body. Fear of injury pervaded much police work. Similarly, the episodic confrontations with the city's minority ethnic groups represented a major contrast to the routine subjugation of lower-class whites. Finally, there were incidents with political connotations when the city police engaged in major confrontations with the unemployed. This was after all a force formed in 1919 from strike-breakers and from those who had taken other men's jobs.

DOMESTICS

You learnt quickly that of all public order work, interventions between husband and wife or in a family squabble, often exacerbated by wider problems of poverty, meant that you were always on a loser.

T. B. You were always taught to be careful of what action you took because if it was husband and wife, you would rest assured that if you did anything about the husband, the wife would turn on you and give evidence against you. You always tried to square it off without taking any action against them. You were always sticking your head in a noose.

T. D. I was called to trouble in Fletcher Street and there was a woman stripped to the waist, knocking hell out of her husband (he was the size of threepence), and the minute I went to deal with her, her husband turned on me: 'There's no black in that.' Occasionally, you would be called into a house and the feller would threaten to do you in. Just off Everton Brow, when I was on nights, I was walking up and this woman was sobbing—she had a baby in her shawl. I said, 'What's the matter, love?' 'He's hit me in the eye.' 'Will you charge him?' 'Yes, I will.' So I went and knocked on the door and he said, 'What do you want?' 'I want a word with you about this woman and this baby.' So I stepped into the passage and he called me out to go out in the street with him. I'd taken off my gloves and I'd put them in between my coat and my trousers and as we struggled that was it. So I locked him up. She came down to the station with me and he was charged with assault and something like 'causing injury to the child'. It was only five weeks old.

When we got into court, she was there and he was called up and the prosecutor said, 'The wife doesn't want to give evidence against him.' So I had to get in the box and give evidence about what had happened but they'd got a solicitor. He said, 'Did you fight with this man?' 'I struggled with him on the street.' 'You didn't fight?' 'No.' 'Did you have your gloves on?' 'No, I took my gloves off.' 'So you went in for a fight?' 'No.' I said: 'Your worship, when I go into a house, I've got to be prepared to write something in my notebook and I can't write with gloves on.' He got fined £2 but the couple were together again. I was sorry for her because she had a real shiner and they were both of the same name but they weren't related.

Intervening in a domestic, in any case, might bring community reaction—local people regarded such matters as having little to do with the state in the shape of the uniformed constable. The Sweeneys again.

T. D. There was a family, the Sweeneys, in Byrom Street, and if you came in contact with them, it meant a fight. They were drunks, a father and two sons, and one morning I was going along a street off Islington—Christmas morning—and there was a man and a woman in front of me and they were quarrelling violently. He gave her a mighty thump which was nothing unusual around that area—but I was so near, I couldn't avoid this. If I could have dodged down a side street, I would have done so—let 'em get on with it. It never did to interfere with between a man and wife. When he turned round—it was one of the Sweeneys—I promptly hit him right away, pulling him into the street and knocking his cap off. By the time he came at me, I'd got my baton out and hit him on top of the head. Well, people around me and they wouldn't let me move hand or foot and they took him away. That was the last I saw of him. They wouldn't let me do any more but they stopped me from being assaulted by him.

In any case, domestics could occasionally result in horrific results, the constable being left to sort out the charnel house. Beat officers were very aware of the maxim: 'If you want to die peacefully, don't get married.'

K. R. I had a murder in my own division—chap stabbed his girlfriend in the throat and was taken away. I got the job of him being charged with GBH [grievous bodily harm]—she lasted a week and died. I was at her bedside. It appeared that the gullet, which is a hard bony substance, was broken and rubbing against each other until eventually it wore through an artery and she was drowned in her own blood. Her name was the same as my mother's—Alice Reade. I had to go to Walton Gaol and bring him out and charge him with murder. I took him through to the Assizes and he was convicted of murder and the poor feller was hanged. I was only a young constable at the time.

Suicides were not just unpleasant to deal with—they also constituted criminal offences. Evidence was required.

A. M. I went to Lark Lane police station one morning, about twelve o'clock. There was an oldish bobby in charge, very reliable but not very bright—and there was a woman there with tears in her eyes—says she's killed her baby. 'Killed a baby, what have you done? Where does she live?' 'Twenty-eight Aigburth Drive.' So I got a bobby to go with me there. The woman there says, 'Nobody's got babies here, nor next door.' So I said to the bobby 'I wonder if she meant 20*a*.' So went to 20*a*. Knocked on the door—no answer. Went round the side—looked in through the window and there was a cot—the baby quite still. So we broke in and—you've seen an egg, when you break an egg—baby's skull was just like that.

I quickly looked round. There was nobody else present. There was a note which I pocketed and went back to the station, leaving the bobby in charge saying: 'Whatever you do, don't let anybody in and don't touch anything.' A CID inspector says: 'I'll come right away—be there in ten minutes.' So he was.

In the meantime, bobby says: 'Sergeant, this woman says she's taken a hundred aspirin—here's the bottle to prove it.' 'That true?—quick give me some salt and a mug.' Half a cup of water and so on. Says to the woman: 'Come with me and you too, bobby.' Into the nearest cell. 'Look—this big strong feller is going to hold you so you can't move, and I'm going to hold your nose so you can't breath through it. When you open your mouth, I'm going to pour this stuff down it to make you sick. Now you can drink it of your own accord, or we can make you.' In the meantime, we had to get a bucket ready to preserve her vomit plus the empty bottle so when the CID came round, we could show it to them. Inspector says, 'I hadn't thought of that.' The ambulance got her to hospital and she was in danger for two days but she pulled through. Went to court and eventually she was detained according to His Majesty's Pleasure.

The other penalty for domestic intervention was the subsequent legal procedures. Most violent deaths involved man or woman being charged with the murder of their 'nearest and dearest'. No one wanted to be involved in a case which might result in a judicial execution.

D. A. I got a call on the radio on the handlebars one day to go to a house in

Watchdale Road. Walking round the garden, I found a man, and a woman with her throat cut. I called the ambulance, blankets round her throat. On the way down, the feller said: 'This is the end of seven years' carry-on. I wish I had finished her off.' Her head was practically hanging off. Through the night in Garston Hospital, they had to call court to take a deposition from her because she was expected to die any minute. But she recovered and he went before the court and they reduced it from attempted murder to felonious wounding and he got a year.

P. P. A lot of suicides then because things were very bad. At one house, the wife and daughter went out shopping and when they came back, they found the husband lying there on the floor with the three children—all got their throats cut and were dead. Lots of suicides when I was on duty on the Dock gates. One week, I got called to a suicide every day—found dead in the water, often weeks after—you can imagine the state they were in when we hauled them out and had to get them identified.

Death at home was something to be avoided.

S. H. On the beat on Longmoor Lane, one day, and a fellow came up to me and says: 'Officer, will you come round. I'm an insurance man and I've got a Mrs So-and-so up the steps above the grocery shop. I collect the money from her but I can't get any answer.' 'But perhaps she's gone out shopping.' 'No, she's an invalid and can't walk.' So I started banging the door down. 'Are you there, Mrs So-and-so?' And I thought: 'If I break this door down and she's out, I'll have to answer for it.' So I decided to risk it and bust the bloody door in. She was on the lavatory seat, stone dead. She was about 15–16 stone. I thought: 'Bloody hell, what can we do? We can't leave her on the lavatory seat.' She wasn't what you call frozen but she was hardened because if you die, you die in the same position that you're in. What a bloody job I had to get her off.

The Instruction Book had little relevance to other, confusing incidents.

S. H. One night on Rice Lane, this woman walked right down the street and right round the block of houses in her sleep. I followed her. She came out and she went in. I had another woman there. She was confused—in fact, bloody barmy. She used to walk the tram-lines every night. Another morning, I was just going off duty at about ten to seven and another fellow pushed his head in the gas oven. I tried to revive him and I got him round, took him into Kirkdale Homes, all old people, and there's all these old fellows on their beds. They were all confused —one fellow playing the tin whistle. He shouts at me, 'Here you are, bobby, have a go.' As soon as you took a confused person in, they used to lock you in as well because otherwise, these other buggers would get out.

Domestic situations were commonly to be avoided. Male police officers often saw it as none of their business if occasionally a man thumped his wife.[2] It was an unpredictable situation in which both parties—or perhaps, the local community—might turn against the intervening constable.[3] At least, when confronted with an angry crowd, the experienced officer could make a fair estimate of the likelihood of injury; in the home, there were no easy indications. Law and Instruction Book, in any case, had little to say about what to do in the domestic dispute. However, the rules could intervene clumsily if suicide or homicide was the result.

BUMPS, SCRATCHES—AND WORSE

There were other kinds of trouble, the unexpected blow, perhaps destroying your police career and leaving you forever embittered with the organization and its leadership. The incidence of accident and injury was nearly on a par with mining. There were several fatalities in the inter-war years.

At the inquest of Wm. Henry Peers (23) a Liverpool police officer, and Military Medallist, it was stated that Peers joined the force in 1919. He was on night duty on the 10th inst., a very stormy night. Late at night, he was found by the Stanely Dock Gate, standing on one foot and in great pain. He said he had been blown down some steps. He told the Police Sergeant that he saw some electric trucks after he had been injured and got on one, and came back to the gate on it.   (*Police Chronicle*, 1921

The jury returned a verdict of 'Manslaughter' at the inquest on P. C. Albert Millington of Liverpool Police who was killed when cycling on duty. P.C. Millington was run into from behind by a car. P.C. Stokes said he found the body lying under the footwalk. There were skid-marks from the car measuring a total length of 124 feet. The fenders of the car were bent, a headlamp broken, the windscreen damaged, and there was a dent in the fabric body. The cycle was damaged at the rear, and a portion of the lamp was found over a wall five feet high. Measurements showed that the body was carried or pushed about 50 feet.

(*Police Review*, 1932)

Inter-personal violence was the other hazard.

P.C. Anderson was busy directing traffic at Liverpool, when a woman stabbed him in the back with a sailor's jack-knife. The blade penetrated his great-coat and tunic and inflicted a severe flesh wound a quarter of an inch long. The Constable fell to his knees, but scrambled up and helped to arrest the assailant, who declared 'I'll do him in yet. Pity the knife did not go in far enough'. It was stated in Court that the woman had a grievance against the Constable for giving evidence against her in a case in which she was convicted for improper conduct.   (*Police Review*, 1927)

P.C. John Gawne of the Liverpool City Police was attacked and injured by a mob when he was attempting to arrest a man. He was thrown to the ground and his face and body were kicked. As the Constable lay semi-conscious, the man he had tried to arrest made a dash for liberty. He was met and recognised by P.C. Monaghan who, after a short chase, cornered him in a court. Meanwhile two civilians had summoned an ambulance and P.C. Gawne was taken to the Liverpool Stanley Hospital.   (*Police Chronicle*, 1937)

Constable C. Brown had a struggle for life last week. While patrolling the quayside at

King's Dock Liverpool, one of the loneliest spots on the eight miles of Dock estate, he slipped on some ice and in the darkness fell into the water. Fog prevented him ascertaining his bearing, and for 20 minutes, hampered by his overcoat and helmet, he swam round the four walls of the dock in an endeavour to locate the one ladder from the water to the quayside. When he discovered it, Brown was so exhausted and numbed by the cold that he was unable to extricate himself. Clinging hold of the bottom rung of the ladder he raised an alarm, and dock gatemen and a policeman ran to the scene. For a time, they were unable to locate the man, and eventually they had to haul him to the quayside with ropes placed under his armpits by a man who descended to the water's edge. By this means, he was raised between 15 and 20 feet. His limbs were useless, and he was taken to the Southern Hospital, where he is detained.   (*Police Chronicle*, 1934)

Some constables lived a charmed life, however, risking much without personal consequence

A plucky rescue of a dog which had been washed under the landing-stage at Liverpool was effected by P.C. Rigby. He had to worm his way while lying flat for 50 yards along three slippery pontoons. Last month P.C. Rigby performed another act of courage and resource. An escaped bull was amok and the Officer chased it into a newspaper van. He threw his greatcoat over its head and ran it into a passage. The Constable was thrown heavily, but others came to his aid and the bull was recaptured.   (*Police Review*, 1926)

Reactions by the authorities to personal injuries could be unpredictable.

W. S. I got a bit of a bad do when I was on Scotland Road—bad pains. The police doctor had to come—smashing little feller. He took me into the Northern Hospital. I had to go down for an appendix. The specialist allowed a student to take over half way through. What does he do? He cuts the nervous system. So I'm paralysed from the neck to the behind. This shoulder comes out of the socket—the pain was terrible. I said, 'I'm getting a pain.' 'It's the draught from the window.' Nobody had realized what had happened. The doctor injects mercury into an artery for the bowels to get moved because the muscles in the seat wouldn't move. I'd to go into the Royal Infirmary. They took me up to theatre and put a plaster of paris jacket on me to try and bring the shoulder back. I was off six months. The police were good to me—sent the wages to the house end of every week. After six months they cut the jacket off. Put an electric wire here—all the muscles had slipped. They are not really back now. Put me on four hours when I got back and transferred me out to a country area.

J. V. Sixteen years in the force and then I got the sack. I was one of the original traffic squad in 1931. The traffic patrols were just starting and I was one of the first—had motor bikes, big, twin Royal Enfields—a cancelled order for the RCMP and taken up by Liverpool. I joined because I had a motor bike already. Then when I was travelling along Dale Street in 1938, there was a bend—never dreaming or going fast—and a chap came over on the other side on driving instructions in a hired car. He came over two sets of tram-lines and belted me into the side car. My leg and knee were broken. Had I not been thrown off my seat, my leg would have been taken off because the car brushed alongside me and took the toe-cap off this boot. I woke in hospital, allowed to walk back to the station. When I walked in, the Super. said, 'Och, man, I thought you were dead.' My face was this colour. I was treated by the surgeon regularly and a car called to take me to the police office.

It was a month before they discovered I had a fracture and within another four weeks, the Medical Officer reported me fit for duty. I said: 'I can't stand upon this. If I step backwards, I'll fall.' He sent me up to Walton Hospital, took an X-Ray and he said 'Come and see me tomorrow.' Next day he said: 'Have you seen a solicitor? You want a bloody good one.' And he told me I had a fracture of the knee. I was seven weeks in hospital and four months in a rest-home. I returned to full duty. After twelve months I was transferred with three others out of the motor patrols and taken before the Medical Board as unfit for duty. They put me off on £50. 4s. a year. I took action over my recommended treatment and when it came to trial, the judge said there was no reason why I should lose my occupation—said I should get in touch with the Federation—you must be joking! I appealed to the Watch Committee but they simply said that my appeal was dismissed. I still only receive £20 a week.

If, domestics were difficult to handle, and personal accidents unpredictable, one other type of 'trouble' was easy to define. In racial matters, there was less confusion.

WHITE ON BLACK (and YELLOW)

The Liverpool City Police has a long, inglorious tradition of racism. Given the history of the city as a major protagonist in the slave trade, its nineteenth-century mercantile exploitation of West Africa and the West Indies, and the effects of the World War in sundering demobbed black servicemen from their homes, by the early 1920s the city had a substantial ethnic minority population.[4] Even in the nineteenth century, children of mixed race—the 'arab' children—were regularly regarded as a major problem, and the police, in common with most other city institutions such as the Workhouse, regularly stereotyped Irish itinerants as feckless and idle.

our worship of the fetish of individual liberty makes our immigration laws so slack that we afford asylum to the physically and mentally degenerate of other nations, which on their side show more common sense by taking our good stuff and rejecting our rubbish.

(Liverpool Head Constable's Report, 1909)

In view of such attitudes anti-police riots by ethnic groups have a long history in Liverpool—from the occasion in 1835 when Irish Catholics and Protestants suspended their own hostilities to hang the Head of the Night Watch in effigy on the gates of the Main Bridewell,[5] to the Toxteth riots of 1981.[6] Police racism had surfaced dramatically with the major race riot in the city in the weeks preceding the Police Strike of 1919.[7] Precipitating events, in particular, the demobilization of large numbers of white British competing for jobs with the small local black community,[8] are minimized and misrepresented in the police evidence in court.

Fierce struggles between Liverpool policemen and a number of coloured men took place in a common lodging house . . . The police, satisfied that it was being run as a gaming house, made a raid shortly before midnight. They arrested fourteen negroes and their white women . . . Some of the coloured men offered violent resistance to arrest.

(*Liverpool Daily Post*, 1919)

In fact, the raid on the common lodging house appears to have been a consequence of a police search for black seamen involved in an earlier affray, when two Scandinavians stabbed a West Indian, when he had refused to give them a cigarette.[9] The report to the Watch Committee on the subsequent race riot, in which many black residences were sacked, ignored any such causal factor and proposed an alternative, reflecting the bigotry institutionalized in the force at the highest levels.

The Head Constable begs to report . . . that for some time, there has been a feeling of animosity between the white and coloured populations of the city. This feeling has probably been engendered by the arrogant and overbearing conduct of the Negro population towards the white; and by the white women who live or cohabit with the black men, boasting to the other women of the superior qualities of the Negroes, as compared with those of white men . . . there have been serious disturbances. In nearly all cases, negroes have been the aggressors.[10]   (Liverpool Head Constable's Report, 1919)

According to one 'experienced' Liverpool police officer: 'The people here understand the negroes . . . They know that most of them are only big children who when they get money like to make a show . . . The negroes would not have been touched but for their relations with white women. This has caused the entire trouble.[11]

    A black Liverpudlian of the period, who had been arrested, beaten up, and then acquitted by the courts, had a different view of the policing of the riots: 'I found that even some members of the Liverpool Police had become so prejudiced against coloured men that their behaviour towards them had become nothing less than hooliganism.'[12]

    Occasionally, the compulsion to racialist imagery and practice gave way to practical police solutions. When an incident could be construed in a different way, when the racial stereotyping was secondary to a parental concern for an absent child, more pragmatic relations were possible.

W. S. We get a report of a girl missing from home—normally we give them a run—don't chase them up right away. So 'Lets go round and see if she's in Selbourne Street—in the black club.' When we get there, there's a coalman—you know how they put coal down into the cellar through a grid. There's a young white girl at the door watching, counting the bags to see that they don't fiddle it. 'Who wants her?' 'We're Plain Clothes—mother says she's missing and we want to see her.' 'Joker!' Joker comes—black feller (leader of a club in Smithdown Road —eventually he stood trial after shooting some bailiffs). 'Come in gentlemen

—you go back and watch the coal' (to the girl). Stood by the fireplace. 'Have a cigar.' Girl comes back through and we follow her into her room. 'Where are you from?' 'I'm from Birmingham'—a photograph of a big buck nigger on the mantelpiece, a bed and coal. 'Are you living with this feller?' 'Yeah.' She goes out and we go and have a look in the door. Different black fellers were coming with different girls, black and white. We couldn't find her—she wasn't there. So we go to Joker's own place then and we're standing. 'Listen Joker, we're looking for a girl. Her people are worried stiff—she's away from home. She's only seventeen.' 'Oh,' he says, 'that's her. Her father's not worried stiff. Her father comes and meets her here and the black fellers buy his drinks.' I says, 'Oh, well, that's enough'. So the poor mother didn't know that the father was going to the club every day and meeting his daughter!

Memories of this period amongst these former officers of the Liverpool City Police were inevitably conflated with later experiences. Distinctions between different ethnic groups were obviously flavoured by more recent disputes over race.[13]

G. E. Coloured people were mostly West Africans off the Elder Dempster boats. They were good, very well-behaved people. Blue Funnel line brought the Chinks. They jumped the ships and never went back. It was only when that Caribbean lot arrived, full of impudence, that caused any trouble. The West Africans never gave any trouble—well-behaved. Used to get into trouble through the white girls. The girls were always chasing them down to the docks on the Elder Dempster boats because they had money and the white girls would go and chase them. Several cases where the girls were only eleven—the parents would come and complain to CID and we'd have to go down and lock up the coloureds—they didn't know anything about them being under age. The coloured feller would just think that she was one of the prostitutes hanging about the Dock gates.

People of mixed race have been an inveterate target for police racism. In phrases that found an echo in police commentary immediately prior to the Toxteth riots of 1981,[14] *the City Police of the period made a relatively unsubtle distinction between blacks and Chinese, with a minority that was not as easily categorized often receiving the most opprobrium.*

The matter of the half-castle population needs attention, as such offsprings are undesirable and when arriving at adult age present a problem, especially in the case of girls; employment is not easy for them, on account of their appearance and sometimes their habits.   (Liverpool Chief Constable's Report to the Watch Committee, 1929)

Racial imagery provided an easy explanation of black–white conflict, concealing the distinctive socio-economic backcloth of post-World War I tension, and the city's historical tradition of mercantile racism. These different influences were conflated with the practical experiences of policing the street and the consequences of the latter for a distinctive view of the different minorities.

Afro-Caribbeans on the Street

The West Indians in particular had not been habituated to the cowed deference with which most lower-class whites regarded the police. Lower-class whites had learnt that 'move on' brooked no argument. Street constables found the West Indian unique in refusing unquestioned obedience. 'Civilized behaviour' was equated with genuflection to the almighty power of the beat constable.

M. B. The people who gave us the most trouble were the blacks—the Jamaican types. They're very arrogant . . . they're stupid, very thick, and the majority have no intention of working. The majority are ready to scrounge off the government as long as they live. They don't live as clean a life as you, and dirtier habits than we have, and they have more violent tempers. The ones that used to get under my skin was the real West Indians. They were arrogant all the time. They would fight us. They weren't civilized—might have been a bit of prejudice by us. They'd fight amongst themselves. If you saw them fighting, you'd leave them to it. I saw one occasion the Plain Clothes people having a rough and tumble with them, bustling them about—couple of these coons off the Elder Dempster. If they'd turned on the PC blokes, they could have murdered them.

Experience was reinforced by later arguments on the composition of a force that was not merely all-male, but also all-white. Deference to the police was a cultural product of the city, not (surprisingly to many beat constables) a universal human attribute. Police racism was in part a consequence of black refusal to adopt the expected role. Given that the core of the police mandate was to control the street, any group that broke with the traditional practice of 'moving-on', was trouble, trouble compounded by the fading stereotypes of Empire.

J. H. The blacks in Toxteth were like currants in a cake. The whites wouldn't stand any of their nonsense, and suddenly, they started pouring in. They even kicked the white people out of the pubs and took over. The country they come from, they go to a certain place, and they all stand around talking and laughing. When they come to this city, we didn't allow any groups of people, black or white, to congregate. 'Come on, on your way.' They didn't like being shifted about. When we were on our own there, I had a few battles because they wouldn't move on.

B. A. There used to be an African hostel—Hill Street. No trouble with coons. The nigs in the hostel were OK. The problem was that unemployment meant that they stood on the street corner—anything from two or three to a dozen. That constituted a nuisance, so I had to go along and hive them off. There's two ways of living—control them or they'll control you.

A black who rose above his or her allotted station in life was a special case for treatment.

T. B. Some of the West Indians were educated. I stopped one fellow—there had been a lot of burglaries, and I saw this fellow coming down Smithdown Road with a suitcase. I didn't stop him because he was a black man but because he was carrying a suitcase. I said, 'What have you got in that suitcase?' He said: 'I'm walking down the King's Highway. It's my own property.' Now, we were going to have some fun with this fellow. So I said: 'You can please yourself. You can either show it to me here, or get round the corner and open the case, and let me have a look at it—or you can open it in the police station. I'm not going to argue about it.' So he spread the case and let me have a look inside. Now that was the type—they stood on their dignity. They pushed you as far as they could. I never seemed to have the same trouble with whites.

We had a few fights with them. When they was drunk, they wanted to show how strong they are—peculiar mentality. They thought that they was better and tougher than anyone else. It was not you personally they had antipathy to. The biggest ones had to show how strong they were and how they weren't afraid of anybody.

P. P. The only trouble we had with the coloured seafaring men—perhaps a woman had two coloured seafaring men going to see her at different times. Well, if they came home at the same time, there was a bit of trouble.

Occasional reservations surfaced.

A. M. They lived their own lives and they didn't interfere with other people. We had a very poor opinion of them but broadly speaking, they behaved very well. They didn't cause any trouble.

Individual problems with the failure of black people to move on might on occasion be compounded by a later police determination to control the street in force. One major affray recorded in immediate post-war city history, in the continuing schismatic police–black people relations, is a so-called 'race riot' which seems to have been precipitated by the unilateral action of one police sergeant.

D. A. I only once had to use my stick in my police service and that was when we had a bit of black trouble. I was a sergeant then, down in C Division, Toxteth. On this particular occasion, the blacks had some idea that they were going to rule the roost down there and they were marching round in a square—Parliament Street, Windsor Street, Upper Stanhope Street, and Birchett Street. They were gathering recruits all the time they were marching around. I was there with about twelve men—twelve PCs—no officers there. I was the only one with rank and I could see the situation developing. Once they got sufficient recruits, they would attack us, instead of us attacking them.

I thought to myself: 'I'm not prepared to sit here and get beat—get man-handled by these people.' So I gathered my men. At Berkeley Street in those days, there were only gas lights—and so I called my men into a dark spot and I said: 'The next time they come round, we got to the attack. Nobody moves until I give the order.' And when they came round, I give the order and we got amongst them. They split up and ran like fury. One black drew a knife on me, so I had to use the sergeant's stick. I banged his arm with it and then they fled into a club—Wilkie's Club in Upper Parliament Street, just right by the Rialto.

They were all prepared for us because by every window they had boxes of empty bottles, beer bottles, and they got in there, closed the door behind them, left us out on the street, and then bombarded us with empty bottles. Then B Division came to our rescue—I was still there with only twelve men—and B Division sent a sergeant and a platoon of men up. The B Division sergeant got struck in the face by a bottle and his face gashed. So we decided then that it was time to go in. We forced the door and went in and drove them all down to the basement and locked them up.

There was a big court case about it but they got away with it—the cases were dismissed (I think they charged them with the wrong thing in Prescot Street Bridewell) I can't recall what caused the trouble in the first place—I wasn't there at the beginning of it. I was sent up and had to act as the situation was developing.

Again, the police officer's view of events is limited to his particular involvement. In fact, the black street demonstration was a self-defensive measure after two days of white attacks on black persons and property.[15] *The very nature of street policing, the compulsion to challenge all who stood their ground, compounded the latent racism fuelled by history and by racial and sexual ideologies.*

The Chinese off the Street

The nuances of police racism—the distinction between those ethnic groups that meant 'trouble' and those that were 'law-abiding'—have been noted by many contemporary writers. Where a group didn't challenge beat work—where deviance was confined to the home and did not occur on the street, and where appropriate deference was displayed—it achieved relative popularity with the beat constable. The Chinese community, not as numerous or as visible as the Afro-Caribbeans,[16] *displayed 'positive' characteristics.*

part of the lure of the Chinaman consists of the notorious fact that he does not get drunk and does not beat his woman, which is more than can be said for many a native suitor.

(Liverpool Head Constable's Report, 1910)

M. B. They're the most gentle people I have come across. There was never any trouble in Chinatown. Opium-smoking and all that but they were very quiet people. More quiet than our own. Always very clean. Always found them quiet and respectful. The Chinese were the finest people I have ever dealt with. They were the most law-abiding, most respectable. They didn't interfere in any shape or form. I had the greatest respect for the Chinese community. They looked after themselves and their own community.

These police views of the Chinese, as stable, family-orientated persons, found support in early Liverpool social surveys describing them as making 'excellent husbands'.[17]

A. M. There used to be a Chinese Centre in Pitt Street. They had a club there and every year they used to hold an annual celebration—the best-behaved people in the whole community. One vice they was on was smoking opium and the gambling. They smoke opium. They do it in their own houses and they don't trade in it. They gamble like billy-o but they gamble in their own houses. On their own premises they might break the law by having other people in but it's just like having large families. All the police liked the Chinese. Never caused any trouble. Never caught a drunk Chinese.

I locked up the only Chinese I ever knew for fighting in the street—wasn't altogether his fault. There was a real buck—he'd set about this Chinese for a start (which I didn't see—it came out in court). I came across the two of them fighting—both in tangles. The simplest thing to do was to lock them both up, which we did and took them both to court the next day. The bucko pleaded guilty. The Chinese said 'Aaaaaaa . . .' 'Can we have an interpreter?' So: 'You're charged with being drunk and disorderly—do you plead guilty or not guilty?' His face lit up. 'Aaaaaaa . . .' Then the interpreter turned round to the magistrate and said: 'He says "Guilty", your Worship'—one of the funniest things I ever saw.

T. D. There was some of the Plain Clothes who tried to pinch them for gambling. To me it was all boloney. I used to have different acquaintances with them. The Chinese girls at night-time who had been working late in the cafés used to be walking home late on, about half past eleven and there'd always be one of their own Chinese behind them, watching them home safe.

T. B. The Chinese were the most inoffensive. I met one with a sack on his back. He had some Indian corn, 'What have you got in there?' 'Just some corn for the chickens.' 'Well, let's have a look.' There was about a third of a sack. Well, you were lucky if, on rations, you got enough to fill a pint mug. So took him and he was cautioned. The shopkeeper who supplied him got into more trouble than him.

It was a patronizing racism, echoed at higher levels.

Twelve Chinese arrested in the Chinese quarter of Liverpool . . . pleaded guilty to the charges of allowing the premises to be used for smoking opium. Mr. Marshall (for the defence): 'If all these men are deported, there would be a shortage of assistance in Liverpool laundries.' (laughter)   (*Liverpool Daily Post*, 1920)

The Chinese played the deferential game well.

P. P. You know that the Chinese have their own Freemasons—the Tongs. They called me in one time, two yards within the doorway, and pulled out a bottle of beer and gave it to me. I didn't drink so took it to the man on the next beat.

Racial policing in Liverpool between the wars was primarily the product of city and national history, compounded by economic and sexual factors. In any case, the ethnic-minority groups socially and geographically occupied that traditional lower-class territory, the inner-city streets, which has always served as a reservoir for police culls.[18] *For the beat police officer, there was also the central factor of the job. Afro-Caribbeans suffered worst from street policing because black culture incorporated twin elements—firstly the street as a place of recreation and secondly the absence of historical conditioning to servility on the street. For the Chinese community, lesser police hostility derived primarily from a learnt deference to police authority and to social and economic pursuits whose location posed no public-order problem to the street patrol.*[19]

Racial troubles were more commonly disputes between individual constables and black people who refused to give way. Less frequent in policing the city were those episodes which involved mass conflicts relating directly to economic interests.

POLICING LABOUR

Three distinct issues characterized City Police relations with industrial labour in the inter-war period. This was a force that had itself emerged from a major industrial conflict: police unionism and its collapse had left its mark. Secondly, the city's economic structure —the dependence upon casual labour—had not given birth to a highly unionized working class. Police–labour conflict was rare, partly because labour lacked industrial muscle. (Nevertheless Liverpool and its environs were affected by national industrial disputes.) Finally, while there were relatively few opportunities for confrontation with organized labour, the Liverpool working class had excelled in the 1920s in its ability to organize the unemployed. Long before the birth of the National Unemployed Workers' Movement,[20] *organizations of the Liverpool unemployed were in sporadic but fierce battles with the City Police.*

Police Unionism

In 1919, the class solidarity expressed by leaders of the City Police was unique in British history.

Mr T. Marston (Police Officers' Union) '. . . asked for assistance in the recognition of their union. The police were one of the most vital arteries by which militarism and secret diplomacy was forced on the people, especially the labour sections. They now stood in the ranks of the workers and declined to be torn from them, but they were fully conscious of their duties to the Public, for they were looking forward to the day when a Labour Government would be in power.'   (*Liverpool Weekly Post*, 1919)

The police union, consisting of sacked strikers, survived in Liverpool for some ten years after the 1919 dismissals. Several of its members—such as Jack Hayes—rose to prominence in Liverpool and national Labour politics.[21] *Hayes himself was metamorphosed into Labour*

MP for the Liverpool Edge Hill constituency and became spokesman for the Police Federation in Parliament.

Home Secretary Joynson-Hicks to Labour Liverpool M.P. Jack Hayes [a former police striker and an ex-leader of the Police Union]: 'it is the duty . . . of the loyal able-bodied citizens, whatever their political complexion, to take a part if need be in protecting the community against acts of violence . . . I . . . support chief officers [in] the enrolment of suitable individuals from any source provided they are approved as suitable . . . A proposal is under the consideration of the Chief Constable [of Liverpool] to enrol, in their individual capacity, a small number of reliable persons who have been members of the Fascisti but these measures have been suspended pending further consideration.'

(*Police Chronicle*, 1925)

Other leaders, such as the former police sergeant Robert Tisseyman, became prominent in local politics. Tisseyman himself provided a reminder by his presence on the City Countil of the continuing problems, as working men, of the rank-and-file police officers.

For those police who retained their jobs, there were rare organized rumblings of discontent. In October 1931, nearly 1,000 officers packed the city's Picton Hall to complain bitterly about the government pay-cuts, and there were further Federation-organized protests in 1933.[22] *For the most part, however, the beat constable was deprived of an outlet for his complaints. Few saw the Police Federation in any way as having the strength to articulate the problems and stresses of street duty. It would occasionally win a few minor concessions from the Watch Committee, but for the most part dared offer no more than token protests.*[23] *The fading of the Police Union—the conscience of the police service—as the number of ex-strikers dwindled, marked the termination of the City Police connection with organized labour and of the ability of the rank and file to have a real say in their conditions of employment.*

Industrial Labour

The General Strike of 1926 serves as an example of police-organized union relations between the wars in Liverpool and its environs. In more industrial cities, less dependent on a casual work-force, overt conflict between the two parties was more common. Officers in industrial cities like Manchester might be more regularly called from the beat to engage in mass confrontation with industrial pickets. In Liverpool, the General Strike brought no such direct confrontations.[24] *However, in the surrounding coalfield of West Lancashire, beat police officers, press-ganged like their successors in 1983–4 to serve as the guardians of the State's conditions of labour, had different experiences.*

Few events in British police history have created more myths than the General Strike. All the orthodox histories wax lyrical about the police role in that dispute.[25] *A central claim is that in no other country could such idyllic football matches between strikers and police have taken place. In Critchley's standard work we find 'both sides . . . played . . . the game according to unwritten rules, as though the standards of Arnold's schoolboys had permeated all classes'.*[26] *Such matches did occur, but equally there were many violent clashes between police and strikers. The policing during the transport strike of 1911, recorded by the labour leader Tom Mann, could hardly disappear within the space of fifteen years: 'If the worst and most ferocious brutes in the world had been on the scene, they would not have displayed such brutality as the Liverpool City Police.'*[27]

In the Lancashire coal-mining communities, there was both violence and calm in police–workers relations (including football matches) during the events of 1926. Critically, relative harmony prevailed only when two conditions were satisfied—when the pickets were not troubled by the employment of 'scabs', and when there was some social affinity between police and striking miners. The presence of many ex-miners amongst the ranks of the police was a soothing lubricant.

D. A. The General Strike was my first week on the beat—I just did what I was told. No thoughts of my own at all but to do as I was told. The boys back home that I had been mining with were all very friendly, despite the strike—all very jealous that I had escaped from the pit, and that they remained with a very dangerous job. That's when I was sending as much money home as I possibly could to support my family, who were on strike.

Physical size and occupation background often determined which Liverpool police were sent to the collieries.

W. S. When the General Strike started in 1926, I'm going down Burns Street on the beat and I'm picked up by a sergeant. He says: 'Listen, Strathearn, you're an old miner. Go home to your lodging. You're going to Sutton Manor [colliery].' Nine of us went from Scotland Road. When we got there, the people at Sutton Manor wouldn't accept us—they didn't like strange bobbies coming in. We had gone to help out Lancashire County. So the fellers from Scotland Road said: 'If they won't accept us, we'll give them a chase. We'll get the batons out and run at them.' There for sixteen weeks. I was the young feller—the other fellers who were with me were married men. I could walk to the colliery, stand outside with the pickets, and explain all about the coal-face and what was going on. This broke the ice. (I'd been injured in a coal-mine before I came down to Liverpool—by a stone in a very bad place. The prop cracked in from the roof. A stone fell on me and damaged me and I lay in bed for a months at the coal-miners's home in the North of Scotland and they thought I was going to get TB. When I went down again, they put me on what they call the tumbler—a big round thing. This is how I could explain to the picket at Sutton Manor. When wheel come up with the bogey of coal, you pulled a lever and the whole contraption went round, dropped the coal down a chute to the wagon, comes round again and it's empty, and it's followed by another, and so on.) We were then accepted at the coal-miners' club. We had our drinks there with the miners. There was one family there—they took to me as a young feller. You didn't have scabs. We got word that we were going home after fourteen weeks. The last night at Sutton Manor, we had a great night. All the Liverpool bobbies and all the Lancashire bobbies—we all went to the miners' club, and on the table you couldn't have dropped a penny for bottles. Got back to my lodgings and somebody suggested a bottle of rum—the old lady had taken to me. Gave me a glass of rum and milk—that was enough for me! So her son-in-law took me into the bedroom, threw me shoes off and put me on the bed. I wake up after a couple of hours and I feel a movement at my back. I looked down to the bottom of the bed and the three daughters are standing there looking at us—the feller who had put me to bed, the son-in-law, was worse than me. He was at the back of me.

D. A. I'd been a miner so they sent me to Golbourne Pit. Billeted in the police station and fed in a nearby café for a couple of months—no extra pay. Lancs County Sergeant came in one day and said 'Can any of you chaps play football?' I said 'Just a bit' He said 'We want a charity match with some of the strikers and we're trying to find a team to play them.' I said 'If I can borrow a kit, I'll play.' I played and we had quite a nice time, and then we tried to arrange another one. But the Football Association stopped it, saying that the football season was over. We used to give some of the older miners a couple of bob to go and have a drink. All the married men got a lorry and they loaded with bags of coal to travel from the pit to drop bags of coal at their homes in Liverpool.

Where there was no common ground, police intimidation maintained a sort of peace.

T. B. When the strikes were on, a hundred of us did seven weeks at Worsley Main, near Wigan. Now and again they came throwing stones at us. But you used to draw your baton and say, 'If you don't bugger out of it, we're coming for you.'

Several expressed sympathy for those other working men.

P. H. Went to the coal-strike in St Helens. Felt sorry for the miners who were living on a pittance. They were starved into submission.

In the city, the united response to the General Strike, together with the political conservatism of many of its leaders, ensured that there was little fratricidal cause for trouble. The Chief Constable notes only seven arrests relating directly to the strike.[28]

A. R. I went on the streets just before the General Strike—something about the General Strike that always impresses me. I went out expecting trouble round every corner. But far from it—it was like a general holiday—it wasn't of course, for the people concerned. There were lots of Special Constables with armlets—professional people, most of them. Most of us had a Special Constable with us. We didn't see anything at all—perhaps one or two processions, which were very orderly, and the whole business was over in a few days.

For most constables, covering for colleagues on strike-related duties, it was memorable only for longer hours and more pay.

T. D. When the General Strike was, we were immediately called into action —twelve hours a day, for seven weeks. I never had so much money in my life—£7. 10s. a week. I was stuck in Liverpool. They put me in charge of Garston Gas Works. Took you about a week to walk round it. I had to deal with any intruders. The only trouble we had was on Saturday nights—the blokes used to go in the pubs and get blotto. It was easy pickings for some of our fellers. They would take anybody in.

P. P. There were bobbies floating around all over the place, drawing on the strength, so much so that I and my little triangular beat was out on six-day beats—two miles this way, two miles that. Once I found some fellows stealing barrels of beer from a dray. What could I do—I was only 100 yards from the bridewell and I nipped down there and asked for help, then back and waited for help. But before it come, the barrels had gone. There were no reserves in the bridewell because of the strike.

It was also an event which clearly reaffirmed the class nature of policing—the reserve army of white-collar workers played its usual Special Constable role.[29]

G. E. The General Strike was a great game, a great time—only lasted about ten days. We had some fun in CID. I was at Garston then. We had about ten Special Constables attached there on reserve. They didn't go out and do any duties at all. They were there in the station always, in case of any rioting. They were all businessmen. I got pally with one. He was a Jewish leather merchant, a very fine feller, and he loved being a Special. I used to take him home from Garston—he lived in Croxteth Road. He was in charge of his own business, had lots of employees. I went home with him, last night of the strike, 'Come for a drink,' the leather merchant says. 'You've been very good, giving me a lift. I want to reward you.' 'You can't reward me—we're not allowed to take money.' So he says, 'What do you fancy as a present?' I was in the front room of his big house. So I says, 'I fancy that'—a Chinese vase. He says, 'Right,' and wraps it up in newspaper, and my daughter has it still—a valuable piece.

The Elder Dempster boats—bananas—were in and out from Garston Dock. They had to discharge their boats because the bananas would go rotten—in those days they didn't have refrigerator ships. They'd put the bananas on green and during the ten days' voyage to Liverpool they'd ripen nicely. Pickets were on the gates, stopping everybody working. They were easily kidded—used to put a gang of dockers (strike-breakers really) on at Speke Goods Station. They'd get in a big freight van there and down the railway line to Garston Dock and go to work that way, so they wouldn't pass any pickets. That's how they kept unloading bananas before they became over-ripe.

Boss of the strikers in the South End here was a feller named Harry Pugh. Used to call him 'King of the Isle of Man' because the Isle of Man was all his province as a labour boss. He was a very good feller. I had several cases on at the time and had to go down to the court to get remands. There were no railway trains, no trams running. I'd have had to jump on a bike to get down to the court—lots of detectives borrowed bikes and rode down. Harry Pugh picked me up every morning and took me down. Press would think we were the biggest enemies—but no. He used to take me down and bring me back to Garston. You kept on good terms with the labour people.

The General Strike encompassed many of the contradictions in the life of the City Police rank and file. Geography, beat location, physical size, and social background determined in part whether the dispute was an event to remember or merely one other form of tedium to be endured. As working men in uniforms, they had to contain affiliations to both the class from which they had come and the organization to which they had sworn an oath. The general passivity and solidarity of the General Strike in Liverpool itself ensured that often, rather than the violent hostility that could have been expected between the police and organized labour, unwritten rules of forbearance and discipline prevailed. For a few officers, it provided light relief from the routine of everyday life. Other matters at the crux of economic relationships, however, were relatively uncomplicated.

Unemployment Demonstrations

Demonstrations of the unemployed were the other major potential flashpoints. Throughout the 1920s and 1930s, the scale of the unemployment problems—varying over time, but always substantial—together with the activities of the unemployed organizers, resulted in episodic confrontations. The Watch Committee records include a stream of complaints against police actions over demonstrations of the unemployed.[30]

Two incidents, in 1921 and 1931, serve as reminders that despite the general placidity of beat life, there were occasions when group solidarity encouraged random, severe violence.

The following police riot is commemorated rather differently by its labour leaders than in police memoirs. Robert Tisseyman, the ex-police sergeant and striker, had led an unemployment protest march into the city's Walker Art Gallery.[31] Police information about this demonstration (like many others of the time) relied heavily on spies, a trade which has traditionally led to much embellishment of reported conspiracies.[32]

G. E. The unemployed held a meeting and decided to march. But they didn't know that we had a chap named Bennett who was a little feller—didn't look like a policeman. He joined the unemployed gang and he was made one of the six leaders of it. He was a serving policeman and he heard the discussion of all the plans. They were going to take over the Town Hall, the St George's Hall, the Walker Art Gallery—he gave us all that news. They met at Islington Square at midnight, marched down and were going to take charge of all these places. But all of us policemen were waiting for them—a big crowd. We dealt with them pretty easily.

Weinberger notes of the affair, a 'close communication between CID in Liverpool and the Home Office . . . In nine closely typed foolscap pages a verbatim report was given of a meeting called by the Liverpool Unemployment Committee, which itself had only been formed the previous week.'[33]

Inside the Art Gallery, more police caused pandemonium. Men yelled aloud as they were batoned down. Others dashed around panic-stricken. A few desperate ones dropped down from an open window into a side street and got away. Those attempting to follow were struck down from behind. The police closed all windows and doors. There were no further escapes. Batons split skull after skull. Men fell where they were hit. The floors streamed with blood. Those lying on it were trampled on by others who were soon flattened out alongside them. Gallery workmen were battered too. The police had gone wild. The old police-striker [Tisseyman], appealing to their decency, had his arm broken and his head smashed.

(George Garret, Liverpool 1921–2)

In response to the police actions in the gallery, the City Recorder sought a public inquiry, only himself to be treated as a leper over succeeding months by the City establishment.

When binding over an unemployed leader in Liverpool, the Recorder said he thought the police used unnecessary violence. Two [of the unemployed] were cruelly and improperly punished. He did not want to palliate the folly of taking possession of public buildings but the police must realise that they had no right to make their hands heavier on the public than was necessary.

(Police Chronicle, 1921)

The official view of the Walker Gallery disturbances was in stark contrast:

Alderman Maxwell . . . stated that the Police did their best under very trying conditions, and but for that promptitude in their action, costly damage, to be afterwards borne by the ratepayers, might have been done to the Gallery. The officers took the precaution to protect the valuables, and personally he could not blame them for what occurred. The utterances of certain men had been becoming more and more threatening, and promptness of action on the part of the Police was sometimes called for.

(Police Review, 1921)

During last week, the unemployed in several big towns got out of hand, and the police had trouble in restoring order. At Liverpool, on Tuesday, the workless attempted to raid the Walker Art Gallery, and the police of the city were obliged to make a baton charge inside the Gallery and about 100 persons were injured . . . the genuine workless are not the men who create riot and disorder, who destroy property and injure innocent civilians. The firebrands who deliberately set themselves to defy law and order are not the real unemployed . . . they are persons who exploit the true working man, and fatten on his troubles and misfortunes. They are the root of all mischief, and their mission is to stir up strife, and set public opinion against the police. No-one in authority in the Police Service, we are quite sure, desires to be other than tolerant and sympathetic towards the genuine unemployed. A police officer is a worker himself, and it is a kindly heart that beats beneath the tunic. He desires as much as any man to see every willing worker in a job, and until that happy state of affairs comes to pass, his influence and protection are on the side of the man whose luck is out. The decent working-classes know and respect the Force. They know that the Constabulary stands between themselves, their wives and children and their little homes, and the spoilers of peace who would turn his country into a Russia if they could . . . the worker who thinks for himself, and is not led away by the wild men, will realise that his own class stand to gain everything by the Law. We hope he will always look upon the Constable as his friend, and go to his assistance when he is assaulted by the cowards of the mob.   (*Police Chronicle*, 1921)

Subsequently

Ex-Sergt. Robert Tisseyman, Liverpool, who was remanded with others in connection with the unemployed riots, has applied to have his recognizance in £50 to appear in Court removed. The Deputy Stipendiary declined to interfere with bail, and Tisseyman surrendered himself into custody.   (*Police Chronicle*, 1921)

Tisseyman had vainly assured his followers that the police, being ex-colleagues of his, would not use violence. But the Police Chronicle'*s picture of the police officer as a tolerant working man, while containing some truths, bore little resemblance to behaviour when the individuality of the street patrol was exchanged for the mass anonymity of a uniformed mob.*

Similarly, there are alternative sources for accounts of the Birkenhead 'Means Test' disturbances ten years later, in which the Liverpool Police played a major part. The Birkenhead Poor Law Commissioners had unilaterally halved Poor Relief, at a time when over a third of the town's population were dependent.

B. T. They had riots over in Birkenhead. We went over there and there was a big riot in Price Street. You were supposed to keep order. When they gathered and started throwing things at you, you had to do something. You were ordered to draw your batons and charge. The little light stick they get nowadays wouldn't hurt anybody. Our sticks were hardwood, heavy, used to slip down your side trousers. You were instructed to use them if you were attacked—weren't allowed to use your fists. There were a few of them throwing things from the balconies at you. You went after them and they all ran in.

There are insiders' accounts of the ferocity of the Birkenhead and Liverpool Police in those tenements.

The worst night of all was Sunday night, 18 September, about 1.30 a.m. We were fast asleep in bed at Morpeth Buildings, having had no sleep the two previous nights and my husband very poorly. My old mother, 68 and paralysed, could not sleep. She was so terrified. I have five children, a daughter 19, one 15, a son 17, one of 12, and one 6. Suddenly, my old mother screeched. She is unable to speak. We were all wakened at the sound of heavy motor vehicles, which turned out to be Black Marias. Lights in the houses were lit. Windows opened to see what was going on. Policemen bawled out 'Lights out' and 'Pull up those . . . windows.' Hordes of police came rushing up the stairs, doors were smashed in, the screams of women and children were terrible. We could hear the thuds of the blows from the batons. Presently our doors were bashed by heavy instruments. My husband got out of bed and, without waiting to put his trousers on, unlocked the door. As he did so, 12 police rushed into the room, knocking him to the floor, his poor head being split open, kicking him as he lay there. We were all in our night clothes. The language of the police was terrible. I tried to prevent them hitting my husband. Then they commenced to baton me all over the arms and body. As they hit me and my Jim, the children and I were screaming, and the police shouted 'Shut up, you parish-fed bastards!'

(Quoted in Hutt, *The Post-War Struggle of the British Working-Class*, 1937, p. 224)

These contrasting accounts from the ground are not unexpected.[34] Each has its own validity. The officer on the street saw only his small piece of the jigsaw—had no real recognition of the total mosaic, no appreciation of the precipitating factors. Nevertheless, as regards the wider struggle and the extent of police savagery, such myopia had its utility.

By the end of their service, most officers had become immune to legitimate working-class protest. In particular, they had been conditioned against those organizations through which working and unemployed people sought to articulate their grievances.

S. H. After leaving the police, I went to work in the Co-op stores—general cleaner. Fellow walks in one day and says, 'You're an ex-policeman, aren't you?' I says; 'What the bloody hell has it got to do with you?' He says, 'Are you in the union?' 'What union?'—he was collecting the union money. He says, 'You're doing someone out of a job.' So I throws the shovel down and says to the manager: 'Give him the bloody job. I don't want it.' Course the fellows who were making the coffins were laughing. I went in and saw the manager: 'Make me cards up. He's asked me to join a union—after thirty years in the police force.'

A working man who had joined the City Police in the 1920s, and who may have had class and trade-union affiliations at the outset, after thirty years' service had invested too much, for self-preservation, in becoming a police servant. Street survival required adopting a persona that rejected communal and class affiliations. The isolation of beat life, under the constraints of a Panopticon discipline, had required that he develop personal strategies of survival. Like the street people, he had sought individual solutions to a collective problem. In policing the street, he had, albeit often reluctantly, imposed the moral order of a different class. Crime—in its popular sense—had been no concern of his. Like those of his fellows in Plain Clothes and in CID, his job had been one of social and economic regulation, sanitizing out those groups, distinguished primarily by class and by geography, but also often by the other social divisions of race, gender, and age.

At the end of the day, the organization had won. The police officer as working man had been moulded like clay into a different being. His class affiliations, especially through organized labour, had been destroyed. The social pressures and isolation of the street patrol, the occasional requirement to act in a quasi-military role against a specific enemy, and the sanctions—disciplinary and financial—of the police organization, meant that the City Police and its paymasters had largely succeeded. Time on the beat, stereotyped interaction with the lower and working classes, had removed the contradictions from the class location of the police officer.

AFTER POLICE

Where did they go? Jim Hawkins's final resting place in Spandau was unique. Most left as soon as they were pensionable—twenty-five or thirty years' service. Problems faced them. They were cushioned with a small pension. But they were also unqualified. The private-security industry was in its infancy. Their only formal credentials were their police-service exams—qualifying them for nothing outside. Most went into jobs where Boy Scout qualities of virtue, reliability, and punctuality were the primary criteria—from furniture representatives to private messengers.

The ex-officers had their own priorities.

P. P. I went into the Inland Revenue. When I thought of retiring, I always said what I wanted is Saturday off, no uniform, and no nights.

M. B. I was only an inspector for three years and then I left. I was approached about taking over security for the Dunlop Rubber Company—which was a far better job than a police inspector. So I retired after twenty-five years. I made up my mind that I wouldn't go a day over that.

D. A. I went to John Holt's, the shipping company, as a messenger. I was only there for a short time when I was chosen to go as a confidential messenger to the Directors, so that I was only dealing with the brass. Used to hear things I'd never have believed. I was made redundant at John Holt's—they were African merchants and Nigeria and Ghana got their independence and, because they were self-supporting, they cut down on John Holt's staff. After that I went to the County Court as a bailiff. The best job I ever had—used to start at nine, stay in the office till about quarter past ten, then go out, and if I wasn't home by quarter past two, the wife was worried.

Others drifted into various legal-related activities—perhaps 'touting' for custom for a solicitor. Some resumed occupations discarded thirty years earlier. The ex-seaman went back to sea for a further nine years. The armature winder resumed a trade that he had been made redundant from in the 1920s.

They were marked men—ironed into habits first developed scuffing the beat on the quarter-hour points, financially different from others because of their pension, and still looked on suspiciously by those who knew what they had once been. Those senior officers who, in the early years of the century, had aimed to mould raw country stock into city police officers had succeeded in one sense. At the end of the thirty years, they were not what they had been. It is one thing, however, to lose your identity, your connection to your home community, and to your social class. It is another to have no new identity on which to fall back. Being ex-police did not help with your later years.

APPENDIX: METHODOLOGY

Oral history as a technique of social investigation in relation to criminal justice has nineteenth-century origins.[1] John Clay and Henry Mayhew drew heavily upon oral testimony as ammunition for penal and social reform.[2] Mayhew himself and, to a greater extent, Charles Booth,[3] drew upon the accounts and records of beat constables. In more recent years, oral police testimony and observation has been used in several sociological and social-historical monographs documenting the experience of policing the city streets.[4] Mayhew and Booth had their own priorities in using police evidence but the central concern of Booth's work was with policing as an occupation—not in relation to crime or to social conditions. The central thrust was, in Maurice Punch's words, to 'demystify police practice by simply viewing it as work'.[5]

More generally, life-history accounts, written as narrative, have detailed the working lives of a variety of occupations.[6] Taking up the apparently humdrum experiences of men and women, they attempted to give a wider social meaning to tasks that, to the outsider, contained little intrinsic worth. A central theme for Fraser was the problem of survival: how individuals constrained by tightly defined work roles develop strategies of survival, to give meaning to the apparently meaningless.

Life-history studies have contributed elsewhere to more specifically criminological work on the social meaning of occupations—Sutherland's pioneering study of the professional thief and Klockars' account of the life-skills of a professional fence.[7] A rather different use of life-history material appears in Samuels and White, where the oral material is utilized to illuminate a 'criminalized' under-class.[8] Finally, there have been texts that have utilized oral material to illustrate the problem of *survival* in stressful contexts—for example, Cohen and Taylor's account of the experience of long-term prisoners.[9]

This narrative of the working lives of rank-and-file police officers in the Liverpool City Police between the World Wars draws selectively upon that tradition. From Booth and Mayhew, it acknowledges the valuable, if qualified, observations on the beat. From sociologists such as Punch, it accepts the importance of studying policing as an occupation in its own right. It takes from Sutherland and Klockars the recognition of the processual career features of the occupation—the snapshots of writers from Punch to Graef, more recently,[10] do not locate episodes within the totality of the individual's experience. From the social historians, it recognizes the requirements for the *contextualization* of police life—especially the need to locate such material within the contradictory class structure. Policing can be studied as an occupation; but only when one recognizes the ambiguous position of the police constable—a member of the working class but also a controller of that class. Finally, *On the Mersey Beat* draws on the approach of Cohen and Taylor in using oral material to document the experiences of individuals under stress, showing how individuals contrive their own survival techniques.

The primary aim of this text has been to elucidate how the class and other cross-pressures were managed, how despite the contradictory class location of these police officers, they survived with elements of humanity, humour, and notions of personal integrity. *On The Mersey Beat* is in only a secondary sense a history of street policing between the wars. The text is more concerned to contribute to the sociology of occupations than to the social history of urban life. The problem of surviving work-life, in the crucible of conflicting class pressures, has been the central focus.

Primary data came from semi-structured interviews with a sample of retired police officers from the old Liverpool City Police. The local branch of the National Association of Retired Police Officers (NARPO) supplied a list of pensioned members. These were already coded according to year of retirement. A sample of thirty-eight was chosen on the basis of entry to the force being prior to 1930. This population was in part skewed in terms of location. A small number of potential respondents were removed from the sample on the basis of geography —residence more than fifty miles from Merseyside.

Of the thirty-eight in the initial sample, only twenty-four interviews were eventually conducted. Six had died in the period (three immediately prior to the interview) between NARPO's most recent listing and the time of the study, in spring 1988. One had died ten years earlier. However, his pension was still being paid in his name to his surviving wife. One had moved without a forwarding address. Four others, in nursing homes or other institutions, were not in a fit state to be interviewed. Two potential respondents declined for unspecified reasons.

The interview schedule was designed on the basis of the author's previously acquired material on the local police,[11] and methodologically was within the established traditions of oral history. The primary focus was on personal biography and specific items indicative of the 'occupational strains' of the interviewees' working lives. Interviews were taped and lasted, on average, one and a quarter hours. A general condition of the use of the interview material included a guarantee of anonymity.

The oral material was supplemented in two ways. All other surviving members of the City Police in the same age cohort (approximately forty) were circulated with a general request for relevant accounts. Some dozen replies of varying quality were received. Secondly, contemporary publications were reviewed for the between-war period—including both local and national, popular and quality press, the in-house police reviews, and certain radical publications.

Several caveats over the validity of the oral data as correct representations of the past are important. Memory amongst such an elderly group of respondents is fallible. As many researchers have found, oral history can lead to unreserved sympathy for the subject. The material is one-sided: those who were policed had little opportunity to contribute.

Memory was not a major problem. Respondents often collapsed the time sequence of their accounts—jumps between the 1920s and 1930s were common. In general, however, more detailed questioning ascertained that the predominant accounts came from the 1920s. On certain key points, secondary data were available to provide one check (although generally, such data were more readily available for the 1930s than for the 1920s). More importantly, where detail appeared to be embroidered with the benefit and nostalgia of hindsight, that process in itself signified the importance of the event. The illustrative anecdote, for example, could make a valuable contribution, emphasizing the way an incident should be understood and interpreted.[12]

Empathy with interviewees is a common problem in such work. Potentially, it can warp accounts, the nuances of the narrative, the awkward topic, being interpreted in a way that favours the respondent. In this study, the bottle of sherry and the family album hardly allowed a stand-off between the two parties. However, not every respondent could be a saint. The interviewer had access to information about the larger picture of policing in the city, for example that some officers in police uniform used their batons on the unemployed in the Walker Art Gallery. Relations with the interviewee were thus not conducted in a vacuum. Material was sieved through structural reservations.

One-sided accounts of police work are common. Within what Howard Becker has called the 'hierarchy of credibility',[13] official accounts are the norm.[14] The respondents' accounts necessarily suffer from that defect. In one sense, however, the perspective is not top–down —these police officers were at the bottom of the policing hierarchy. But to paraphrase Alvin Gouldner in the debate with Becker,[15] beneath every underdog is another underdog. One person's subordination is another's domination. *On the Mersey Beat* is inevitably both partisan and partial in its depiction of the urban lower classes of the city. However, though the focus is on police officers, this account is *not* intended primarily as a history of policing. It is above all else a depiction of occupational survival under stress. The lower classes—for good or ill—are the dummy players in that presentation.

NOTES

INTRODUCTION

1. See R. Reiner, 'The Police in the Class Structure', *Journal of Law and Society* 5: 2 (1978) and A. Hunt, *Class and Class Structure* (London, 1977) on the complex arguments in relation to the class affiliations of rank-and-file police officers.

2. The best accessible exposition of the idealized form of the early Metropolitan Police beat system is in James Grant's Report in J. Tobias, *Nineteenth Century Crime: Prevention and Punishment* (Newton Abbot, 1972), 115–16.

3. My thanks to Ron Noon for this critical contribution to distinguishing between the police and the policed.

4. There is considerable literature on the male police view on women—as policewomen, as suspects, and as victims. Two perceptions dominate: most women are traditionally seen as being the wife of a man, with rights deriving from the man, not as possessing personal rights. Alternatively, gender is neutered by the woman being included with the class of people who lie at the foot of the social ladder whom Gordon Lee termed 'police property': Gordon Lee, 'Some Structural Aspects of Police Deviance' in C. Shearing (ed.), *Organisational Police Deviance* (Toronto, 1981). In the latter case, no rights are assumed, and the woman as police property—as in the case of the suspected prostitute—is presumed guilty until proved innocent. In the words of a senior officer of the North-West Mounted Police, defending his force against a bastardy charge, 'Irish Ruby is the common property of the police.' Amongst much other literature on women and policing, see S. Ehrlich-Martin, *Breaking and Entering* (Berkeley, Calif., 1980).

5. See Appendix on the methodological techniques and problems of this study.

6. The best account on the origins, life, and demise of the Police and Prison Officers' Union is in V. L. Allen, 'The National Union of Police and Prison Officers', *Economic History Review*, 11: 1 (1958), 133–43.

7. For an outline history of the Liverpool City Police's relations with industrial labour see M. E. Brogden, *The Police: Autonomy and Consent* (London, 1982), ch. 7.

8. M. E. Brogden, 'Troubles in Toxteth, 1909', *Police Review*, Aug. (1983).

9. D. Jones, *The Social Survey of Merseyside* (Liverpool, 1934).

10. Ibid.

11. See J. White, *The Worst Street in North London* (London, 1976) for a quite excellent analysis of the class structure of the urban poor in between-the-wars England.

12. D. Jones, *Social Survey*.

13. Ibid.

14. There is considerable literature on the Panopticon structure and its implications for social control in Victorian England. Among the best, see M. Ignatieff, 'State, Civil Society, and Total Institutions', in S. Cohen and A. Scull (eds), *Social Control and the State* (London, 1983). For the present-day implications, see S. Cohen, *Visions of Social Control* (London, 1985).

CHAPTER 1

1. In 1913, only one in five of Metropolitan police officers had been born in London. R. B. Fosdick, *European Police Systems* (London, 1914).

2. The Main Bridewell, the central police station, adjacent to the Magistrates' (Police) Courts, could keep prisoners for longer periods than a small local bridewell with its overnight lock-up.

3. See Brogden, *The Police*, ch. 8 for a development of this critique.

4. See C. Steedman, *Policing the Victorian Community* (London, 1984) on the origins of county police officers in the third quarter of the 19th cent. However, her evidence is of limited application to the Liverpool situation—given both the period and the county context —half a century later. On the parallels with the myriad of British colonial police forces, formed variously on Metropolitan Police and Irish Constabulary models, see M. E. Brogden. 'An Act to Colonise the Interior Lands of the Island', *International Journal of the Sociology of Law*, 15: 2 (1987).

5. W. Miller, *Cops and Bobbies* (Chicago, 1977).

6. R. Bean, 'Police Unrest, Unionisation and the 1919 Strike in Liverpool', *Journal of Contemporary History*, 15 (1980), 633–53.

7. Ibid.

8. A prime example of that tradition of police families is the continuing presence of a rump of Catholic police officers within the Protestant-dominated Royal Ulster Constabulary.

9. R. Pagot Arnot, *The Miners: Years of Struggle* (London, 1953).

10. See M. E. Brogden, 'Interviews at Armthorpe', in R. Samuel, B. Bloomfield, and G. Bonas (eds), *The Enemy Within: Pit Villages and the Miners' Strike of 1984–1985* (London, 1986) on more contemporary problems of surviving a miners' strike.

11. See Steedman, *Policing*, 85 for a criticism of the assumption that Victorian policing was an avenue of self-improvement.

12. See the many other examples of 'strangers policing strangers', in Brogden, 'An Act'.

13. E. C. Cox, *Police and Crime in India* (London, 1977), 147.

14. E. Dep, *A History of the Ceylon Police* (Colombo, 1979), 17.

15. Brogden, *The Police*.

16. For the best detail on the causes and course of the Police Strike, see Allen, 'Union of Police' and Bean, 'Police Unrest'; and for local colour, A. V. Sellwood, *Police Strike, 1919* (London, 1978) and G. W. Reynolds and A. Judge, *The Night the Police Went on Strike* (London, 1968).

17. See P. L. F. Garner, *Policing the Liverpool General Transport Strike* (Liverpool, 1984) and T. Mann, *Tom Mann's Memoirs* (London, 1967). Pitch-and-toss is an old working-class street game of chance. It involves two participants each throwing a coin against a wall. The one whose coin lands nearest to the wall then tosses the coin in the air and calls 'heads' or 'tails'. If successful, he wins both coins.

18. Reynolds and Judge, *Police on Strike*.

19. Quoted in P. Ayers, *The Liverpool Docklands* (Liverpool, 1989).

20. The Union—consisting of ex-strikers—reportedly continued in existence until shortly after World War II. Allen, 'Union of Police'.

21. Committee Appointed to Enquire into the Claims of Men Dismissed from the Police and Prison Services on Account of the Strike of 1919, *Report*, Cmd.2297 (London, 1924).

22. Chief Constable's Annual Report, Liverpool City Police (1926). See A. Judge, *A Man Apart* (London, 1972), 36, for a comment on recruitment between the wars.

23. 'From all this came across, insidiously but strongly, a picture of society with a sharp division between "them" and "us"'. Comment on police training by Robert Bradley, 'The Copper', in R. Fraser, *Work* (London, 1968), 189. See, among several others, the analysis on present-day police socialization in training and the development of the 'canteen culture'

in N. Fielding, *Joining Forces* (London, 1988) and M. E. Brogden, and D. Graham, 'Police Education: The Hidden Curricula', in Fieldhouse, R. (ed.) *The Political Education of State Servants* (Manchester, 1988) on the partisan character of police education today.

24. Quoted in C. Jeffries, *The Colonial Police* (London, 1952), 155.

25. See Chapter 5. The social history of women and policing in Britain has yet to be written. For some Liverpool material for the period between the wars, see Committee on the Employment of Women on Police Duties, *Minutes of Evidence*, Cmd. 1133 (London, 1921) and Home Office Departmental Committee on the Employment of Women Police Constables, Cmd. 2224, *Minutes of Evidence*, 1924. In the latter, Everett, the Liverpool Chief Constable, argued fiercely—in opposition to the Commissioner of the Metropolitan Police in particular—that the voluntary Women Preventive Patrols (funded by the Watch Committee) would lose their effectiveness with women and children if they had police powers, 'chiefly for the reasons that as private individuals, they have far greater freedom of action than they would have as Constables'. In Liverpool, one of the last major forces to accept women constables, a pressure group had lobbied without avail since 1922. They were only formally given police powers in 1945.

26. A series of cartoons in *Police Review* in the mid-1930s repeatedly demonstrates the 'voluntary' contributions of the police wife to the county force. See also T. A. Critchley, *A History of Police in England and Wales, 900–1966* (London, 1978) on the problems of police wives, and M. Cain, *Society and the Policeman's Role* (London, 1973), ch. 5 on the experiences of police life more recently.

27. The most recent manifestation of this housing problem has arisen over the substitution of the Poll Tax for the household rates in mainland Britain. Under the rating system, the local Police Authority was responsible for taxes on the house. As the Poll Tax is a personal charge, it falls on the police officer himself.

28. A more extreme account of police children's experiences—on this occasion during a mining strike—appears in S. Humphries, *Hooligans or Rebels: An Oral History of Working-Class Youth, 1889–1937* (London, 1981): 'We had an awful life. A policeman's daughter or a policeman's son . . . they were all against you . . . the other children'd chase you and pelt you with stones . . . They used to have fun chasing us; we was just "Bobby's child". You were outsiders, really, being policemen's children.'

29. Bean, 'Police Unrest'.

30. There are numerous sources on the nature of the police occupational or 'canteen' culture—for example, R. Reiner, *The Politics of the Police* (Brighton, 1985), ch. 3, and M. E. Brogden, T. Jefferson, and S. Walklate, *Introducing Policework* (London, 1988), ch. 2.

31. See, e.g., the accounts of police comradeship during the miners' strike of 1984–5 in R. Graef, *Talking Blues* (London, 1989) and how officers came to terms with their contradictory experiences.

32. See Critchley, *History of Police* on the social isolation of police officers as recorded in the 1908 Select Committee *Report*.

33. For example, the racism and chauvinism in the Metropolitan Police documented in a Policy Studies Institute report: D. J. Smith, *Police and People in London* (Aldershot, 1985).

CHAPTER 2

1. The surveillance features of the beat are best illustrated in detail in Charles Booth's *Life and Labour in London* which uses police notebooks as a major source of data about the life of the

London poor. The beat system gave the police a unique position to observe and document lower-class life. In Liverpool, the system had changed little from when it was first mapped out by Head Constable Whitty and Watch Committee Chairman Walmsley in 1835 in their original plan for the New Police.

2. Ignatieff, 'State, Civil Society'.

3. A remarkably different perspective on night beat work during the period appears in Harry Daley's autobiographical account of his career in the Metropolitan Police. Daley's account would have been given short shrift by these Liverpool ex-constables: H. Daley, *This Small Cloud* (London, 1986), 141. A different account of a police homosexual relationship (with a Liverpool street kid) between the wars is contained in J. Robinson, *Teardrops on my Drum* (London, 1986).

4. See M. Cain, 'On the Beat: Interactions and Relations in Rural and Urban Forces' in S. Cohen (ed.), *Images of Deviance* (Harmondsworth, 1973) on the easing devices on the night patrol.

5. See P. Manning, *Police Work* (Cambridge, Mass., 1977) on the importance of ritual and dramatic presentation in police work in his account of a police funeral.

6. Cain, 'On the Beat', 55, for a more recent description, and S. Holdaway, *Inside the British Police* (Oxford, 1983).

7. See A. Judge, A Man Apart (London, 1972), 57, for an insider's account of post-war beat initiation.

8. Holdaway, *British Police*.

9. See National Association for the Care and Resettlement of Offenders, *Briefing*, 87 (July 1987).

10. Cain, 'On the Beat', 69.

11. B. Jackson, *Working-Class Community* (London, 1968) has given a perceptive taste of working-class and middle-class views of policing in 1950s, suggesting the earlier relationship still held fast after World War II.

12. Cain, 'On the Beat'.

13. Tobias, *Nineteenth Century Crime*.

14. S. Holdaway, 'Changes in Urban Policing', *British Journal of Sociology*, 28: 2 (1977), 119–37, gives a stark and more recent example of the way police officers from other divisions are drawn into a car chase outside their organization patch.

15. B. Howell, *The Police in Late Victorian Bristol* (Bristol, 1988) notes for the late Victorian era a case of a constable being given 7 days' hard labour for being absent for 2 days without leave.

16. Liverpool Watch Committee Minutes, 1839.

17. See the account of the Michael Cavenaugh affair in Kirkby (in 1979) in *Daily Telegraph*, Aug. 19, 1979.

18. The Liverpool Head Constable's Address of 1852 is eulogized by police historians for its exemplary exhortations on such matters. Critchley, *History of Police*, 147–50.

19. Although no incidents quite as dramatic as Harry Daley's initiation in London with a berserk steam wagon. Daley, *Small Cloud*, 87–8.

20. One only has to recall the British Crime Survey (1984) comment that the patrolling constable catches a burglar in the course of the act only once every 15 years.

21. S. Harring, *Policing a Class Society* (New Brunswick, NJ, 1983).

22. See the example given by Cain, 'On the Beat'.

23. Laurie Taylor gives a different (apocryphal) account of a bored sweet factory worker enlivening the day by writing 'Fuck off' all the way through a stick of Blackpool rock.

L. Taylor, 'Industrial Sabotage: Motives and Meanings', in S. Cohen (ed.), *Images of Deviance* (Harmondsworth, 1973).

CHAPTER 3

1. Liverpool Watch Committee, Minutes, 1843.
2. Miller, *Cops and Bobbies* and P. Thurmond Smith, *Policing in Victorian London* (London, 1985).
3. The official data on punishments conceal more than they display. Actual dismissals were rare. In the 1930s, for example, the number of outright sackings rarely rose into double figures out of a force of nearly 2,000 men. However, that figure conceals the number of men to whom it was informally indicated that they had no future in the force. The City Police did not keep figures for most such involuntary resignations. In the immediate post-war years, 1920–2 (admittedly in the unique post-Strike context), one in six recruits were not allowed to complete their probationary year. They were not, however, regarded as 'dismissed'. Similarly, minor punishments could be meted out by the local superintendent and not noted in the public records.
4. Critchley, *History of Police* notes the ritualistic nature of HMIC inspections for the period. After 1913, the records of such inspection were proscribed from public scrutiny, and were not available publicly again until 1989.
5. See Manning, *Police Work*, ch. 1 on police symbolism.
6. See Critchley, *History of Police*, 152 on how little this petty discipline had changed since the 1880s. Smith, *Policing Victorian London*, 49, notes an incident from the 1850s when a constable was compelled to resign from the Metropolitan Police for continuing to live with his wife, after he had found a man in bed with her.
7. *Liverpool Daily Post*, 1932.
8. R. Mark, *Policing a Perplexed Society* (London, 1977).
9. Cain, 'On the Beat', 160.
10. Disciplinary powers of the chief officer embodied in the Police Discipline Regulations, were formalized for the first time by the Police Act 1919, s. 4(1). Appeals against discipline were universally agreed under the Police (Appeals) Act 1927.
11. The Victorian Watch Committee Minutes contain no examples of an appeal resulting in a variation on the Chief Constable's decisions between the wars: Liverpool Committee Minutes, 1836–72—see Brogden, *The Police*. The previous disciplinary powers of the Watch Committee under the Municipal Corporations Act 1882, s. 191(4) did not give a formal right of appeal but, in practice, officers were often given such a token opportunity. Prior to 1914, the committee had been more likely to increase a penalty than to diminish it: Bean, 'Police Unrest'.
12. See R. Reiner, *The Blue-Coated Worker* (Cambridge, 1978) on the development of the 'blue 'flu' technique.
13. See Cain, *Society and Policeman's Role*, ch. 6.
14. Chief Constable's Annual Report, Liverpool City Police (1928).
15. J. M., see Hart, *The British Police* (London, 1951) on the effect on the police of the austerity pay-cuts. The cuts that precipitated the Invergordon mutiny in the navy had their own, lesser, repercussion in the police service.
16. See Critchley, *History of Police*, 205–8 on the Trenchard scheme and on the reactions to it. A proposal for direct entry was being discussed again in 1990.
17. Bean, 'Police Unrest'.
18. Ibid.

19. Such concerns are hardly absent from the police in the last decade. See S. Knight, *The Brotherhood* (London, 1984).

20. A 1920 letter in *Police Review* complains bitterly and at length about such promotion practices in the Liverpool City Police.

21. For more recent examples of attempts to develop direct entry schemes, see B. Whitaker, *The Police in Society* (London, 1979), 216.

22. M. Jones, *Organisational Aspects of Police Behaviour* (Farnborough, 1980) provides a specific example from Merseyside in the late 1970s of beat work receiving rhetorical support but being treated in practice as a reservoir upon which other departments drew at will.

23. Cain, *Society and the Policeman's Role*, 163 comments: 'Formal rewards of compliments, commendations, and merit stripes—often accompanied by a small financial reward—were highly prized by the men.'

CHAPTER 4

1. See Brogden *et al.*, *Introducing Policework* for contrary views of crime-fighting versus order-maintenance functions in the British police.

2. Noted in Harring, *Policing Class Society*. See Daley, *Small Cloud*, 118 for a London example.

3. Chief Constable's Annual Reports, 1860–1930, Liverpool City Police.

4. Quoted in Brogden, *The Police*.

5. M. E. Brogden, 'From Henry III to Liverpool 8' *International Journal of the Sociology of Law*, Winter (1984).

6. See D. McBarnet, *Conviction* (London, 1981), R. Ericson, and P. Baranek, *The Ordering of Justice* (Toronto, 1984) and M. McConville, and J. Baldwin, *Courts, Prosecution, and Conviction* (Oxford, 1981) on the current debate over the permissive features of English criminal law.

7. See W. Chambliss, 'A Sociological Analysis of the Law of Vagrancy', *Social Problems*, 11 (1964), 67–77; S. Hall, C. Critcher, T. Jefferson, J. Clarke, and B. Roberts, *Policing the Crisis* (London, 1978), and Brogden, 'From Henry III' on the history of inquisitorial street legislation in Britain and its implementation against the lower social classes.

8. Liverpool Watch Committee, Minutes, 1839.

9. Humphries, *Hooligans or Rebels*, 203, gives a London example from the period of the kids' reaction to the police over football: 'We used to have a policeman who used to stop us playing football round the back wall . . . I don't know why, 'cos we wasn't hurting anything 'cos there was the dock wall and there was only one or two houses and then a factory, but he insisted upon us stopping playing football round there. And the football was a sack made up of sawdust and rags . . . I remember some dockers gave us a football and, oh, we was tops then. And when old Bloodnut come on, he started his beat, he pinched our ball, and he knifed it, pierced it. So what we did in vengeance, coppers in those days used to have to go on duty in the winter with their very heavy tarpaulin cape, so we pinched his tarpaulin cape. We know where they used to leave it . . . And we chucked it over Hermitage Bridge. He done our football, we done his cape.'

10. A caseball was the normal term for the old leather-panelled football, before the introduction of plastic balls.

11. Ayers, *Liverpool Docklands*.

12. For recent studies that treat the Magistrates' Courts as a 'Guilty Plea' system—where nearly all defendants are processed into Guilt findings, see P. Carlen, *Magistrates' Justice* (London, 1977), J. Baldwin and J. McLean, *Defendants in the Criminal Process* (London, 1976), and McConville and Baldwin, *Courts, Prosecution.*

13. On the rhetoric of police professionalism and its influences for police autonomy, see R. Ericson, and C. Shearing, 'The Scientification of Police Work', in G. Böhme and N. Stehr (eds.), *The Impact of Scientific Knowledge on Social Structures* (Dordrecht, 1987).

14. See J. Skolnick, *Justice without Trial* (New York, 1966) for an early statement on the peacekeeping versus law enforcement issue.

15. See R. Clarke and M. Hough, *The Effectiveness of Policing* (Farnborough, 1980) on the problems of measuring police effectiveness.

16. Daley, *Small Cloud*, 104, demonstrates the absurdity of this practice when as a probationer he was cautioned on his low arrest rate and sent out (complete with a piece of wire to check on motor-cycle silencers) with an experienced sergeant to arrest all and sundry. They conclude the day by severely cautioning small boys for kicking a paper ball in the street.

17. J. Van Maanen, 'Working the Street', in Jacob, H. (ed.), *The Potential for Reform of Criminal Justice* (Beverly Hills, Calif., 1974) and E. Bittner, *The Functions of Police in Modern Society* (Washington, DC 1970).

18. E. Bittner, 'Florence Nightingale in Pursuit of Willie Sutton', in Jacob, *Potential for Reform*.

19. See e.g. R. Roberts, *The Classic Slum* (London, 1973) for account of slum policing in Edwardian Salford, and White, *Worst Street* for slum policing in London in the 1920s and 1930s.

20. Quoted in Ayers, *Liverpool Docklands*.

21. Brogden, *The Police*, ch. 2.

22. For a discussion of such recipe rules in police work, see Ericson and Baranek, *Ordering of Justice*, M. Punch, *Policing the Inner City* (London, 1979) has discussed the way such rules are transmitted by more experienced officers to the younger through metaphors and allegorical stories.

23. See P. Cohen, 'Policing the Working-Class City', in B. Fine (ed.), *Capitalism and the Rule of Law* (London, 1979), Humphries, *Hooligans or Rebels*, G. Pearson, *Hooligan* (London, 1983).

24. See Nott Bower, *Fifty-Two Years*.

25. Humphries, *Hooligans or Rebels*, 146.

26. See H. Parker, *View from the Boys* (Newton Abbot, 1974) and O. Gill, *Luke Street* (London, 1977) for examples some 50 years later on Merseyside. Gill, in Birkenhead, describes the Bonfire Night festivities as mainly important as a display of ritual conflict between the police and street kids.

27. There is an increasing sociological literature on the question of 'policing and consent', and especially on the relationship between the police and the working and lower classes. Amongst several others, see Brogden, *The Police* and Pearson, *Hooligan*.

28. For a greater variety of examples of the relationship of individual street people and the police, see White, *Worst Street* and for an earlier period, R. Samuel, *East End Underworld: Chapters in the Life of Arthur Harding* (London, 1981).

29. See White, *Worst Street* on the contradictoriness of lower-class culture.

30. Ibid.

31. Clive Emsley has provided a useful antidote to the orthodox emphasis on control by 'moral authority' in an important account of the use of violence by police officers in the nineteenth century: C. Emsley, '"The Thump of Wood on a Swede Turnip": Police Violence in Nineteenth Century England', *Criminal Justice History*, 6 (1984), 125–49.

32. Detail of such conflicts with the police appears in the unique Police (Toxteth) Enquiry (1909). On this and other such incidents see Brogden, 'Troubles in Toxteth' and P. J.

Waller, *Democracy and Sectarianism* (Liverpool, 1981) for a history of sectarian relations within the city. As early as 1835, conflicts between Irish Catholics and Protestants in the city had metamorphosed into a unified grand assault on the then police, the Night Watch, and the hanging of an effigy of its commander, Whitty, later to become the first Head Constable of the City Police, on the gates of the Main Bridewell.

33. See R. Graef, *Talking Blues* (London, 1989), 227–8.

34. A summary of the literature on police corruption today is given in M. Punch, *Conduct Unbecoming: The Social Construction of Police Deviance and Control* (London, 1985). See Daley, *Small Cloud*, 107–8 on similar evidence of the low level of normal corruption—apart from bookmaking and a few prostitution rackets in the Metropolitan Police. Beat constables rarely met anybody who could afford to pay a bribe.

35. See Daley, *Small Cloud* for similar corruption evidence on the Metropolitan CID.

36. M. E. Brogden, 'Rules, Regulations, and Christmas Boxes', paper presented to Conference on Crime, Law, and History, University of Warwick, 1983.

37. See the summaries of the revisionist literature on policing in Reiner, *Politics of Police* and Brogden *et al.*, *Introducing Policework*.

CHAPTER 5

1. See G. Stedman Jones, *Outcast London* (London, 1971) on the relationship between work and leisure.

2. G. C. Allen, *The Import Trade of the Port of Liverpool* (Liverpool, 1946).

3. See White, *Worst Street* for the most detailed description of participants in street economy.

4. See M. E. Brogden, 'Policing a Nineteenth Century Mercantile Economy', paper presented to Annual European Conference on Critical Legal Studies. University of Kent, 1984, on the nature of the secondary economy in the city in earlier years.

5. See D. Jones, *Social Survey*, on the numbers of casual workers attached to the Docks, especially on the stands of dockers waiting for hire.

6. There were regular campaigns in the late nineteenth century against the city's 'vice' problems by the liberal middle class. One illustration of that campaigning—and one that has ramifications in debates over questions of police accountability—is the order in 1890 to the then Head Constable, Nott Bower, by a reforming Watch Committee 'to proceed against all brothels, without any delay'. On this, see e.g. Brogden, *The Police*, ch. 2. Amongst many pamphlets on the crusade against lower-class vice, see R. Armstrong, *The Deadly Shame of Liverpool: An Appeal to Municipal Voters* (n.p., 1890). Similar Victorian crusades were waged against street betting in the city—see e.g. the articles in the *Porcupine*, 18 (1887), and in the *Liverpool Review*, 1883–6.

7. E. Blackwell in Royal Commission on Lotteries and Betting, *Minutes of Evidence*, Cmd. 4341 (London, 1932–3), 33.

8. T. Bigham, Deputy Commissioner, Metropolitan Police, ibid. 35.

9. Royal Commission on Police Powers and Procedures, *Report*, Cmd, 3297 (London, 1929).

10. Chief Constable Caldwell, Annual Report, Liverpool City Police (1922).

11. Money could readily be inserted into these special bags but a key was needed to extract it.

12. See Daley, *Small Cloud*, 94–5 for other examples.

13. These look-outs had numerous local titles. In White's Islington, *Worst Street*, 118, for example, they became 'doggers-out'.

14. Ayers, *Liverpool Docklands*, p. 67.

15. Woods, J., *Growin' Up* (Preston, 1989), 65.

16. Bigham, e.g. as n. 8 above.

17. See e.g. C. Smart, *Feminism and the Power of Law* (London, 1989).

18. P. McHugh, *Prostitutes and Victorian Social Reform* (London, 1980). For the best overview of the more recent experience of prostitutes with the police, see E. McLeod, 'Man-made laws for men? The Street Prostitutes' Campaign against Control', in B. Hutter and G. Williams (eds.), *Controlling Women* (London, 1981).

19. See Graef, *Talking Blues*, for a more recent example.

20. Samuel, *East End Underworld*; White, *Worst Street*.

21. J. H. Bagot, *Juvenile Delinquency* (London, 1941).

22. See e.g. G. Honeycombe, *Adam's Tale* (London, 1975).

23. On the detective craft, see R. Ericson, *Making Crime: A Study of Detective Work* (Toronto, 1981).

24. W. Nott Bower, *Fifty-Two Years a Policeman* (London, 1926).

25. See R. Allason, *The Branch; A History of the Metropolitan Special Branch* (London, 1987) for a wider account of the same Sinn Fein episode.

26. B. Behan, *Borstal Boy* (London, 1958).

27. See P. Gill, 'Clearing-up Street Crime: the Big "Con"', *Journal of Law and Society*, 14: 2, (1987) on the continuing use of write-offs in Liverpool.

28. Royal Commission on Police Powers, *Report*.

29. Ibid. 102.

30. Brogden *et al.*, *Introducing Policework*, 78.

31. Royal Commission on Police Powers, *Report*.

32. J. Moylan, *Scotland Yard* (London, 1934).

CHAPTER 6

1. In the present-day literature, see esp. S. Edwards, *The Police Response to Domestic Violence* (London, 1986). See Graef, *Talking Blues*, 156–8 for present-day examples of police reluctance to be involved in domestics.

2. T. Faragher, 'The Police Response to Violence against Women in the Home', in J. Pahl, (ed.), *Private Violence and Public Policy* (London, 1981). Until the Domestic Violence and Matrimonial Proceedings Act, 1977, there was no legal requirement for the police to intervene in the private sphere: an Englishman's home between the wars was not just his castle, it could also be his private wife-beating fief.

3. M. Chatterton, 'Organisational Relationships and Processes in Police Work: A Case Study or Urban Policing', Ph.D. thesis, Manchester University, 1975.

4. I. Law, and J. Henfrey, *A History of Race and Racialism in Liverpool, 1660–1950* (Liverpool, 1981).

5. M. E. Brogden, 'Law, Riot, and Labour Disputes', paper presented to North-West Labour History Annual Conference, Liverpool, 1982.

6. See amongst several others, Brogden, *The Police*, Appendix on the Toxteth riots, 1981.

7. R. May, and R. Cohen, 'The Interaction between Race and Colonialism: A Case Study of the Liverpool Race Riots of 1919', *Race and Class*, 16 (1974–5).

8. Variously estimated as between 2,000 and 5,000: P. Fryer, *Staying Power: The History of Black People in Britain* (London, 1984).

9. Ibid.

10. Quoted in Brogden, *The Police*.

11. Quoted in Fryer, *Staying Power*, 302.

12. E. Marke, *Old Man Trouble* (London, 1973).

13. See the Policy Studies Institute report on the Metropolitan Police for more recent evidence of how police culture makes similar racial distinctions: D. V. Smith, *Police and People in London* (Aldershot, 1985).

14. See e.g. M. Young, 'On the Mersey Beat', *Listener*, 2 Nov. 1978.

15. Fryer, *Staying Power*, 367–71.

16. I. L. Lynn, *The Chinese Community in Liverpool* (Liverpool, 1982).

17. D. Jones, *Social Survey*, 'Population'.

18. See J. Davis, 'From "Rookeries" to "Communities": Race, Poverty, and Policing in London', *History Workshop*, 27, Spring (1989), 66–85.

19. Police relations with the Chinese were not all sweetness and light. Note the complaint by Liverpool workers over the action by City Police officers against striking Chinese seamen: Liverpool Watch Committee Minutes, 18 Oct. 1933.

20. On the origins of the NUWM see W. Hannington, *Unemployed Struggles, 1919–1936* (London, 1977).

21. Not all the leaders were radicalized. One, W. Hughes became a leading anti-communist militant in the city: Bean, 'Police Unrest'.

22. Liverpool Watch Committee Minutes, 1931 and Nov. 1933.

23. See e.g. the agreed request for more police housing: Liverpool Watch Committee Minutes, 18 June 1925. This was more than counterbalanced by the frequent rejections of Police Federation-supported appeals against dismissals, e.g. Watch Committee Minutes, 25 May 1926, 7 Sept. 1926, 15 Nov. 1927, 28 Aug. 1928 and 13 Jan. 1929.

24. D. E. Baines and R. Bean, 'The General Strike on Merseyside', in J. R. Harris (ed.), *Liverpool and Merseyside* (London, 1969).

25. For a commentary on the national picture in the various police histories see Brogden, *The Police*.

26. Critchley, *History of Police*.

27. Mann, *Memoirs*, 220.

28. Baines and Bean, 'General Strike'.

29. See Brogden, *The Police*, ch. 7.

30. Complaints from Labour and union organizations over police conduct were regularly dismissed by the Watch Committee, e.g. complaint by the Independent Labour Party, 8 Feb. 1921; from many labour organizations in relation to the Walker Art Gallery troubles, 11 Oct. 1921. A Flag Day was given to the Anti-Communist Union, 28 Nov. 1922 but not to the Labour Party (requested through its representative, Hayes, the ex-police striker turned MP), 13 July 1926. Alderman John Braddock complained of police attacks on the unemployed but the Assistant Chief Constable retorted that the demonstration had been 'Communist-inspired' and that his men behaved 'impeccably', 26 May. Several labour organizations complained over the use of the City Police against the unemployed and strikers in Birkenhead and Burnley, but the letters were rejected, 27 Sept. 1932. Alderman Braddock complained over the refusal to hold a police enquiry into their harassment of him, 27 Feb. 1934. For oral history material on the experience of Liverpool workers, employed and unemployed, with the Liverpool City Police, see T. Lane, 'Some Merseyside militants of the 1930s' in H. R. Hikins (ed.), *Building the Union* (Liverpool, 1973).

31. G. Garret, *Liverpool 1921–2* ([Liverpool], n.d.).

32. See the account of the *agent provocateur* Sergeant Popay of the Metropolitan Police in Critchley, *History of Police*. On police spying on the NUWM, see Hannington, *Unemployed Struggles*, 8, and R. Hayburn, 'Police and the Hunger Marchers', *International Review of Social History*, 17 (1972).

33. B. Weinberger, 'Police Perceptions of Labour in the Inter-War Years', in F. Snyder, and D. Hay, (eds.), *Labour, Law, and Crime* (London, 1987).
34. Quoted in A. Hutt, *The Post-War Struggle of the British Working-Class* (London, 1937). See also Lane, 'Merseyside Militants'.

APPENDIX

1. See J. Bennett, *Oral History and Delinquency* (London, 1981).
2. Ironically, in the latter case, apparently influenced by the oral testimonies to the Royal Commission of 1839 that gave birth to the County Police in England and Wales. See ibid.
3. C. Booth, *Life and Labour of the People of London* (London, 1902); see also Stedman Jones, *Outcast London*.
4. M. Punch, *Policing the Inner City* (London, 1979); J. Rubinstein, J., *City Police* (New York, 1973) and Chatterton, 'Organisational Relationships'.
5. Punch, *Policing the Inner City*.
6. S. Terkel, *Working* (New York, 1975); Fraser, *Work*.
7. E. Sutherland, *The Professional Thief* (Chicago, 1937); Klockars, C., *The Professional Fence* (London, 1974).
8. Samuel, *East End Underworld*; White, *Worst Street*.
9. S. Cohen, and L. Taylor, *Psychological Survival* (London, 1972).
10. Graef, *Talking Blues*.
11. Brogden, *The Police*; 'Troubles in Toxteth'; 'From Henry III to Liverpool 8'.
12. Punch, *Policing the Inner City*.
13. H. S. Becker, 'Whose Side Are We On?' *Social Problems*, 14 (1967), 239–47.
14. See Bennett, *Oral History* for similar examples in the case of Charles Booth.
15. A. Gouldner, 'The Sociologist as Partisan', *American Sociologist*, May (1968).

BIBLIOGRAPHY

(Asterisks indicate books for readers wishing to pursue the subject further.)

Allason, R., *The Branch: A History of the Metropolitan Police Special Branch* (London, 1987).

Allen, G. C., *The Import Trade of the Port of Liverpool* (Liverpool, 1946).

Allen, V. L., 'The National Union of Police and Prison Officers', *Economic History Review*, 11: 1 (1958), 133–43.

Armstrong, R., *The Deadly Shame of Liverpool: An Appeal to Municipal Voters* (n.p., 1890).

Arnot, R. Pagot, *The Miners: Years of Struggle* (London, 1953).

Ayers, P., *The Liverpool Docklands* (Liverpool, 1989).

Bagot, J. H., *Juvenile Delinquency: A Comparative Study of the Position in Liverpool and Merseyside* (London, 1941).

Baines, D. E., and Bean, R., 'The General Strike on Merseyside, 1926', in J. R. Harris (ed.), *Liverpool and Merseyside* (London, 1969).

Baldwin, J., and McLean, J., *Defendants in the Criminal Process* (London, 1976).

Banton, M., *The Policeman in the Community* (London, 1964).

Bean, R., 'Police Unrest, Unionisation and the 1919 Strike in Liverpool', *Journal of Contemporary History*, 15 (1980), 633–53.

Becker, H. S., 'Whose Side Are We On?', *Social Problems*, 14 (1967), 239–47.

Behan, B., *Borstal Boy* (London, 1958).

Bennett, J., *Oral History and Delinquency: The Rhetoric of Criminology* (London, 1981).

Bittner, E., *The Functions of the Police in Modern Society* (Washington, DC, 1970).

——, 'Florence Nightingale in Pursuit of Willie Sutton', in H. Jacob (ed.), *The Potential for Reform of Criminal Justice* (Beverly Hills, Calif., 1974).

Brogden, M. E., *The Police: Autonomy and Consent* (London, 1982).*

——, 'Law, Riot, and Labour Disputes', paper presented to North-West Labour History Annual Conference, Liverpool, 1982.

——, 'Rules, Regulations, and Christmas Boxes', paper presented to Conference on Law, Crime, and History, University of Warwick, 1983.

——, 'Troubles in Toxteth, 1909', *Police Review*, Aug. (1983).

——, 'Policing a Nineteenth Century Mercantile Economy', paper presented to Annual European Conference on Critical Legal Studies, University of Kent, 1984.

——, 'From Henry III to Liverpool 8: The Complex Unity of Police Street Powers', *International Journal of the Sociology of Law*, Winter (1984).

——, 'An Act to Colonise the Interior Lands of the Island', *International Journal of the Sociology of Law*, 15:2 (1987).

—— and Graham, D., 'Police Education: The Hidden Curricula', in R. Fieldhouse (ed.), *The Political Education of State Servants* (Manchester, 1988), 72–98.

——, Jefferson, T., and Walklate, S., *Introducing Policework* (London, 1988).*

Cain, M., *Society and the Policeman's Role* (London, 1973).

——, 'On the Beat: Interactions and Relations in Rural and Urban Forces', in S. Cohen (ed.), *Images of Deviance* (Harmondsworth, 1973), 62–97.

Carlen, P., *Magistrates' Justice* (London, 1977).

Chambliss, W., 'A Sociological Analysis of the Law of Vagrancy', *Social Problems*, 11 (1964), 67–77.

Chatterton, M., 'Organisational Relationships and Processes in Police Work: A Case Study of Urban Policing', Ph.D. Thesis, Manchester University, 1975.

Clarke, R., and Hough, M., *The Effectiveness of Policing* (Farnborough, 1980).

——— ———, *Crime and Police Effectiveness* (London, 1984).

Cohen, P., 'Policing the Working-Class City', in B. Fine (ed.), *Capitalism and the Rule of Law* (London, 1979).

Cohen, S., *Visions of Social Control* (London, 1985).

——— and Taylor, L., *Psychological Survival* (London, 1972).

Cox, E. C., *Police and Crime in India* (London, 1977).

Craggs, S., *The Chinese Community in Liverpool: An Historical Study* (Liverpool, 1982).

Critchley, T. A., *A History of Police in England and Wales, 900–1966* (London, 1978).*

Daley, H., *This Small Cloud* (London, 1986).*

Davis, J. 'From "Rookeries" to "Communities": Race, Poverty, and Policing in London, 1850–1985', *History Workshop*, 27, Spring (1989), 66–85.

Dep, E., *A History of the Ceylon Police* (Colombo, 1979).

Edwards, S., *The Police Response to Domestic Violence* (London, 1986).

Ehrlich-Martin, S., *Breaking and Entering: Police Women on Patrol* (Berkeley, Calif., 1980).

Emsley, C., '"The Thump of Wood on a Swede Turnip": Police Violence in Nineteenth Century England', *Criminal Justice History* (1984), 125–49.

Ericson, R., *Making Crime: A Study of Police Patrol Work* (Toronto, 1981).

———, *Reproducing Order: A Study of Police Patrol Work* (Toronto, 1982).

———and Baranek, P., *The Ordering of Justice* (Toronto, 1984).

———and Shearing, C., 'The Scientification of Police Work', in G. Böhme and N. Stehr (eds.), *The Impact of Scientific Knowledge on Social Structures* (Dordrecht, 1987).

Faragher, T., 'The Police Response to Violence against Women in the Home', in J. Pahl, (ed.), *Private Violence and Public Policy* (London, 1981).

Fielding, N., *Joining Forces* (London, 1988).

Fraser, R., *Work* (London, 1968).

Fryer, P., *Staying Power: The History of Black People in Britain* (London, 1984).

Garner, P. L. F., *Policing the Liverpool General Transport Strike* (Liverpool, 1984).

Garret, G., *Liverpool 1921–2* ([Liverpool], n.d.).

Gill, O., *Luke Street* (London, 1977).

Gill, P., 'Clearing-up Crime: The Big "Con"', *Journal of Law and Society*, 14: 2 (1987).

Geary, R., *Policing Industrial Disputes* (Cambridge, 1985).

Gouldner, A., 'The Sociologist as Partisan', *The American Sociologist*, May (1968).

Graef, R., *Talking Blues* (London, 1989).

Hall, S., Critcher, C., Jefferson, T., Clarke, J., and Roberts, B., *Policing the Crisis* (London, 1978).

Hannington, W., *Unemployed Struggles 1919–1936* (London, 1977).

Harring, S., *Policing a Class Society* (New Brunswick, NJ, 1983).

Hart, J. M., *The British Police* (London, 1951).

Hayburn, R., 'Police and the Hunger Marchers', *International Review of Social History*, 17 (1972).

Holdaway, S., 'Changes in Urban Policing', *British Journal of Sociology*, 28: 2 (1977), 119–37.

———, *Inside the British Police* (Oxford, 1983).

Honeycombe, G., *Adam's Tale* (London, 1975).

Hough, M. and Mayhew, P., *The British Crime Survey: First Report* (London, 1983).

Howell, B., *The Police in Late Victorian Bristol* (Bristol, 1988).

Humphries, S., *Hooligans or Rebels: An Oral History of Working-Class Youth, 1889–1937* (London, 1981).*

Hunt, A., *Class and Class Structure* (London, 1977).

Hutt, A., *The Post-War Struggle of the British Working-Class* (London, 1937).

Ignatieff, M., 'State, Civil Society, and Total Institutions', in S. Cohen and A. Scull (eds.), *Social Control and the State* (London, 1983).

Jackson, B., *Working-Class Community* (London, 1968).

Jeffries, C., *The Colonial Police* (London, 1952).

Jones, D. (ed.), *The Social Survey of Merseyside* (Liverpool, 1934).

Jones, M., *Organisational Aspects of Police Behaviour* (Farnborough, 1980).

——, and Winkler, J., 'Policing in a Riotous City', *Journal of Law and Society*, 9: 1 (1982).

Judge, A., *A Man Apart* (London, 1972).

Klockars, C., *The Professional Fence* (London, 1974).

Knight, S., *The Brotherhood* (London, 1984)

Lane, T., 'Some Merseyside Militants of the 1930s', in H. R. Hikins (ed.), *Building the Union* (Liverpool, 1973).

Law, I. and Henfrey, J., *A History of Race and Racialism in Liverpool, 1660–1950* (Liverpool, 1981).

Lee, G. A., 'Some Structural Aspects of Police Deviance in Relation to Minority Groups', in C. Shearing (ed.), *Organisational Police Deviance* (Toronto, 1981).

Lynn, I. L., *The Chinese Community in Liverpool* (Liverpool, 1982).

McBarnet, D., *Conviction* (London, 1981).

McConville, M. and Baldwin, J., *Courts, Prosecution, and Conviction* (Oxford, 1981).

McHugh, P., *Prostitutes and Victorian Social Reform* (London, 1980).

McIlroy, J., 'Police and Pickets: The Law against the Miners', in H. Beynon (ed.), *Digging Deeper* (London, 1985), 101–22.

McLeod, E., 'Man-Made Laws for Men? The Street Prostitutes' Campaign against Control', in B. Hutter, and G. William (eds.), *Controlling Women* (London, 1981).

Mann, T., *Tom Mann's Memoirs* (London, 1967).

Manning, P., *Police Work* (Cambridge, Mass., 1977).*

Mark, R., *Policing a Perplexed Society* (London, 1977).

——, *In the Office of Constable* (London, 1978).

Marke, E., *Old Man Trouble* (London, 1973).

May, R. and Cohen, R., 'The Interaction between Race and Colonialism: A Case Study of the Liverpool Race Riots of 1919', *Race and Class*, 16 (1974–5).

Miller, W., *Cops and Bobbies* (Chicago, 1977).*

Moylan, J., *Scotland Yard* (London, 1934).

Nott Bower, W., *Fifty-Two Years a Policeman* (London, 1926).

Parker, H., *View from the Boys* (Newton Abbot, 1974).

Pearson, G., *Hooligan* (London, 1983).

Punch, M., *Policing the Inner City* (London, 1979).*

——, *Conduct Unbecoming: The Social Construction of Police Deviance and Control* (London, 1985).

Reiner, R., *The Blue-Coated Worker* (Cambridge, 1978).

——, 'The Police in the Class Structure', *Journal of Law and Society*, 5: 2 (1978).

——, *The Politics of the Police* (Brighton, 1985).

Reynolds, G. W., and Judge, A., *The Night the Police Went on Strike* (London, 1968).*

Roberts, R., *The Classic Slum* (London, 1973).

Rubinstein, J., *City Police* (New York, 1973).*

Samuel, R., *East End Underworld: Chapters in the Life of Arthur Harding* (London, 1981).*

——, Bloomfield, B., and Bonas, G. (eds.), *The Enemy Within: Pit Villages and the Miners' Strike of 1984–1985* (London, 1986).

Scraton, P., *Causes for Concern* (London, 1984).

——, *The State of the Police* (London, 1985).

Sellwood, A. V., *Police Strike, 1919* (London, 1978).

Skolnick, J., *Justice without Trial* (New York, 1966).

Smart, C., *Feminism and the Power of Law* (London, 1989).

Smith, P. Thurmond, *Policing Victorian London* (London, 1985).

Solmes, A., *The English Policeman* (London, 1935).

Stedman Jones, G., *Outcast London: A Study in the Relationship between Classes in Victorian London* (London, 1971).

Steedman, C., *Policing the Victorian Community* (London, 1984).*

Sutherland, E., *The Professional Thief* (Chicago, 1937).

Taylor, L., 'Industrial Sabotage: Motives and Meanings', in S. Cohen (ed.), *Images of Deviance* (Harmondsworth, 1973).

Terkel, S., *Working* (New York, 1975).

Tobias, J. J., *Nineteenth Century Crime: Prevention and Punishment* (Newton Abbot, 1972).

Van Maanen, J., 'Working the Street', in H. Jacob (ed.), *The Potential for Reform of Criminal Justice* (Beverly Hills, Calif., 1974).

Weinberger, B., 'Police Perceptions of Labour in the Inter-War Period', in F. Snyder and D. Hay (eds.), *Labour, Law, and Crime* (London, 1987).

Waller, P. J., *Democracy and Sectarianism* (Liverpool, 1981).

Whitaker, B., *The Police in Society* (London, 1979).

White, J., *The Worst Street in North London* (London, 1976).*

Woods, J., *Growin' Up* (Preston, 1989).

Select Committee on Police Forces Weekly Rest-Day, *Report and Minutes of Evidence*, PP IX (London, 1908).

Committee on the Employment of Women on Police Duties, *Minutes of Evidence*, Cmd. 1133 (London, 1921).

Home Office Departmental Committee on the Employment of Women Police Constables, *Report and Minutes of Evidence*, Cmd. 2224 (London, 1924).

Committee Appointed to Enquire into the Claims of Men Dismissed from the Police and Prison Service on Account of the Strike of 1919, *Report* Cmd. 2297 (London, 1924).

Desbrough Committee on the Police Service, *Reports*, Cmd. 874 and Cmd. 574 (London, 1919).

Royal Commission on Police Powers and Procedure, *Report*, Cmd. 3297 (London, 1929).

Royal Commission on Lotteries and Betting, *Minutes of Evidence* Cmd. 4341 (London, 1932–3).

Royal Commission on the Police, *Evidence* and *Appendices* (London, 1963).

SUBJECT INDEX

INTERVIEWEE INDEX

* written communication.